The Pleasure
of Birds

The Pleasure of Birds

An Audubon Treasury

Edited by LES LINE

Drawings by Chuck Ripper

Published in cooperation with the National Audubon Society
by J. B. LIPPINCOTT COMPANY · Philadelphia and New York

All of the material in this book originally appeared in somewhat different form in *Audubon* magazine. Copyright © 1966, 1967, 1968, 1969, 1970, 1971, 1972, 1973, 1974 by the National Audubon Society.

Grateful acknowledgment is made to the following publishers and authors for permission to use and adapt material which subsequently appeared in book form:

"The Bird Habit" is reprinted by permission of Doubleday/Natural History Press from *This Bright Land*. Copyright © 1972 by Brooks Atkinson.

"Birds of an Old Farm" is reprinted by permission of Dodd, Mead & Company, Inc., from *A Naturalist Buys an Old Farm*. Copyright © 1974 by Edwin Way Teale.

"Little Auk! Little Auk!" is reprinted by permission of Little, Brown and Company from *In Defense of Nature*. Copyright © 1969 by John Hay.

"The Power of the Owl" is reprinted by permission of Four Winds Press from *The Nightwatchers*. Copyright © 1971 by Peter Parnall and Angus Cameron.

U.S. Library of Congress Cataloging in Publication Data

Main entry under title:

The Pleasure of birds: an *Audubon* treasury.

"Material . . . originally appeared in somewhat different form in Audubon magazine."
1. Birds—Addresses, essays, lectures. I. Line, Les. II. Audubon magazine.
QL676.P7   598.2   75–17948
ISBN–0–397–01065–6

OTHER BOOKS BY LES LINE

Puffin Island
Mystery of the Everglades
What We Save Now (*Editor*)
The Sea Has Wings
Seasons
Dining on a Sunbeam
The Floor of the Forest
This Good Earth (*Editor*)

For Eugene E. Kenaga,
my guide in the ways
and wonders of birds

CONTENTS

Audubon's Photographers
Portfolio One follows page 63
Portfolio Two follows page 127

FOREWORD

"The observation of birds," the eminent British ornithologist James Fisher once wrote, "may be a superstition, a tradition, an art, a science, a pleasure, a hobby, or a bore; this depends entirely on the nature of the observer."

The nature of this observer should be obvious from the title I have chosen for a collection of twenty-five articles and eighteen color photographs gleaned from the pages of *Audubon* during the years of my editorship. Birds, to me, are a pleasure.

But in truth, the element of pleasure can be found in each of the categories cited by Fisher. The proof is at hand. The contributors to this book, among them some of the foremost naturalist authors and photographers in the world, consider the superstition of birds, the tradition of birds, the art of birds, the science of birds, the hobby of birds (which, if carried to the extreme, can become a bore). And from page to page there is a unifying theme: the pleasure of birds.

The theme is quickly apparent in most of the selections, beginning with Brooks Atkinson's opening essay on "The Bird Habit," which serves as an introduction to the entire anthology, for no words that I could put to paper would better answer the question he poses: Why birds? But it is present, albeit in a perverse way, even when George Laycock recalls the plume-hunters' slaughter of seabirds on a remote Pacific islet. After all, the albatrosses of Laysan were butchered so that fashionable ladies could have the pleasure of wearing feathered hats.

The choice of contents for *The Pleasure of Birds* is a personal one, and reaches back only as far as the spring of 1966, when I assumed the helm of a magazine that previously had many distinguished editors. Also, in an effort to represent as many authors as possible, I resisted the temptation to include more than a single chapter from any one writer whose work frequently appears in *Audubon*. Thus some longtime readers may be disappointed that their favorite bird stories are not found herein. I ask them to be patient. Enough treasures remain to fill several more volumes.

Finally, any applause that this anthology merits belongs to the twenty-five authors and fourteen photographers who graciously gave us permission to include their work, and to artist Chuck Ripper, whose sensitive drawings, made specifically for this book, decorate these pages. Nor can I overlook the contributions of my colleagues on the *Audubon* staff who helped to shepherd these stories and pictures to their original publication.

LES LINE
Editor, AUDUBON

THE BIRD HABIT,
BY BROOKS ATKINSON

The fascination that birds hold for millions of people is difficult to explain to someone who hasn't been similarly seduced. This thoughtful essay, better than any before it, conveys the many reasons why the lure of the bird often becomes irresistible.

Why birds? In the field of natural history there are many bountiful subjects—plants, trees, stars, butterflies, wild animals, fish. Any one of these miniature worlds helps the amateur to find his place in the universe. I am not qualified to speak for the professionals, although I suspect that the spiritual overtones are the same. But it is good for everyone to have his imagination stimulated. Life has become so mechanized, life is so lacking in flavor, that anything learned about anything rescues people from the boredom of civil obedience. In a technological age the man who knows where the bergamot grows in some brushy back field or knows when and where to look for the Pleiades is a revolutionary. He has published his declaration of independence. He can no longer be conveniently catalogued or efficiently computerized or checked off as a safe statistic.

I would not therefore celebrate birds above any other hobby that is spontaneous and disinterested. They all fulfill the basic test of hobbies that was proposed by that lovable sage, Aldo Leopold: A hobby, he thought, must be "in large degree useless, inefficient, laborious, or irrelevant." If it shows a profit it is no longer a hobby but part of the rat race that continuously debases mankind.

I speak a good word for birds because they have been a part of my marginal experience ever since I was in grade school. Why birds? There are all sorts of reasons. Many birds are extraordinarily beautiful; that is the reason most commonly given. In the temperate zone of northeastern America, where I live, the spectacular beauty of the Baltimore oriole and the fiery plumage of the scarlet tanager and the splendor of most of the warblers would be unbelievable if they were not common facts of wildlife. If the robin were not so familiar, his beauty of plumage and song and his lively personality would also be wondered at. The Maryland yellowthroat with his stunning black mask would seem normal in a tropical jungle, where gorgeous birds, like toucans and parrots, tumble and scream through the dense foliage. But to see not one but several yellowthroats every day in the dry, dusty brush along a stretch of road and to hear their modest serenade is to be startled by the extravagant beauty of nature—a beauty that is all the more remarkable because it is as common as the white daisy, the scrub oak, and the gray squirrel.

Not that birds have to be beautiful in order to be interesting. Some of them, like the pelican or the cormorant, are grotesque or ugly and obviously have not been designed to enrapture human observers. But it is chastening to remember that human values may be irrelevant here. We are not the final judges of the beauty of the natural world. The vulture, which staggers through the sky as it patrols the ground, and the California condor, with its snakelike neck and hooked beak, and the roseate spoonbill, with its monstrous beak, and the surf scoter or "skunk-head coot," with its hideous bill and nostril formation, represent an order of life that has its own functional laws.

To human beings there is something offensive about the feeding habits of vultures and condors—crows, too, in some cases. They tear strips of rancid meat off decomposed carcasses. We regard putrid meat as loathsome and injurious to health. In this respect our instinctive reaction to the feeding habits of vultures and condors coincides with self-interest. But the family of scavengers performs its mission in life with considerable stateliness, skill, and composure—all of which are elements of beauty. Vultures and condors, it is significant to remember, probably do not regard live human beings as beautiful. They prefer corpses.

Nor are most birds' songs beautiful according to the arbitrary standards of human beings. The dry rasp of the chipping sparrow, the monotonous iterations of the red-eyed vireo, and the futile little buzz of the prairie warbler have no esthetic distinction. But again we are not qualified to make definitive judgments, for these birds do not sing to enchant us. They are communicating in the codes of their world—communicating affection, fright, or warning in the conduct of their community life. They are also sometimes communicating content and joyousness. For I am sure that those professional ornithologists are wrong who declare that bird song is exclusively functional. Some of it, like the long rambling rhapsody of the brown thrasher on a sublime morning in the breeding season, expresses a sense of well-being.

Esthetically, the thrasher's song and similar songs by catbirds, red-winged blackbirds, and grackles are not beautiful in the sense that the hermit thrush, the rose-breasted grosbeak, the purple finch, the goldfinch, and the robin express ecstasy in a melodious style. But no matter. Bird songs are not intended to enchant human beings. They are parts of the dialogue of the bird world, which keeps many secrets.

And this leads us to a fundamental factor in the fascination of birds. The essential part of their being eludes us. Although they coexist with us on this eroded planet, they live independently of us with a self-sufficiency that is almost a rebuke. In the world of birds a symposium on the purpose of life would be inconceivable. They do not need it. We are not that self-reliant. To prop up our egos we have to reassure ourselves about our importance to the universe by arranging seminars in which we argue basic questions. We are the ones who have lost our way. Birds do not have to consult the Bible in order to obey the mandate to increase and multiply, nor do they have to worry about a population explosion. They do not have to define a purpose.

The bird and human worlds are not entirely separate. Bluebirds, tree swallows, and house wrens occupy houses that we provide for them. In several other ways birds associate with our world without actually joining it—using birdbaths and feeding trays. Chickadees definitely enjoy human society. But the deepest part of the life of the birds takes place in secret, where human eyes rarely see it. The Arctic tern bypasses human civilization twice a year; the sandhill crane posts sentinels against human invasion. Our grand achievements in the refinement and organization of knowledge and the development of atomic fission mean nothing in the life cycle of birds. On Midway atoll the albatrosses that have nested there for centuries cannot seem to learn that in a technological age jet planes take precedence over birds.

The success of birds in the proliferation of life challenges our view of ourselves. Their life began before human beings started to walk upright. They have a longer history on this planet than we have. When I see a hermit thrush in a New York City park during migration time or a flight of blue jays in the center hedges of upper Broadway, I think of the centuries during which their ancestors migrated over the same terrain when it was composed of woods, ponds, and ledges. Is it possible that the races of birds have not noticed that something fundamental has changed? When I see a string of wild geese flying and honking above the piers, loft buildings, and luxury apartment houses of modern Manhattan, I wonder if they notice that the landscape has changed in the last three centuries.

One of the four things that King Solomon could not understand was "the way of an eagle in the sky." Here we are well on in the twentieth century with similar problems and areas of ignorance. We do not know much about the inner drives of birds. We are still baffled by the purposes, the origins, and methods of bird migration. No simple explanations account for all the variations. It is no disparagement of ornithological knowledge to have a sardonic fondness for unanswered questions. Why do so many herons migrate northward after the breeding season? Why do bobolinks start south in July before the harvest has begun? Why do the swallows form up in August and go south while there is still more of their food available than there is in April when they come north? Why do the evening grosbeaks migrate east rather than south?

Not that birds succeed more consistently than men do. Some species, like the passenger pigeon and the heath hen, have failed conspicuously. Some, like the starlings, succeed so sensationally that they threaten to consume their environment, as we do. As country people in the nineteenth century held the passenger pigeon in low esteem because of its voracity and filthiness, so we look at the starling with distaste and some anxiety. But what we think of them is hardly more than gossip that will be forgotten in a century or two. The civilization of birds endureth forever. Nothing we think affects the vast, endless, mysterious cavalcade of birds that began millions of years ago, has survived the vicissitudes of this irascible earth, and will go longer than we shall.

An interest in birds helps to put the past into perspective. Our America is radically different from the America of Audubon and Thoreau. Our roads and buildings are different; the automobile has changed our life profoundly; airplanes have sharply divided the old from the new. But the mergansers we see in the river and the song sparrows we listen to with gratitude in March are for all practical purposes identical with the birds Audubon and Thoreau saw and listened to. They are links to the past of America. We feel closer to Audubon and Thoreau when we participate in the America they knew. The birds that today flourish in Stratford-on-Avon in England provide a firmer link to Shakespeare than his plays do; the plays are more dated than the doves, wrens, cuckoos, falcons, and owls that he knew and to which he referred in his plays and poems.

Although we know that swallows do not hibernate by laying themselves up in mud during the winter, Gilbert White's mild and thoughtful observations of the birds he knew on the South Downs of Hampshire in the eighteenth century dramatize history and draw a familiar portrait of a sweet-minded clergyman. "Martins in general were remarkably late this year," he wrote to a correspondent in the year in which Cornwallis surrendered to George Washington in Yorktown. How much more contemporary White's ordinary remark seems than that illustrious fact of American history. Birds do not recognize wars; their scale of values is more celestial. During World War I birds kept their rendezvous with life in the torn and shattered fields of France, and birdwatchers in uniform saw and identified them. In Flanders fields the Canadian poet John McCrae heard "the larks still bravely singing." In a marsh near the Somme River, where the fighting was interminable, John Kieran, wearing an American soldier's uniform, noted an abundance of coots and herons, as if he were making his morning rounds in Van Cortlandt Park in New York City. Some ornithologists who survived World War II look back with satisfaction on the new birds they saw overseas. As civilians they might never have visited so many wild and obscure Pacific islands, where the Asiatic birds refused to take sides between belligerents.

Flight is the genius of birds. If they could not take off so spontaneously and make such casual use of air and sky they would not stimulate the imagination of the birdwatcher so effectively. To earthbound watchers a bird's flight endows him with an otherworldly quality that is close to spirit. Nothing else in nature has the capacity to leap off the ground with so much skill and virtuosity.

More than a century ago Thoreau could take smug satisfaction in his belief that since men could not fly they could not contaminate the sky. The Wright Brothers destroyed that argument in 1903. Today men cannot only fly—they can fly high and far enough to assassinate 130,000 civilians on the ground and return home safely from the scene of disaster. Men can fly faster than birds; 175 to 200 miles an hour seems to be about the top speed of birds. Men can climb higher in the sky; 15,000 feet is a great altitude for birds, although the Mount Everest expedition of 1924 saw yellow-billed choughs up to 27,000 feet. Men can also cover greater distances at sustained speeds of several hundred miles an hour. By mechanically reproducing the physical fundamentals of bird flight, men have made astounding progress in extending technological ingenuity into the sky.

But flight is an acquired characteristic of man —the result of study, skill, and will. In comparison with birds, planes are clumsy. Only a few birds, like the California condor, have so much difficulty in getting off the ground, and none of them have to be as cautious about returning as planes have to be. Nothing men have accomplished in the laboratory and factory equals the ease with which the kingbird takes off from his perch to snatch an insect in the air and then casually returns, or the lazy circling of a hawk in the sky, or the silent facility with which the black-billed cuckoo plunges through the foliage and manages to keep out of sight while he is in action. All gulls are marvelous fliers. No plane equals the flight of the tiny ruby-throated hummingbird that darts through the dooryard so swiftly that he is almost invisible, that can hang in one place by hovering before a flower, and that can fly backwards. During the migration season this miniature bird flies more than six hundred miles over the open ocean to Bermuda or five hundred miles over the Gulf of Mexico to Yucatan. All this amazing speed and endurance come from an oval egg about as big as the end of a man's little finger.

The noiseless, spectral flight of the barred owl at dusk is so far beyond human experience that we can only wonder at and envy it. It takes thousands of men and millions of dollars to build a plane that can leave the ground. But everything the barred owl needs to have and to know in order to fly he acquires without effort from the egg. The perpendicular plunge of the gannet into the sea, the swirling race of the chimney swift in the evening, and the loping hop of the pileated woodpecker constitute the poetry of flight. Airplanes are prose by comparison.

If hunting were not one of the primitive instincts, birdwatching would lose much of its appeal. In birdwatching nothing gets killed. The pleasure of the chase survives; the cruelty of death is eliminated. It was not always that way. Before good binoculars were available birds were shot with impunity and also with a good deal of professional pride by people who were fond of them or were studying them. In many cases shooting was the only method of identification. By today's standards Audubon's competitive shooting in Florida was wanton and barbaric. No doubt birds in those days seemed to be inexhaustible in numbers, particularly in Florida, which was an unsettled part of the continent. But as a competitive hunter Audubon shared the callous, brutish attitude toward birds that was widespread in the first half of the nineteenth century.

In the second half of that century W. H. Hudson shot birds for money in Buenos Aires. He earned a meager living by collecting bird skins for the Zoological Society of London. During this period he had one experience that sounds unnerving. An oriole that he shot but did not immediately kill fell into a stream. Floating on the surface of the water the oriole resumed his sweet song and continued singing in Hudson's hand after he had been recovered from the stream. At that time and in that place Hudson seems not to have been pained by the artless singing of a bird he had fatally wounded. He was a professional collector earning a living in the field. Except by license, shooting most birds today is not only unlawful but an offense against the "reverence for life" that Dr. Albert Schweitzer's blunt phrase has made a canon of civilized behavior. As we neutralize the harshness of nature through science and technology, we revere the beauties of nature more passionately. The gunner is the modern barbarian.

Hunting for birds with binoculars in fields and woods, in swamps, on the shore, and at sea is one of the most beguiling aspects of an interest in birds. Plants and trees remain in definite places; they can be revisited at will. But not birds. Birds are elusive because they move around freely in their summer environment, to say nothing of their formidable migrations. The pair of hawks I saw twice on the mountain last week and was unable to identify I have not been lucky enough to see again, although I have patrolled the area repeatedly. Nor have I been able to see a bird I feel sure is a yellow-throated vireo. I can hear him talking rather slowly, and I suspect that he is not a red-eyed vireo, one of our commonest birds. But I cannot see him because the midsummer foliage at the top of the trees is thick and because his movement through the foliage is languid. If he were easy to see, like the robins and towhees, I should probably be less eager to see him.

For the pleasure of hunting does not depend upon success. It is enough to be out-of-doors on some mission—to enjoy the broken radiance of the morning sunshine in the oak and hemlock woods or the glowing splendor of the bird's-foot trefoil in the fields, or to smell the pungent odor of the sea and hear the crash of surf, or to walk under the lofty canopy of the redwoods, where birds are almost impossible to see, or to look off across the green floor of Yosemite Valley from a parapet on Glacier Point. Days out-of-doors are the bright particles of birdwatching because they are never empty or routine. The birdwatcher shares them with deer, raccoons, rabbits, and squirrels, which he is likely to see, and with bears, wildcats, and foxes, which he rarely sees. If a family of ruffed grouse explodes at his feet he knows he is in the thick of things.

My skills in the identification of birds are indifferent. If I am afield with a skillful birdwatcher I am seldom the first to see a bird or identify it. Neither my vision nor my mind is up to the standard of the experts, who invariably have orderly ways of observing the visible universe. But I have had hundreds of glorious days out-of-doors. Even if Ian and Eben McMillan had not introduced me to twelve of the forty extant condors on Hopper Mountain in California one winter, the excursion would have been memorable—the vivid canyons that drop off sharply, the dry rangelands, the salt-encrusted Carrizo Plain, where a flock of sandhill cranes was gathered, the ponderosa pines, the live oaks, the brilliant winter sky at night.

If I had not been fascinated by birds I should never have had a close look at a king vulture, which the resident ornithologist pointed out to me in the slippery, streaming jungle of Barro Colorado Island in the Panama Canal, or made the acquaintance of the white ibis off the coast of Florida during a standard Audubon tour. Nor would I have seen European goldfinches and cream-coloured coursers in the Jordan Valley, where Bedouins live, or watched and listened to the nuptial flight of the woodcock on a peaceful evening in Connecticut, or seen oystercatchers hawking over Cobb Island off Virginia, or, by chance, found a great horned owl perched close to the trunk of a huge beech tree in my own woods one Labor Day. All these birds were wonderful to see. But I also remember with pleasure the settings in which I saw them—the texture of the days, the bulk of the trees, the steep pitch of the trails, the glare of beach sand, the glimmer of running water.

To hunt successfully is not necessarily to win. It is to watch and listen, stop and stroll, sit and wait, to see what has been seen before and also to hope for something new, as in the instances of a Philadelphia vireo or a blue-winged warbler in a copse across the road, where I had never seen them before. To see a chance visitor like these is to be obsessed with the illusion that every other field and clump of trees is also concealing rare birds. If a hunter moves slowly and quietly and looks in all directions, half convinced that something of single interest is lurking nearby, he will never return without some trophy, if it is only a fruited hop hornbeam branch or a stalk of elecampane. The main thing is to be out-of-doors.

No one is more cosmopolitan than a birdwatcher; he is at home in any part of the world. Men have long dreamed of creating "one world," in Wendell Willkie's wistful phrase. In 1945 representatives of several nations, in a state of solemn euphoria, organized the United Nations to foster peaceful relations everywhere. But all the thought, goodwill, and manpower squandered on that organization have not silenced the guns or grounded the bombers or opened the borders between nations. The thousands of white wagtails that visit Israel in the winter also visit Jordan and Syria with an innocence that makes the UN look clumsy and inept.

It can be a traumatic experience for a human being to cross from Israel to Jordan. The transit requires documents and interrogation. Machine guns are in place; armed guards block the road. You are a potential enemy if you attempt to cross the lines. But all the white wagtail has to do is to hop over the boundary and take up residence in Jordan or Israel, as the case may be. The same birds visit or live in both places because birds do not recognize political demarcations. They were flying through Palestine and nesting in Jerusalem long before the Arabs and the Jews started shooting at each other after World War II. The handsome bulbul lives without prejudice on both sides of the border. The voice of the turtledove that delighted Solomon is still heard in both lands. Birds have learned something about freedom of movement that men cannot seem to understand. To see the same birds in Israel and Jordan is to recognize the absurdity of political nationalism and to be irritated by and have contempt for the ludicrous rituals of border-crossing. What is it that men are so afraid of?

Even if the world were not divided into quarrelsome segments by hostile governments and armies, birdwatching would still make all parts of the world seem familiar and hospitable. The mid-Atlantic in early winter is not alien or desolate. The fulmars, the shearwaters, and the petrels make it look like a pleasant rolling meadow. They use it as casually as the bobolinks use the hay-fields of northeastern America. The mid-Pacific is not lonely. Black-footed and Laysan albatrosses glide across it in all weather. They use it as naturally as we use croplands. The Salween River Valley in China is not hostile territory. The gloriously bedizened hoopoe perches on the roofs of straw houses there and calls to everyone within hearing; and the magpie inhabits the villages. The celebrated Pripet Marshes in Russia swarm with ducks and plover, as our marshes do. Nothing in nature speaks a foreign language.

When abroad I have never had the leisure to concentrate on birdwatching, and usually I have been stationed in cities. But except in the Soviet Union, where binoculars raise troublesome questions (I left mine in Helsinki the last time), I have always had birdwatching in the back of my mind. It destroys the formality of foreign cities, as it destroys the formality of cities at home. Excepting once, I have never had the good fortune to go in the field with a native birdwatcher, and my list of identified species overseas is brief. There was no bird society in Israel when I was there, although there was a wildlife organization that included birds. In Jordan the only birdwatchers I met or heard about were American and British. Countries without great natural resources do not idolize nature. They have to exploit nature in order to survive—not only birds but animals, plants, trees, water, and land. If an Arab or Israeli boy sees a bird he may throw a stone at it or try to catch it to sell. He is at about the same cultural level as the stupid gunners in Los Angeles who shoot condors. In most of the countries I have visited for one reason or another, I have had to blunder around among the birds without the guidance of native people.

But I remember with great enjoyment one snowy Saturday afternoon in Stockholm when a Swedish birdwatcher quixotically took me in tow. Arriving from Finland about noon at a hotel on the inlet and across from the royal palace, I saw hundreds of gulls, geese, and ducks feeding, flying, and swimming on the icy water and gabbling loudly among themselves. After checking into the hotel I took my binoculars and a copy of *A Field Guide to the Birds of Britain and Europe,* crossed the snowy street to the edge of the water, and started to look at the birds systematically. Most of them were gulls and other water birds that I thought I either knew or could identify by referring to the bird guide. I didn't have to. An amiable Swede in a dark overcoat and fur hat joggled my elbow and pointed to the sky over the royal palace. "Sparrow hawk," he said—that is, the European sparrow hawk, not ours.

The Swede did not have much English and I had no Swedish—the humiliating situation in which most Americans find themselves abroad. But the situation did not require many words. Like music, painting, and ballet, birdwatching has no language. My Swedish host led me across the street to a boat landing where about ten busy young men were spending their Saturday afternoon banding geese. Among the birds my host pointed out to me was a white-fronted goose, which was for me a new species, or "life bird." In the heart of a capital city in a foreign country at an inhospitable time of year, I found myself in a familiar and sociable environment. I have never seen so many birds in the East River of Manhattan, and I have never found a birdwatcher there.

To be interested in birds is to look around one corner of civilization and to get not so much a glimpse of cosmic truth as a shadowy impression—half between dread and hope. Who are we, where are we and why? These are the sovereign questions that knowledge limited to human experience cannot begin to answer. Robinson Jeffers had more confidence in birds than in men. Bitter over the depravities of human society he wrote: "The unsocial birds are the greater race." I am less certain that the comparison is relevant. Birds are not only unhuman; they are inhuman. By the ethical and moral standards human society has improvised out of all sorts of experience, birds do not rank high. House sparrows drove the wren away from his box this year out of pure malice, it seemed to me, since the house sparrows were already nesting in another box fifty yards away. Starlings drove the tree swallows out of the swallow box but did not use it themselves. They nested in our kitchen flue, where they were both noisy and filthy. A grackle systematically polluted the birdbath by dropping into it the excrement he removed from his nest ten yards away. Unalloyed perversion, it seemed to me.

We cannot look to nature for ethical guidance. Even plants, which cannot move away from fixed positions, are at war with one another and exterminate the weak. Civilization tries to preserve the weak; mercy and charity are ideals we have created and which to some extent we profess. I do not look at birds uncritically. In the United States and in most European countries the human race extends to them more goodwill than they extend among themselves. If it were not for the bounty of birdwatchers who put out food and water, many birds would not survive the savage weather. However, we are eroding their system of values by imposing ours on them, exempting them from their ecological mission of hunting for their own food; our bounty diminishes their independence.

But any hobby is a means of liberation from the stale repetition of civil life. To hunt for birds in the field is to hear the distant, muffled ticking of the great clock of the universe. To human beings these units of time are staggering. It is believed by some professionals that the annual migration of birds repeats every year the advances and retreats of the several glaciers of the Pleistocene epoch. But I doubt it. Although the Pleistocene lasted more than a million years, it constituted less than a hundredth part of the age of birds. The glaciers were incidents. Bird life preceded the glaciers by millions of years.

That is the kind of speculative mathematics a birdwatcher is dealing with when he hears the geese going over in the fall. Something bigger than anything we know is happening.

BIRD IS A VERB,
BY MARGARET CHENEY

Birdwatchers are a long-suffering lot, accustomed to being misunderstood and even mocked by friends, relatives, colleagues, and strangers. Fortunately, most birdwatchers also have a sense of humor about their hobby and the varied paths down which it leads them.

It is almost impossible now to believe how much I did not see before I began seeing birds or what I failed to hear before I began hearing their songs and signals—not just hearing them, you know, but *hearing* them. Oddly, as soon as I began to see, I also began to hear. This enhancement of awareness would seem to conflict with the notion that blind persons hear better *because* they are sightless.

Soon I shall be turning to some other form of addiction. But wherever in the future my path is crossed by a bird, especially a bird with which I am unfamiliar, I shall spring to a crouching position and catch my breath. At any messages the bird may broadcast, whether of exultation, pride of plumage, lust, eggs, fledglings, nest construction, seeds, or secrets of migration, whether of property rights or disaffection—you may be sure that my ears will prick up. If I am speaking, I'll break my sentence in midair. Should I be listening to humankind, my eyes will glaze and I'll sink back in my seat.

With Rat I'll exclaim, "O, Mole! The beauty of it! The merry bubble and joy, the thin, clear, happy call of the distant piping! Such music I never dreamed of . . ."

I learned to watch birds and to miss them when they went somewhere else. I read the literature and did my bit to fog the lenses of those who would like to make birds tedious, who are fretful until every living creature has been wrung out and tagged and forced to yield up its contribution to the jolly old knowledge explosion. Any breathtaking new facts I accumulated were inadvertent and may or may not be divulged.

As a birdwatcher I was a minibuff, although it is by its nature a training ground for megabuffs. Anyone who thinks to birdwatch either frivolously (as of course I did at the start) or desultorily soon finds he has trifled with strong medicine. Without conscious thought, I began to notice such things as that the cedar waxwings left last week. Had they heard that a thousand yammering house finches were due in town today? On checking around, I discovered that the waxwings left only after picking every pyracantha bush in the neighborhood clean of its bright red berries; that the berries achieve a certain fermentation around the holiday season, and that the waxwings were stoned silly when they pulled out, which helped to explain their behavior. Chances were they created a hazard on the Pacific Flyway, the great freeway in the sky of the migratory Western species. And where were my crows? Yes. I even became proprietary about crows.

You cannot dabble in birds without becoming involved with their habits and habitats. Once you get into oceans and fields, you are lured as by the mother killdeer feigning a broken wing on into the broad range of conservation problems. You have to become an expert about farmers and pesticides, hunters and licenses and preserves, fossil-fuel powerplants, nuclear powerplants, air pollution, thermal pollution, offshore oil drilling, industrial chemicals, and sewage outfalls. You must learn the ways of Congressional committees and grow skilled at protest tactics. You should be prepared to have your home bugged and your phone wiretapped, to be gassed from a helicopter or thrown into jail. If you write a letter to Pacific Gas & Electric Company protesting the filthy smog from its

Moss Landing plant, expect to have a cross burned on your lawn. (Mind you, I don't say it's going to happen; but just be prepared.) If the birds you most dote on happen to be pelagic, be prepared also to become excruciatingly—although inexpertly—involved with everything else that lives in the ocean, from plankton to whales.

I discovered that I could not go into birds without being driven by a sense of the transitory nature of nature, by the expectation of imminent loss. What the buff does, therefore, that the garden variety of scientist fails to do, is hurl himself into absorbing as much as he can about everything, knowing he skims the surface, and enjoying it through every spongelike nerve ending.

The buff resolves not to be put down, either by experts or youth.

The former invariably preface their writings with a stern warning against anthropomorphizing. Birds are not just little human beings in feathers. Birds do not think. Birds act from instinct. No matter how closely the actions of birds may remind you of your neighbor, or of people you meet on the freeway and in department stores—forget it. Instinct. For example, those birds that make a habit of going around puncturing other birds' eggs or pushing them out of the nest—instinct, pure instinct.

Now as to youth: In relative silence, as birdwatcher and mother, I have suffered the attacks of the young on the character, life-performance, and institutions of me and my peers. I see much that is vile in the world and mean to go on blaming others more severely than myself. But I should not dream of castigating—say—the Pacific Ocean.

Yet my own child, when I pointed out to her the majestic power and immensity of the Pacific ("Look how big it is," I said), at once criticized it as a "suburban" ocean. Of Monterey Bay, she claimed that when you looked at it from almost any direction, you could see land on the other side. "This," she said contemptuously, "makes it seem like it's only a lake."

The Big Sur coastline she found more rewardingly dramatic, whereas in fact it is merely melodramatic, a case of God not knowing where to stop.

When I first discovered the thrill of watching birds through binoculars, I had some foolish notion of cementing togetherness with Vicki. "Just take a look through these," I said, handing her the glasses. "It's a whole fresh world, a new dimension, like being Columbus and discovering curves. Take a close-up at that violet-green swallow on the wire in front of Mrs. Fouts' house."

She accepted the glasses and I was gratified by the intentness she brought to bear in the direction indicated. Just as I thought we were about to *share an interest,* she handed them back.

"Guess what Mrs. Fouts has on her grocery list," she said. "She's got tomatoes and milk and two pounds of sugar and a can of frozen orange juice . . ."

I snatched the glasses. She said, "It's *nice* that you've got a hobby."

So this is what we are up against, we noble buffs. If experts and infants had their way, we should soon become as extinct as the passenger pigeon, the dodo, and the great auk. As it is, our position is roughly as chancy as that of the whooping crane, the California condor, and the Kirtland's warbler.

The scorn of experts and youth is to us as pesticides to the peregrine falcon, the brown pelican, the cormorant, the murre, the shearwater, and all those others. Our eggs grow thin-shelled and unviable. We may be the last of our kind.

TSI-LICK! GOES THE HENSLOW'S, BY GEORGE PLIMPTON

Bird-listing—running up a score of species you have seen and identified, as distinguished from the simple joys of birdwatching—is a sport. Like baseball, football, hockey, or golf, bird-listing has its fanatical followers, its records to be broken. Like the World Series, Super Bowl, Stanley Cup, or Masters, bird-listing also has its championship playoff. Who better to report on this event than the Walter Mitty of sports journalism?

I should admit at the outset that my credentials as a birdwatcher are slightly sketchy. True, birdwatching *is* a hobby, and if pressed I tell people that I truly enjoy it: on picnics I pack along a pair of binoculars and the Peterson field guide. But I am not very good at it. Identification of even a mildly rare bird or a confusing fall warbler is a heavy, painstaking business, with considerable riffling through the Peterson, and then a numbing of spirit since I am never really *sure*. As a birder I have often thought of myself as rather like a tone-deaf person with just a lesson or two in his background who enjoys playing the flute—it's probably mildly pleasurable, but the results are uncertain.

Pressure to better myself as a birder has been consistently exacted on me by my younger brother and sister, who are both good birdwatchers and can hardly wait for fall and the possibility of being confused by warblers during the migration.

Sometimes, when we are all going somewhere in a car, they involve me in a birding quiz which utilizes the Peterson guide. My sister will say, opening the book at random, "All right, the two of you, see if you can guess this one."

She summarizes: "4¾ to 5¼ inches in length. O.K.? The bird is short-tailed and flat-headed with a big pale bill; finely streaked below. The head is olive-colored and striped, and the wings are reddish. Its flight is low and jerky with a twisting motion of the tail . . ."

"Got it," snaps my brother. "A cinch."

My sister looks at me.

"Well, it's not a brant goose," I say.

"That's very perceptive," she says.

"What's its call?" I ask, indulging in a holding action since I've never been able to remember or indeed hear in my inner ear the dreamy *tseeeee-tsaaays* or the syrupy *zzzchuwunks* that pepper Peterson's descriptions.

My sister reads directly from the book. "This bird 'perches atop a weed, from which it utters one of the poorest vocal efforts of any bird; throwing back its head, it ejects a hiccoughing *tsi-lick*. As if to practice this "song" so that it might not always remain at the bottom of the list, it often hiccoughs all night long.' "

"You're making that up," I say in astonishment. "That doesn't sound like Peterson at all."

"An absolute cinch," says my brother. "You *must* know."

I decide to take a guess. "A red-eyed vireo."

Both of them groan.

"What is it, Oakes?" my sister asks.

"Henslow's sparrow."

"Of course," she says smugly.

Despite such shortcomings, I was invited to participate in the National Audubon Society's annual Christmas Bird Count. I accepted with alacrity, if only in the hope of improving my birdwatching ability, and perhaps, at the least, so I could do better in the Peterson contest with my brother and sister.

For the uninitiated, the Christmas Bird Count was originated in 1900 by the editor of *Bird-Lore* magazine, Frank M. Chapman, who wished to organize a substitute for a traditional Christmastime wildlife slaughter known as the "side hunt," in which the gentry would "choose sides" and spend a day in the woods and fields blazing at everything that moved to increase their team's total toward the grand accounting at the end of the day.

Chapman's first Christmas count involved twenty-seven people and twenty-five localities. The largest list of birds spotted came from Pacific Grove, California (36 species), and Chapman himself reported the second largest (18 species) from Englewood, New Jersey. Those pioneer bird counters could not have been particularly proficient since the 1972 count near Pacific Grove was 179, and the New Jersey count nearest to Englewood was 72.

From its modest beginnings, the Audubon Christmas Bird Count has mushroomed over seven decades. Today, during the two-week Christmas period, some 20,000 observers are involved. The participating teams (each has one day of search time allowed and is confined to an area with a fifteen-mile diameter) number over 1,000.

Over the past few years the competition for the greatest number of species has been between three areas in California (San Diego, Santa Barbara, and Point Reyes, where in 1971 a huge army of 193 observers was mustered); Cocoa Beach, Florida, where the late Allan Cruickshank was the field marshal; and Freeport, Texas, a relatively new count which was organized in 1957 by ornithologist Victor Emanuel, who worked at the job until, in 1971, Freeport set the Christmas Bird Count record of 226 species, an astounding total considering the limitations of the fifteen-mile circle of land and water.

The Freeport count was the one I decided to join. Emanuel was described to me as being young, eager, and perhaps best known in birdwatching circles for his observations of the Eskimo curlew on Galveston Island in 1959. I told him nothing of my birding inadequacies. A week before Christmas I flew to Houston and drove down to the Freeport area, arriving in the late evening at an A-frame beach house on the Gulf of Mexico (appropriately called "The Royal Tern") just in time to hear Emanuel give a peptalk to his team. His group was young—many of them in their twenties, quite a few beards among them—and an overall mood of intense dedication prevailed, as if a guerrilla operation were afoot.

Emanuel's pep rally essentially sounded as follows: "All right, let's try to get *both* cormorants, the double-crested and the olivaceous. Get close. Compare. It's the only way. The green heron is a problem bird, and so is the yellow-crowned night heron. And the least bittern, a tremendous problem! We've only had it once. Flush him out. He lurks in the cattail areas. Leap up and down. Clap your hands. That sort of behavior will get him up. Ross' goose? I'm concerned. We only had four last year. Look in the sky every once in a while for the ibis soaring. Search among the green-winged teal for the cinnamon." He ran his finger down the list through the ducks. "An oldsquaw would be very nice. The hooded merganser is a problem. Hawks! Cooper's and sharp-shinned —not easy at *all*. You people in the woods, make a special effort. Look at all the buteos for the Harlan's. The caracara is a big problem, especially if they're held down by the rain; but they might be flying around. Rails? We're relying on you people in the marsh buggy for the rails, and the purple gallinule as well. As for shorebirds, last year we did not do well at all."

"We did our best," someone called out from the shadows.

"Emanuel's right. We missed the marbled godwit," a bearded man said from the corner.

Emanuel continued as if he hadn't heard: "We have a barn owl staked out. Keep an eye out for the screech owl. We have often missed him. There ought to be some groove-billed anis around. Can't miss *them*. They have weird, comical calls and they look, when they move around, like they're going to fall apart. Check every flicker for the red-shafted. Say's phoebe might be around. Check the ditches. Bewick's wren, a *big* problem bird." He tapped his list. "Now," he said. "I'm very worried about the warblers. Last year we were lucky with vireos; we got five different species, and we got seventeen out of the possible twenty warblers. The cold weather is going to drive the insect-eaters like warblers farther south. So I am not at all sanguine about the vireos and warblers. I'd be surprised if we get more than ten. Check every myrtle warbler for the bright-yellow throat that's going to mean Audubon's." He paused. "Now, meadowlarks," he said. "Keep your ears open for the western meadowlark's song. It's quite different from the eastern's, and it's the only way to distinguish between the two species."

Someone interrupted from the back of the room. "Do you realize that the eastern has learned to *imitate* the western?"

Shouts and cries of "Shut up, Ben!" The man next to me whispered that it was Ben Feltner, a great birding rival of Emanuel's, the first man to spot the famous Galveston Island Eskimo curlew, then thought to be extinct.

Emanuel continued unperturbed. "The sparrow that'll give us the most problem is probably the lark. Search the edges of the brush. It's been missed, and it's very upsetting to miss. Henslow's is another." My heart jumped. My sister's voice, reading from Peterson, sang in my head. "It's better than a groove-billed ani to find a Henslow's," Emanuel was saying, "a *devil* of a bird. Watch for those reddish wings."

What a moment, I thought, to make an impression—to call out to that roomful of experts, "And don't forget that twisting tail in flight, and that soft hiccough, the *tsi-lick* that marks the Henslow's." I stirred, but said nothing.

"Longspurs," Emanuel was continuing. "This might be a year for longspurs with the cold snap bringing them in." He folded the list. "Well, that's the end. Good luck to all of you. Don't forget to look behind you. Too many bird-watchers forget to do that—to see what it is that they've stirred up while walking through. My own prognosis is that if we bird well and hard, we'll beat 200 tomorrow, and possibly even get up to 220, but it will take some doing."

A few hands clapped sharply in the back of the room, and someone offered up an exhortatory cry: "Down with Cocoa Beach!"

"I've got them psyched up," Emanuel said to me as people got up from the floor and began to stir around. "They have to be. It's not only Cocoa Beach I'm worried about, but San Diego. It's all very nerve-racking."

"I can sense that," I said truthfully. "I feel as though I've been spying on a professional football team's locker room before the Big Game."

"No one's going to get much sleep," Emanuel said.

"Absolutely not."

The next day, on the run, I kept notes. Victor Emanuel kept me with him as a partner. (Most teams covering the twelve areas of the Freeport count worked as pairs or trios.) Emanuel's personal plan was to hit as many areas as he could to see how his teams were working. My notes, somewhat helter-skelter, read as follows:

"Eight cars crowded with birdwatchers are moving slowly down a cart track, bouncing in the ruts, and then the line turns into a field bordering a large pond. It is barely light. Rhode Island Reds are crowing from a nearby barn. From the farmer's bedroom window the cars moving slowly in a row through the dawn half-light must suggest a sinister procession of some sort—a Mafia burial ceremony.

"The horizon toward the Gulf sparkles with the constellation of lights that mark the superstructures of the oil refineries, illuminating the tall steamlike plumes of smoke. Electric pylons are everywhere. Quite incongruous to think that this highly visible industrial tangle can contain such a rich variety of birdlife. I mention it to Emanuel. He has just whispered to me that the year before a least grebe had turned up in this area. At my comment I could see his face wince in the dim light and he snorted. He tells me that only a fraction of the wildlife John James Audubon observed when he visited the Texas coast remained. But still it is a birder's paradise. Why is that so?

"'Trees,' he said, 'large and thick enough to contain and hold the eastern birds; and yet the area is far enough south to get southern and western birds. The cover is so good that the area gets more warblers in its count than Corpus Christi does, which is much farther to the south. Furthermore, there is great diversity—cattle grazing land, the beaches, swampland, ditches, and the Gulf. Since the count started in 1957, the same basic 136 species have turned up every year—which gives you some idea of the huge diversity of the regular bird population.'"

I am tagging along having a good time. I am in awe of Emanuel. Just a flash of wing, or the mildest of sounds, and he has himself an identification. He is so intense that I rarely ask questions. But he shows me things. I have gazed upon the groove-billed ani. True, the bird does fly as if it were about to come apart at the seams. A black wing fluttering down here, a foot there. I have done nothing on my own. Early in the dawn I saw a woodcock flutter across the road, but I was too intimidated to say anything about it. I know the woodcock from New England. Then, at the pond where we were peering at the barely discernible shapes of the ducks beginning to stir out on the slate-black water, the experts rattling them off (gadwall, canvasback, pintail, et al.), someone said, "Oh, did anyone spot the woodcocks coming across the road from the pasture?" And I said "Yes!" like an explosion. "Absolutely!"

Emanuel caught the despairing eagerness in my voice. He has a nice gift for hyperbole. "That's a terrific bird," he said to me. "Well done!"

We got in Emanuel's car and headed for another area he wanted to bird. I asked him about the Eskimo curlew. He said he hadn't been the first to see the one that had caused all the excitement. On March 22, 1959, two Houston birders—Dudley Deaver and Ben Feltner, the fellow I saw at the peptalk the evening before, wearing the blue jay insignia on his field jacket—had been birding on Galveston Island looking for their first whimbrel, or Hudsonian curlew. In a flock of long-billed curlews they noticed a smallish curlew which they assumed was the whimbrel. But there was something odd about it. It had a very buffy look, and most noticeable was a bill much thinner and shorter than the whimbrel's. With considerable excitement they realized they might be looking at a bird which had last been collected in the United States near Norfolk, Nebraska, on April 17, 1915, and which had been categorized as "probably extinct." The only uncertainty lay in Ludlow Griscom's description in Peterson's field guide that the leg color of the Eskimo curlew was dark green. The legs of the curlew they were looking at on Galveston Island were slaty gray.

Two weeks later they took Emanuel out to see what *he* thought. They discovered the little curlew several miles from where Deaver and Feltner had made the original sighting. "You can imagine how exciting that was," Emanuel told me. "Damn, it was like seeing a dinosaur."

Emanuel was also bothered by the leg color, but some research disclosed that not all reports described the Eskimo curlew's legs as dark green. A number of authorities put them down as a "dull slate color" or "grayish blue."

The curlew returned to Galveston for four years in a row. A number of Texas birders got a chance to look at it—on one occasion from about 100 feet away through a 30-power telescope, powerful enough to fill the eyepiece with the bird. All of the experts were convinced. It was a time, Emanuel told me, that he thinks back on a lot.

We met a birder named Dave Smith, who had come in from Wheeling, West Virginia, because he felt his home turf was so limited. Emanuel said, "Hell, I thought you'd come out here for the glory of the Freeport count."

"No," Smith said. "There's not enough swamps in Wheeling."

I asked Emanuel what he considers the qualities of a great birder, and he began talking about Jim Tucker. "He is a superb birder. He found us the red-necked grebe at the Texas City dike. He is a vegetarian. He never sleeps. He's got terrific, keen hearing, and since hearing a bird counts just as much as seeing one, that's a grand asset. He eats a cracker and keeps going. He stays out on a bird-count day until 11 P.M. and he's critical of people who aren't out at midnight at the start, so they can spot, say, a sanderling in the moonlight on the beach, or catch the calls of a migrant bird overhead. One of his most extraordinary feats was to lead a party that spotted 229 species in a single day in Texas, a new national record.

"Now his partner is Roland Wauer. He has the great gift of being able to pick up birds through his binoculars rather than scanning with his eyes. You can imagine what an advantage that is, being able to scan for birds through the binoculars. He'll look down a ravine with his glasses and he'll say, 'Oh, wow, there ought to be a gray vireo in here somewhere,' and he'll *find* it. That's quite a team, those two."

At lunch, which we were having in a restaurant near the beach (not as much roughing-it as I expected), a balding gentleman assigned to count on the beaches came rushing up behind Victor Emanuel, who was bending over a cup of soup at the counter, and cried out: "Oregon junco!"

Emanuel started at the sharp explosion of sound behind him. Then, when he had spun around on his stool, he seemed skeptical.

"But it had pinkish sides," the gentleman said proudly. "It didn't look at *all* like the slate-colored junco. There were a lot of *those* around, maybe 50 or 60, but this fellow was a single junco playing around in the ruts of the road just off the beach."

Emanuel said, "Sometimes the slate-coloreds have pinkish sides."

"Oh," said the balding man. He looked crestfallen.

"No harm in reporting it at the tabulation dinner tonight. The jury will decide."

"I'll think about it," said the man. "I wouldn't want to be taken for a fool."

Emanuel has just given me a lesson on how to tell the difference between Sprague's pipit and the water pipit. Both have the habit of rising vertically out of the gorselike shrubbery of the hummocky country hereabouts, fluttering quite high, as if to look to the horizon to see if anything's of interest, then dropping back quite abruptly to the place where they started from. It's the method of descent that is different. The Sprague's closes its wings at the apogee of its climb and falls like a stone until it is just above the ground, where it brakes abruptly and banks into a bush. The water pipit, on the other hand, drops from the top of its flight in bouncy stages, like a ball tumbling down steep stairs.

"That's a great thing to know," I said. "I'm not sure it's a piece of knowledge I can do very much with. I mean it's not a distinction of daily usage."

Just then, a pipit sprang up in front of us, fluttering up and then dropped sharply back to earth.

"Sprague's," I said.

"Absolutely brilliant," said Emanuel. "You see, you never know."

Emanuel had to take an hour out of birdwatching to be honored at a chamber of commerce meeting. A punch was served and chocolate-chip cookies. A number of birders were there, looking uncomfortable, minds on their lists and anxious to move on.

An official of the chamber rapped for silence. He had an American flag on his lapel. He said in a clear, sincere, municipal voice that the community was proud to have the great Freeport bird count in its area. Texas was number *one*, as everyone was aware, but the nearest municipality, Houston, had been letting everybody down with the Houston Oilers, and the Houston Astros, and the Houston Rockets, who were not displaying the Texas winning spirit worth a damn. It was refreshing to know that at least the bird-count team was number one. He called out, "We've got to be number one in something!"

He looked (rather desperately, I thought) at Emanuel, who nodded vaguely and said they had a very good chance to be.

"Well, go and *bust* them," the official said, with a gesture that slopped some of the fruit punch out of his glass. "What we might do," he went on, "is put some sort of statue around here to show that this area is number one in birds. A big, tall stone, or maybe a *brass* bird." The muscles of his face subsided in reflection. The buzz of conversation rose around the room.

With the official greeting over, a number of the townspeople came up to offer suggestions. I heard one person saying to a member of the count team, "I just promise you—there was a falcon, a big tall falcon, sitting on a branch behind the bank. Sure'n shootin' you rush over and he's there to be spotted. Big tall fellah." The birdwatchers listened politely. Emanuel nudged me and said that it was often worthwhile. The Freeport count, he said, had always relied on the "hummingbird lady," who had a feeding station to which three kinds of hummingbirds had come the previous year. She didn't know enough to distinguish one from another, but the birds came to her, and they'd had a count team in her garden which came back with the ruby-throated, the buff-bellied, and the rufous. Of course, that had been a warm Christmas. Still, a team was assigned the "hummingbird lady," and they'd be making their report at the tabulation dinner.

A somewhat brassy female reporter came up to David Marrack, a British-born birdwatcher, and asked: "I am hearing that the warblers—is that the right word—are off. Is that bad news for you bird-hunters . . . I mean *watchers?*"

Marrack replied: "The cold has destroyed the insects. *Quod*—no warblers."

"I beg your pardon."

He inspected her. "It's too bloody *cold,*" he announced clearly.

We are running through cottonwood thickets looking for Harris' sparrow—the biggest of the sparrows, which summers in the subarctic forests (Emanuel tells me) and winters in the central plains, west to north Texas. With the cold weather, a specimen should be in the vicinity, most likely in amongst the white-crowned sparrows. Every once in a while in our search we step around the whitened bones of a cow skeleton—drowned, I suppose, by the flooding of the creek that flows by just beyond the trees.

In midafternoon Emanuel spots a bird in the top of a tree. He begins swaying back and forth in his excitement. "Oh my." Without taking his eyes from his binoculars, he motions me forward.

"A Harris' sparrow?" I ask.

"It's better," he whispers. "Much better. It's a rose-breasted grosbeak. No one else will get this. Oh terrific. It's only been seen once before on the count." We stared at the bird. I could see the wash of pink at its throat. When it flew, the sun made it blaze, and then, oddly, a barn owl floated out of the trees behind it.

An hour later. What has happened has eclipsed the excitement of the rose-breasted grosbeak. The two of us had not been seeing much, winding down after the long day, and I was trailing along behind Emanuel, idly speculating about what sort of a bird he most closely resembled. It is not an uncommon speculation. William Faulkner once said he would like to be a buzzard because nothing hates him or envies him or wants him and he could eat anything. I myself have always opted for hadedah ibis, a large African wading bird that springs into the air when flushed from a riverbed with a haunting loud bellow, which gives it its name, and defecates wildly into the water below. It is not so much the latter habit that I envy as the *habitat* of the bird, to be able to perch on the smooth bark of the acacia and overlook the swift water of the river and see what comes down to it, that great variety of life, and what happens.

I had no intention of pressing Emanuel on such a fancy, but my own speculation, watching him peer this way and that through the shrubbery, furtive and yet sleek, is that he might pass . . . well, as a brown thrasher.

Just then, he froze in front of me, staring at a spot twenty or thirty feet in front of him. His bird glasses came up. "Oh my," I heard him whisper. "Wait until I tell Ben."

"Is it Harris' sparrow?" I asked.

"My God, no, look . . . It's the magnolia warbler. Oh, Ben is going to die, absolutely die! Don't you see? It's a first for the count." He was almost breathless with excitement.

I spotted the warbler through my glasses. Beside me Emanuel kept up a running whispering commentary. "My first thought was that it was a myrtle warbler. Then I saw yellow underneath, and I knew we had something good. White eye-ring, very delicate yellow pip over the beak. No doubt. Oh, wow! It will *kill* Ben. Green back. Two wing bars, one short, one long. White in tail. Very prominent. Very beautiful."

He took out a pad of paper and began writing down a description of the warbler, which was now fluttering about in a bush in front of us.

"He's feeding well. The magnolia is very common in migration, but it's never lingered like this. It's such a joy to find a warbler in winter."

Just then the bird flew. "Ah!" cried Emanuel happily. "The white flash in the tail. That's the absolute clincher." He turned, his eyes shining with excitement.

"Oh, yes," I said. I struggled for something else to say. "That's the damnedest thing I ever saw," I said.

Wow! This was all beginning to go to *my* head. The sun was starting to go down. I found that I had been absolutely exhausted by Emanuel's enthusiasm.

The tabulation dinner was held at a roadside cafe called Jack's Restaurant in the town of Angleton, which is about halfway between Freeport and Houston. Almost all of the bird-count teams (55 people altogether) were there. We sat at long tables arranged in rows along three sides of a brightly lighted banquet room with red-and-green Christmas crepe pinned up between the light fixtures. The place was taut with expectation. Some of the birders gossiped about what they had seen; others affected a smug air of superiority and mystery, containing themselves until the tabulation. I overheard Emanuel saying to Ben Feltner, "I got a bird's never been on the Freeport list."

"You're kidding," said Ben.

Emanuel grinned enormously. "You'll jump out of your seat."

"What is it?"

33

"I won't tell you. It's a warbler."

Ben stared at him. "Come on."

"You'll have to wait," Emanuel said.

After the dinner Emanuel began the proceedings with a short speech. He announced that the panel that would rule on questionable sightings would consist of himself, Ben Feltner, and Jim Tucker. He said that it was important to maintain the integrity of the Freeport count, and that the panel would strive for a high degree of accuracy. It was important that the judgments be made right away, that very evening, so that those birdwatchers who had accidentals or rare sightings to offer should be prepared to substantiate them. He hoped no one would be *defensive* about his birds; it was a necessary procedure.

Emanuel's master list was divided into three categories—the regular species (birds seen on practically every Freeport count); the essential species (birds seen on most counts but which were present in low numbers and required hard work to locate, and are the keys to a successful high count); and finally the bonus birds, which are rare and not to be expected at all.

Emanuel rattled his list, looked down at it, and began—calling out the name of a bird and looking around the room for someone to raise a hand in acknowledgment that the bird had been seen. Some of the acknowledgments produced cries of delight—and often the team responsible, sitting together at the table, slapped each other's hands like the delighted gestures of ballplayers running back to the bench after a touchdown.

Sometimes, though, a missed bird, especially if it was an "essential" species, brought cries of woe.

"Horned grebe?" Emanuel looked around. No hands were up. Dismay.

"Ross' goose? Black duck? Goldeneye?" Gloom.

But then Dennis Shepler heightened spirits considerably by putting his hand up for the cinnamon teal. "Three males, two females," he said. Shouts of approbation.

"Bald eagle?"

A hand went up. Pandemonium! The birder described it as a single adult, soaring over the lake. Emanuel cried out, "Wonderful, marvelous." Spirits were lifted; some good-natured badinage began—the eagle team being joshed for sighting "a crated bird." "They brought it with them!" someone shouted happily.

The tabulation went on. No hummingbirds had been seen at the "hummingbird lady's" feeder. Horrified cries. Emanuel shook his head. He paused before going on, as if someone would surely recollect that small buzz of color and announce it. He waited, then disconsolately went on. A caracara had been seen. Abruptly the mood shifted again. Shouts of delight. One of the team responsible said they had watched the caracara catch a shrike and eat it. More shouts of glee. I wondered moodily if the shrike would be remembered in the count.

"Peregrine falcon?" Two had been seen, but no pigeon hawks were acknowledged. Groans. The marsh-buggy team got a solid round of hand-clapping for having flushed up a yellow rail.

The climax of emotion came with the approach of the count to the plateau of 200. When a few hands went up for the parula warbler, the 200th bird identified, the entire room rose amidst a storm of clapping and cheering.

At 203 the master list was done, and it was time for the birdwatchers to stand up and offer bonus species. The room quieted down. The 204th species was a pyrrhuloxia, a bird I had never even heard of. The birder, who was an expert from New Jersey, stood and described the specimen in a soft and very difficult stutter, everyone at the tables leaning forward in sympathy with his effort to get his description out. He talked about the bird's yellow bill and its loose crest and how he'd seen it in the salt cedars. One heavily bearded birder astounded everyone by announcing *four* bonus birds—my old pal the Henslow's sparrow, a fish crow, an eastern wood pewee, and the Philadelphia vireo. Each was described; he said he had flushed the sparrow out of dry grass. He didn't mention the hiccoughing song. A Swainson's hawk was 209. Then Emanuel himself rose and announced his two prizes, the rose-breasted grosbeak and the magnolia warbler, grinning in triumph at Ben Feltner as he described the latter. Feltner's eyebrows went up. He pulled at his beard. It was difficult to tell how he was taking it. Emanuel said that I had been along with him and was there for verification; I gave a slight nod at Feltner and looked very arch. There was a tumult of applause when Emanuel sat down.

The 215th, and last, bird offered was a Harlan's hawk. The birdwatcher was quizzed quite sharply by the panel. The hawk was in the light phase, he said, and the sun shone through the tail, which was completely pale except for a black marking toward the end. No, he hadn't seen the back of the bird. It was paler than a red-tailed. The panel looked skeptical; Emanuel tapped a spoon against his front teeth.

Emanuel's panel then disappeared to discuss not only the bonus birds but questionable sightings from the master list. They came back and Emanuel announced that seven birds had not been allowed. He did not say which seven —that might have embarrassed some people who may simply have been over-zealous.

The balding man from the beach had his Oregon junco accepted. I grinned at him, and he came over. "Good news, eh?" he said. "Well, *I* was confident. I know the Oregon junco very well; I've trapped them, and banded them, and maybe the jury took that into consideration. There're not many people around who know the Oregon junco like I do, *nosir!*"

Afterwards Emanuel told me the sort of process the panel had gone through. "Well, we knocked out the olivaceous cormorant from the master list; we'll have to assume it was a double-crested. The spotter didn't mention the white border along the pouch, which is an essential field mark, and besides, it's very difficult to distinguish the olivaceous unless you get a size comparison with the double-crested. So we let it go. We dropped the gray-cheeked thrush because the observer who saw it hasn't had that much experience and his description wasn't right. It's *not* uniform brown with a grayish tail. And it's extremely rare in winter. We also dropped the yellow-throated vireo because the observer didn't emphasize the vireo's slower and skulkier movements. He probably saw a pine warbler. Then from the bonus birds we voted out the Philadelphia vireo, and also the sighting of the wood pewee because it's easily confused with the eastern phoebe. As for that fish crow, well, heavens, his voice is unmistakable, that nasal *cah*, and that essential was never mentioned. The Harlan's hawk just didn't sound right either; it could have been a red-tailed."

He went through the list, ticking off the disallowed birds with obvious sorrow. Some of the votes of the panel had not been unanimous, and every rejection lowered the chances of winning the bird-count championship. "Let's see," he said. "That's 208 birds. I'm scared," he said. "We'll have to keep our fingers crossed."

A few days later, Emanuel called me in New York to tell me how Freeport had fared in competition with other high-count areas. He recapitulated that the areas that bothered him competitively were the three major California counts. To his delight he had found that the cold weather had hurt these California counts as much as it had Freeport's and that San Diego and Santa Barbara were tied with only 195 species.

That left Cocoa Beach, Florida, to be worried about. Two years before, Cocoa Beach had beaten out Freeport by just one species, 205 to 204. Emanuel decided he was going to wait until after the count period ended (January 1st) before calling Allan Cruickshank, his counterpart, to find out what their total was. In the meantime he was going off to Mexico to take his mind off the competition by doing some birding down there. His special loves are hawks, and there are two hawks in Mexico he would just about fall down and die to see—the orange-breasted falcon, which hangs around ruins (he told me), and the black-collared or chestnut hawk.

In mid-January he wrote me a letter in which he said that the Mexico trip had been an astounding success. He had not seen his two hawks, but his letter was lively with accounts of sightings of flocks of military macaws, "a veritable din of squawking as a magnificent flock came pouring over the side of the mountain."

He wrote that on his return he had gone back down to Freeport on December 31st with a friend from Tennessee "to show him some birds." While there he decided to drop in on the "hummingbird lady" to find out what had happened on count day. She was sitting with her mother in the parlor watching the Dallas Cowboys on television. "Well," she said, "*certainly* two kinds of hummingbirds had turned up that day." Emanuel's eyes widened. The hummingbirds came to the feeder every morning at 8:00 A.M. ("You could almost set your clock by them"), and that day was no exception. She had seen them a number of times. The trouble was that the ladies from the count team hadn't arrived until midafternoon, when the birds had left the feeder for the last time. Emanuel gave a whoop at this, making the mother, who was idly watching the Cowboys standing around during a timeout, start in her seat, and he forthwith boosted the Freeport count to 209.

It turned out to be a fortuitous visit—since a January 7th call to Cruickshank produced the information that the Cocoa Beach count was also 209. Thus the two leading bird-count areas in the country were matched in an unprecedented tie.

I wrote Emanuel a short letter of congratulations. I told him that I was proud to have been on a championship team, even if their triumph had to be shared. I didn't tell him that I myself had had a birdwatcher's triumph of sorts recently. I had found myself seated next to a lady at dinner who had begun talking about birds quite without my prompting (the dining room had framed Audubon prints on the wall, perhaps that was why), and she said that the trouble with people who enjoyed birdwatching was that so many of them were unbearably *pretentious*. "Now take those disgusting people who take so much stock in that ritual of the Christmas Bird Count . . ."

"What a coincidence," I said. "I was on the Freeport count."

She was very arch.

"Oh?"

Something stirred in my memory. "I'll bet you can't *guess* what we turned up," I said. "Perched on a weed, its head thrown back, and uttering the feeblest of hiccoughing noises, a sort of *tsi-lick*. Are those enough hints for you?" She looked at me with a gaze of distaste. "Flattish head, as I recall," I went on, "with a tail that twists in flight. Why that's *Henslow's sparrow*," I said quickly, in case she knew enough to interrupt me.

I hitched my chair forward. "How are you on pipits?" I asked. "Would you care to hear a rather nice field characteristic that'll straighten them out for you. Let's start with Sprague's," I said in a strong voice that turned heads at the table . . .

Quite at the other end of the Audubon Christmas Bird Count scale are those reports from locales with limited birdwatching possibilities. I thought it would be interesting to compare the plethora of Freeport with the miniscule counts from such places as Nome, Alaska, for example, where in 1970 eight people went out from 9:00 A.M. to 2:30 P.M. in a wind-chill factor of −40° and worked with as much zeal as the Freeport people to collect a total of three birds—the willow ptarmigan, common raven, and McKay's bunting. The bunting caused considerable excitement. Apparently, the only other bird the Nome contingent had a good chance of seeing was the common eider. I decided, however, that going to a place where the most species one could hope to find was *four* was perhaps overextending the notion of comparing bird counts, and I opted instead for a less insidious contrast—the pelagic trip aboard the ferry *Bluenose* which plies the 95 miles of the Bay of Fundy between Bar Harbor, Maine, and Yarmouth, Nova Scotia.

My host was Edward Thompson, who met me at the Bangor airport. He turned out to be a chemical engineer, a specialist in the physical properties of polymers, which (as I understood his explanation as he drove homeward) have something to do with molecules. He had the car heat on, but I found myself rubbing my mittened hands to keep them warm. The snow squeaked under the tires. The temperature was 9°, Thompson told me, but that was like being in a furnace room compared to what it was going to be like on the *Bluenose* the next day. The wind-chill factor would be many degrees below zero since it was the custom for the bird-count team to stand in the open of the *Bluenose* bow—no self-coddling behavior such as trying to spot birds through the big plate glass windows of the passengers' lounge.

"Oh," I said.

"We had a fellow come out one year who had a battery-heated suit," Thompson said. "It had a huge battery on the belt. He was very uneasy about it. He thought if he got any spray on him he was going to short-circuit. It was rough, with the spray coming over the bow, and he spent a lot of the voyage in the lounge, with the passengers looking at him curiously."

"I can imagine," I said.

We reached the Thompson home, and he introduced me to his wife, Deborah. She was an art historian and archeologist foremost, with birds somewhat far down the list, I assumed from the slightly bemused look that appeared on her face when I announced how much I was looking forward to the boat trip the next day.

Apparently the past week had been frantic with the bird count going on. The big competition between the Deer Isle group and the Mount Desert birders had been won by Mount Desert this year—much to Ed Thompson's dismay (he closed his fist and smacked it against his knee), though of course Mount Desert had a much bigger land mass and more feeders. They could be expected to win. Last year (Thompson recalled with relish) their feeders had let them down, and six species they should have nailed down had never showed up.

"Does a dead bird count?" I asked. "I mean if you ran over a bird with your car . . . ?"

"I think most Christmas-count birders would rush to give it mouth-to-mouth resuscitation," his wife said. "If it budged at all, it'd go on the list." Her attitude was unclear to me.

The telephone rang. Thompson answered it and his face fell slightly, and then brightened. "Goodness!" he said.

He hung up and rejoined us. "Well, the bad news is that the weather is probably going to be good." He saw the relief (my sea legs are questionable) and then the surprise register on my face. "You're more likely to see pelagic birds in stormy weather," he explained. "The wind picks them up off the water. Now the good news is this: a woman in Ellsworth who lives next door to the library has been noticing a bird at her feeder for the last four days which looked like a small robin. After three days of burrowing around in her Peterson guide she finally got up enough nerve to get an authoritative bird-watcher over and, sure enough, what she had there was a varied thrush."

I tried to make an appropriate expression of surprise.

"Oh-ho," I said.

"Yes," Thompson said, "its range is strictly western . . . really quite an accidental. We ought to be able to get it on the Ellsworth bird-count list."

His wife began laying out the dinner plates—five places. "We're expecting a couple from California," she said.

"We don't know them," Thompson said. "He's a doctor. It's their first trip to the East. Apparently he's working on his life-list. He asked if he and his wife could join us for the *Bluenose* trip."

His wife made a face and said she didn't really approve of this sort of life-list birder devoted solely to the numbers. "I'm very skeptical," she said.

Her husband argued that it was too early to make any judgments about their visitors. "We know so little about them," he said. "They sent us a Christmas card. That's the only evidence so far."

He went and fetched it from the mantelpiece. It showed the doctor and his wife birding on the Galápagos Islands. In the foreground was a somewhat startled-looking blue-footed booby sitting on what passes for its nest, while in the background were the couple. It was difficult to tell much about them. The doctor was almost hidden by a large tropical hat, and both he and his wife, who was wearing dark glasses, were slightly out of focus. The booby was *very* much in focus. The card read, "Greetings. Blue-footed Boobies, Hood Island, June 1972."

Thompson's wife said, "Of course, the really intense birdwatchers don't send Christmas cards. They're too busy watching birds—they'd be out in the field somewhere."

"Have you ever seen a blue-footed booby?" I asked.

The Thompsons looked at each other fondly. "We saw the blue-footed booby on, of all places, a recreation lake in Pasadena, California," Thompson said. "The word had whizzed around that there was a booby out there—and we rented a little boat that had foot paddles and we pumped way out to see it."

I asked Thompson what his rarest sighting had been in his own area. He said it was a yellow-nosed albatross he had seen from the *Bluenose* in June 1967.

"Oh, my. The albatross was in flight and cut diagonally across the bow of the ship . . . an absolutely spectacular sight," he said. "I had the bird in view for a good half-minute, by far and away my best sighting. *Really* accidental, with no tropical storm to blow it up from the south, nothing to suggest *why* the bird was there. Quite extraordinary. I submitted the record to *Audubon Field Notes*, but the editor for the region was unknown to me, and I to him, and my report was never published. I didn't take it particularly personally. I'd had the good fortune to make the sighting, and that in itself was enough."

Just then the doctor and his wife arrived by taxi—stepping into the vestibule and stomping their feet and whistling their relief to be in from the cold.

"Ouch," said the doctor. He rose up and down swiftly on his toes. He was a small, lively man. Dinner was ready, and almost as soon as he drew up his chair under him the doctor began talking about his life-list. It totaled 553 birds at the moment, which wasn't much compared to some of the people who had been at it for years, but he and his wife had just come up from the Southeast, which had been a great success. "We just *wiped out* Florida!" he exclaimed.

I asked how many birds one could possibly find in the continental United States, what the ultimate number on a life-list might be.

It was hard to pinpoint (I was told), because obviously "accidentals" and introduced species made the top figure fluctuate, but it would be in the neighborhood of 780. Joe Taylor from Rochester, New York, was the top man in the country at the moment, in fact the only 700 man there was.

The doctor leaned back and sighed with admiration. "Think of that," he whispered. "To reach that 700 plateau. Goodness! Of course, once you get over 675, people call in with sightings and you've got to have the wherewithal and the ability to rush off and *get* there—wherever it is." His voice squeaked with excitement. Perched on the edge of his chair, he seemed poised for flight himself. "Think of those phone calls coming in! 'Mr. Taylor, we think we have . . .' Oh, my! He must have a suitcase packed and ready right by his front door."

"Are you allowed to count introduced birds on your list?" I asked.

"Why," the doctor said in some heat, "if you disallowed introduced species, a birdwatcher would be hard-pressed to get over 600 different species on his life-list—pheasant, English sparrow, monk parakeet, the list is simply *huge!* And it gets bigger every year. People throw a caged bird or two in the air to see what happens . . . and if you throw enough of the same species, they're going to get together and breed. The canary-winged parakeet is doing well, so is the red-whiskered bulbul, *really* well; the blue-gray tanager . . ."

Thompson said that he had seen a toucan being chased down a Miami street by a blue jay.

"Of course," said the doctor. "On Vancouver there're crested mynas and skylarks, and they've been around for seventy years. The European tree sparrow has been breeding around St. Louis for a century. Everyone counts it on their list. We went down to Delray in Florida and saw two hill mynas. There's a woman down there who practically makes a career of showing off these mynas —people come from all over the country and knock on her door. She takes 'em out back somewhere and guarantees a sighting, but the fact is that the mynas are breeding and spreading so fast that I suspect they'll put her out of business. I've been told there are 1,500 of them in the area . . . certainly a countable bird."

The doctor looked at Thompson. "What about the lesser black-backed gull?" he asked abruptly. "Do I have a chance of seeing him tomorrow?"

"Terribly rare," Thompson said. "More of a possibility in Nova Scotia than here. Really rare. I've only seen one." He put his fingertips together. "Other than the pelagic birds you'll see tomorrow, there are a number of others you'll want for your list. You'll go to Newburyport for your snowy owl. You'll want an Ipswich sparrow. Plum Island for him. It's a good place, though of course there're others."

"Well, it's like sex," the doctor said brightly. "You take it where you can get it."

"Yes," said Thompson vaguely.

"What about other owls," the doctor's wife asked. "Do you have anything else in owls? A hawk owl?"

"There've been two spottings of hawk owls in the last eight years," Thompson said. "A terrible cold would have to drive them down from the Arctic. In Quebec and Montreal, sightings are routine. But in New England, no . . . not at all."

"Boreal owl?"

"Gee, darling, you know better than that!" the doctor exclaimed. "No, no, no."

"Well, in fact," Thompson said sympathetically, "there are breeding records from back in 18-something-or-other of a pair of boreal owls up north somewhere. Let me see. How about the great gray? We can offer you the great gray owl."

"No, we wouldn't go out of our way for that. We have him," the doctor said. "We got him on the town dump at Fort Klamath, Oregon. We photographed him, and we baited him with black mice so we'd get nice contrast in the picture. We got the black mice from a friend of mine who's a biologist."

The doctor began talking about the purity of the life-list and how indispensable one's own integrity was to keeping a good list. "I've begun to sanitize my own life-list," he said. "It has been *agonizing*. I removed both the Hammond's and the dusky flycatchers. It was almost like losing two patients," he said. "But I just wasn't sure."

"Well, I've got them on *my* list," his wife said stoutly.

"That's totally inexcusable, since we both saw them, or what we *thought* was them, at the same time," the doctor said.

"Well, you've got the red-billed pigeon on *your* list," his wife replied quickly.

"It's not unreasonable," the doctor said. "It's not a *perfect* red-billed pigeon—in fact I took it off for a while—but then I listened to it again and put it back on."

I asked, "You found it again? The red-billed pigeon?"

The doctor looked startled. "No, no," he said. "I listened to it on my tape recorder—I have a Norelco with me *always*—and I had enough sounds on there to make me feel quite comfortable about keeping it on my list."

"Where'd you see the red-billed pigeon?" asked Thompson.

"In Texas. Early in May. No white in the corner of the tail, which is very short. I was *quite* sure."

"They like tall old trees," Thompson pointed out, "the heights, not low down."

The doctor shook his head, "No, that's not true. The red-billed flies low, and keeps low."

Ed Thompson went on as if he had not heard ("You get quite a few sightings when the Rio Grande floods"), but it was obvious a gauntlet had been thrown down. The two of them got into a heated dispute about the difference between whistling and trumpeter swans. The doctor said it was very difficult. Thompson was quite scornful, citing the trumpeter's size. "But he's *massive* in comparison."

Then they got going on buntings. "You can find all four kinds in Norman, Oklahoma," the doctor said. "They've got the lesser prairie chicken there."

"No, no, no." Thompson jumped in. "Much more in *western* Oklahoma."

"Well . . ." said the doctor, shaking his head, and I could see that he was mustering his arguments.

I decided that was just a fine time to leave them—the issue of the locale of the lesser prairie chicken having been joined—and I excused myself and sneaked up to bed. I'm not even sure they were aware of my departure.

Here are my notes for the next day. I wrote them at some length in the relative warmth of the lounge of the *Bluenose*, retreating there from the bow, where the six birdwatchers—to whom I would occasionally murmur, "Well, I really must go and write something down about this. Excuse me."—peered out through their wool masks at the empty surface of the gray sea. And buffeted by the winds I would skitter across the steel deck by the big winches to the inside companionway with its set of double doors to the lounge. After a while, when my hands began to recover from the cold, and the fingers could work, I wrote in the notebooks . . .

———————— ◆ ————————

The *Bluenose* is passing Egg Rock on the way to open water. I am dressed in thermal underwear, three sweaters, a suit coat, an Arctic sheepskin overcoat, and a red ski hat with tassel, but no face mask, which is a mistake. Everyone else has one—the breath condensing in a circle of frost around the opening for the mouth. The doctor is wearing a jacket he designed especially for birding—a pocket for his tape recorder, another for a little camera, a side pocket for bird guides, notebooks, and pencils, and a pouch in back for "lunch." Certainly he doesn't want to miss a trick. During breakfast (which we had aboard the *Bluenose* at dockside) he took out the tape recorder and I heard him whisper into it: "We are having breakfast in the *Bluenose* saloon."

The sea is covered with sea mist, scudding before a 15-knot wind. The visibility is extremely poor. We are up in the bow of the *Bluenose*. The ship's foghorn goes off behind us every minute or so—making the group jump in unison. Ed Thompson says the fog may help us see birds since we won't flush them off the water until we're right on top of them. To this writing (9:30 A.M.) we have seen the common loon (a distinctive whippy motion of the wings hauls the bird off the water), common eider, black-legged kittiwake, black guillemots, oldsquaw, and common goldeneye—almost all viewed from a considerable distance, specks against the gray smoking swells.

The doctor leans into the wind like a figurehead. From time to time he speaks into his machine. He has two lifers so far to add to his list—the eider and the great black-backed gull. I heard him say into the recorder: "The black-backed gull—100 yards away settling into water—very large, feet pinkish . . ." He saw me looking at him, and he turned away, his voice lowering, as if he had a secret to impart to his machine.

The lounge of the *Bluenose* is depressing. The ocean is not rough, but many passengers are lying on their backs on the red plastic-covered benches, rolling slowly back and forth to the ship's motion. I have just been up to the bridge to see the captain and ask him his impressions of the Christmas Bird Count people. We can look down on them through the glass of the wheelhouse and see them huddled together—a forlorn group that continues to start slightly at the sudden rattling bellow of the foghorn above us. The captain, who was born in Newfoundland, said that he felt sorry for the birders sometimes, but that over the years he had become conditioned to their self-induced misery. "I've had as many as thirty of them up there in the bow—crouched up there in the wind—all the way over and all the way back. I don't get it, frankly. I can see hunting birds, but freezing yourself to death looking at them out here . . . well, I just don't know. The chief officer is our birdman, and he's been trying to explain it to me for years. I've only seen one birdwatcher who had any sense. He had these binoculars which had one of the sections converted into a whiskey flask. That's right. I could look down and see him. He'd have the glasses up to his eyes for a while, and then I'd see him unscrew one of his eyepieces, and then he'd look around, cageylike, to be sure no one was seeing, and he'd tilt his head back and take a big quick drink out of his binoculars, God's truth."

Bill Russell, one of our group, was saying into the teeth of that awful wind sweeping over the bow that there are two grand joys to pelagic birding: *First*, the oceans are linked, and the sighting of any seabird from wherever is thus possible. The only barrier is the figure-eight configuration of the Sargasso Sea—that dead birdless area, probably the only one of the seas devoid of winds, which birds enjoy and need. And then *second*, pelagic birders can see vast distances—none of this being cooped up in a thicket trying to focus on a warbler nine feet away. He swung his arms back and forth and peered into the mists.

My own feeling about viewing pelagic birds, at least in these frigid wastes, is less euphuistic. All of the Alcidae, which are the most interesting birds out here—the puffins, auks, guillemots, dovekies, et al.—fly low to the water; their flight is hurried and their mien somehow furtive, flying away from us in their fluttery flight as if harried by the enormous iron tonnage intruding on their domain. But Russell loves them. He spots one. "Alcids!" he shouts as he peers forward to distinguish its species.

The doctor has just seen his first puffin, but his viewing was obscured by the sea mists and not distinct enough for him to mark the puffin down on his life-list. He is very self-righteous about it. "Absolutely not," he says, "I didn't see it clearly enough. It has to be done right. It's like losing one's virginity. The circumstances must be right!"

A cry has gone up that a glaucous gull is trailing the ship, gliding above the wake, and our group has fled aft from the bow to see it, led by the doctor scampering down the lee companionway in front of us, his hand at the flap of his recording-machine pocket.

How odd it must seem from the bridge—this sudden flight of the birders from their huddled cluster in the bow . . . as if, peering into the mists, we had seen something awful up ahead, a collision imminent.

We saw the glaucous gull, and slowly, after we had our fill of him, we straggled back to the bow . . . victims of a false alarm, it must have seemed to the officers on the bridge of the *Bluenose,* with whatever had terrified us and sent us scampering aft now proved to be harmless, perhaps a phantasmagoria created by the swirling sea mists ahead.

I looked up. The officers' faces were impassive behind the glass.

The doctor now has five lifers. In addition to his common eider and the great black-backed gull, he has added three Alcids—the thick-billed murre, the black guillemot, and the dovekie. He continues to torture himself not only with his puffin sighting (he has not seen another) but with the question of what to do with his Iceland gull, which he'd seen just at the Yarmouth harbor entrance, ripping down the wind drafts, hanging briefly over the funnel of the *Bluenose* before disappearing astern. The problem was not identification but whether he could put the gull on a list restricted to the United States. "We're too near Nova Scotia," he said mournfully. "I don't think I can do it."

Ed Thompson was sympathetic. "Some authorities say that territorial waters extend to whatever distance the needs of the birder require."

43

"Oh dear, I don't know. I don't know," the doctor said. He began speaking into his machine.

We will be docking shortly at Yarmouth. My plan is to leave the birders (who have logged 23 species and will make the return trip to try to increase their count—poised once more in the bow of the *Bluenose*) and fly to Boston. I feel guilty not seeing the whole adventure through, though perhaps not unduly so: the cold has seized me cruelly—the shaking and shivering, and a strange fluted squeakiness of voice by now having become a chronic condition, unchanged even by the relative warmth of the ship's lounge. I stamp my feet. The passengers, now beginning to stir and look chirpy after their queasiness, look over curiously.

One of them came over and asked politely if I was staying in Yarmouth long.

"No," I said without thinking. "I'm flying right out—to Boston."

The passenger's jaw, which was working on gum, stopped moving. He was considering the odd paradox of someone taking a six-hour ocean voyage from the continental United States in order to take a plane flight directly back into it.

"I'm a birder," I said.

It did not help matters. His hand drifted up and toyed with the collar of his windbreaker.

I continued: "We've been looking at the durres and the mauks." I had been meaning to say murres and auks, but had I got it right it would not have soothed his ruffled state of mind. His eyes were glazed.

"I saw a dovekie," I said.

He cleared his throat, and I thought he was going to say something. He never got it out. I turned away. I knew he was staring at me. It's one of the conditions of birdwatching—to have one's back stared at.

BIRDS OF AN OLD FARM,
BY EDWIN WAY TEALE

Take a farm in New England that is returning to the wilds. Add a naturalist with an insatiable curiosity about the lives of the creatures who share his land. The result is an enduring chronicle of the ways of commonplace birds that the listers, to their loss, give scarcely a glance.

During the long days of spring at Trail Wood—as in *My Old Kentucky Home*—"the birds make music all the day." Before five o'clock in the morning, their dawn chorus begins. We awaken to the voices of wood thrush and veery, bluebird and robin, purple finch and catbird and scarlet tanager, yellowthroat and field sparrow, rose-breasted grosbeak and northern oriole. From the weed-tangles along the stone walls of the pastures comes the clear, carrying whistle of the bobwhite; from the brookside trees the *switch-you* song of the chestnut-sided warbler; from across the pond the hoarse, repeated call of the great crested flycatcher. Between 45 and 50 species of wild birds, almost every spring, nest within singing distance of the house. Twice barn swallows have constructed their mud nests and reared their broods on top of the projecting floodlight just outside the kitchen door.

At the end of his voyage to the New World, Christopher Columbus reported to King Ferdinand and Queen Isabella that, among the islands of the Caribbean, he had found himself surrounded by "birds of a thousand sorts." During these days of full birdsong in the spring, there are times, on this New England farm, when we experience a similar impression.

When we arrived at Trail Wood, one of our earliest ambitions was to record as many species of birds for our Hampton, Connecticut, farm as Gilbert White listed for his English parish of Selborne. In 1774, writing to Thomas Pennant, White reported the total for his Hampshire countryside was "more than 120 species." We began our list the day we arrived.

The first bird was a phoebe nesting in the garage, the second a red-shouldered hawk, the third a flicker, the fourth a towhee, the fifth a meadowlark. These early birds came fast: mourning dove, chimney swift, Cooper's hawk, barn swallow, catbird, woodcock, nighthawk. The 90th bird on the list was a pine siskin attracted by food scattered on the snow in January. The 100th passed high above us on May 11, 1961. Shaped like a cross, moving swiftly under a cloudy sky, this late migrant was a loon returning to some remote pond among the forests and mountains of the North. Only on this one occasion have we caught sight of this most ancient of North American birds winging its way across our sky at Trail Wood.

Beyond the hundred-mark, additions came more slowly. Number 101 was a Canada warbler, 102 a magnolia warbler, 105 a spotted sandpiper, 110 the first mallard duck to alight on our pond. A hermit thrush in the woods, a bank swallow flying overhead, an American bittern by the pond raised the total toward 120. It was on June 16th, in our second year at Trail Wood, that we added our 120th bird, a Nashville warbler that was singing in an elm tree below Juniper Hill.

Since then the count has crept upward to equal and surpass White's Selborne list. On October 28, 1964, bird number 128 took its place on the list, a pileated woodpecker seen near Whippoorwill Spring. Our list now stands at 144.

One of the last additions was a coot that arrived in the fall, fed with the mallards during more than a week of fine weather, and took off in the night ahead of an all-day storm. Another was a rare Harris' sparrow that had gone astray during its migration south. The third was the most surprising of all, the last bird we expected to see at the time we saw it. It was large, white, yellow-billed, a great egret stalking about beside our pond during a brief thaw in mid-January.

Among these many birds of many species, certain individuals, seen during odd or special moments in their lives stand out in memory. One was a brown thrasher on the wall under the hickory trees. When I first caught sight of it, it was stuffing food into the gaping mouth of a fledgling cowbird that had just left the nest where its egg had been deposited. I saw the thrasher arrive with a large angleworm, which it pushed into the young bird's mouth. Most of the worm hung down on either side of its bill. Unable to swallow it, it dropped it on the wall. The brown thrasher snatched it up and thrust it into the open mouth once more. The results were the same. Over and over, five, ten, fifteen times, the process was repeated. After the fifteenth time, the brown thrasher swallowed the worm itself.

A robin with a woolly bear provides another memory. The bird picked up the spine-clad caterpillar in the grass. For a full five minutes, before it swallowed it, we watched it pound the larva on the ground, turning it this way and that, breaking off the stiff hairs that covered its body. Then there was the forlorn little myrtle warbler that my wife Nellie discovered on a burdock plant one autumn afternoon. Somehow it had become entangled among the burs. How long it had been imprisoned there, with one wing held outstretched, we have no way of knowing. But in its fright, as Nellie reached out a hand to help it, it redoubled its struggles and tore itself free.

I also remember how one April morning when bluebirds were nesting in one of the weathered bird boxes near the brook, I saw a flicker, in the full flush of his springtime exuberance, swoop down, cling to the side of the nesting box and commence a trip-hammer tattoo with its bill on the wood. The hollow interior, like a hollow limb, reverberated with the sound. The loud, rolling signal of the woodpecker carried across the yard. But it lasted for only a few seconds. Out rushed the indignant bluebird and drove the flicker away.

Day after day and week after week, one year, a male song sparrow fought its reflection in the rear windows of our middle shed. Beyond the lilac bush, three sheds are linked together in a line. The first holds our car, the second our fireplace wood in winter, and the third, a former cowshed, forms a combined workshop and storage place. The windows at the rear face west onto the overgrown edge of the pasture. Apparently, in this particular year, a pair of song sparrows raised two broods in quick succession close to the buildings. Guarding his nesting territory against intruders, the male spotted his reflection in the windows of the middle shed, mistook it for an invading male, and flew to the attack. At times this bewitched bird shifted from one window to another, fighting as many as four imaginary enemies at one time.

I first noticed it on May 18th. It was whacking the glass with its bill with such force I heard the sound 100 feet away. I looked at the second hand of my wristwatch and counted the strokes. At their slowest they were coming at the rate of more than one a second; at their fastest the bird was raining 90 strokes a minute on its image on the glass. I wondered how long it would be before its bill wore away. I was still wondering that weeks later. For through the rest of May and all through the month of June and on through much of July the little bird continued to attack the panes of glass. As early as seven-thirty in the morning and as late as seven o'clock in the evening I would find it belaboring this phantom rival, its unvanquished enemy, its own reflection.

Never before or since have I encountered so pugnacious a sparrow. Throughout the day, it returned at intervals to the attack. On July 27th I saw it make its last onslaught. On that evening I heard it singing on the ridgepole of the shed. It seemed master of all it surveyed. For 71 days it had been engaged in its frantic, one-sided assault. How many times, during those days, had it struck its bill against the glass? Its shadowy enemy was illusory but the hard surface of the pane was not. When I calculated the average number of strokes at 50 a minute and the total time spent at the windows in the course of a day at two hours—both of which figures seem extremely low—I discovered that, during the ten weeks of its long enchantment, the song sparrow had battered its bill against the windowpanes in excess of 400,000 times.

All through the spring and summer, we leave one of the wide doors of the middle shed blocked open for the phoebes to come and go. Once when a brown thrasher flew inside the shed and blundered about from window to window, unable to find its way out again, I caught it in a butterfly net and released it outside. Barn swallows and robins, as well as phoebes, have nested in the middle shed. One June, when a robin nest was overflowing with young almost ready to fly, one of the nestlings prematurely launched itself out and fluttered down to a corner of the shed. I learned again, that morning, the mistake of trying to put a baby bird back in the nest under such circumstances. When I attempted it, all the rest of the brood exploded in different directions. No amount of putting them back in the nest would make the nestlings stay there. A link had been snapped. The urge to stay had been superseded by the urge to leave the nest. In trying to return the first bird, I had only increased the labor of the parents. Instead of feeding the brood together on the nest, they now had to feed the young birds separately on the floor.

Although we have encountered the dense, feathery cushions of Schreber's cedar moss only in one place at Trail Wood, it is this moss that appears every year, in the nests of our phoebes. This same primitive plant, I am told, is used in the nests of these birds along the coast of Maine. One spring, a pair of phoebes building a nest in the middle shed reduced the labor involved by taking a shortcut. Instead of gathering fresh material from the woods, they stripped the dry, last-year's Schreber's moss from a nest in the workshop shed next door. Curiously, one of the most unusual nests we have encountered in Hampton also has its link with this species of moss. A mile or so from us, one year, chickadees nested in an unused rural mailbox, coming and going through a narrow opening in the front. When the box was opened it was found to have the floor covered deeply with a soft wall-to-wall carpeting of green. This carpet was formed entirely of Schreber's moss.

Not only are many species of birds expert botanists at nesting time but they all, even individuals that never made a nest before, exhibit an inborn capacity for selecting the most suitable material from all the plant fibers, twigs, hairs, and grasses around them. We see orioles ripping long, tough strips from the dry stems of last year's milkweed plants and chipping sparrows hunting for hairs shed by animals. Sometimes the nests of these sparrows are made largely of fragrant sweet vernal grass. Occasionally one will be lined with the reddish hair of a deer, at other times with long hairs from a cow's tail found caught on barbed-wire fences. I have one unusual nest given to me by Bert Inman, who lives at the south end of Hampton. It is lined with the soft blond hair of his young daughter, Jane. When, on a warm day, her mother cut her hair under an apple tree in the yard, a chipping sparrow collected the discarded material as a windfall in completing the small cup of its nearby nest.

Along Veery Lane, on an April day, Nellie came upon a chickadee hopping this way and that over the ground. It was furtively gathering, as lining for its nest, small tufts of rabbit fur that lay scattered on the path. New materials, the innovations of technology, are increasingly finding their way into the nests of birds. Wood thrushes have made use of soda straws in place of twigs, and great crested flycatchers have employed strips of cellophane in place of snake skins. Several times, sheets of plastic material Nellie tied to bushes in the woods to mark special wildflowers have disappeared. We suspect the flycatchers. Not long ago, when I opened one of our nesting boxes, I discovered several narrow ribbons of aluminum foil among the dry grasses of a tree swallow's nest.

Perhaps they were used as a substitute for feathers. For, whenever possible, such swallows line the inner cups of their nests with white feathers, most often those of chickens. Along the coast, gull feathers are employed. Nellie and I, each spring, watch the birds toying with feathers in the air, dropping them while on the wing, swooping and catching them again in their bills. They never seem to tire of this sport as they work toward their nesting sites.

I am reminded of an amusing incident that occurred at the entrance of one of our bird boxes on a morning in May. Carrying a larger feather than usual, more than five inches long, a tree swallow flew toward the box. It held the feather crosswise in its bill. At the entrance hole, an inch and a half in diameter, it was brought up short. It circled, dropped the feather, caught it in a new position and tried again. Time after time we saw it approach the hole, but always it was blocked by the feather held crosswise. It never did overcome the difficulty and finally abandoned its feather. However, the tiny brain of the house wren has found the solution to the problem. We have watched these midgets come speeding in, clutching surprisingly long twigs in their slender bills. Without pausing but with a quick sidewise jerk of their heads, they turn the twigs lengthwise at the last instant and pass through the opening with ease.

Each morning during the nesting season we crush up the shells of our breakfast eggs and scatter the fragments on the driveway outside the kitchen door. Within minutes birds alight to feed on these particles rich in calcium carbonate. Usually the first to arrive are barn and tree swallows. I remember one barn swallow that came back nine times—no sooner taking wing than circling back to feed again—before its craving for eggshells was satisfied. Aside from the swallows, a surprising variety of other birds are drawn to the fragments. They include kingbirds, bluebirds, orioles, house sparrows, great crested flycatchers, blue jays, flickers, and goldfinches. Whenever we can tell the sexes apart, the visitors have always been females. Usually the last in the season to arrive are the goldfinches. It is normally well along in August before these late-nesting little finches begin to show an interest in our source of calcium carbonate.

Secretiveness is part of the nesting season for many of our birds. We notice now silent and furtive the blue jays become, how our chickadees and tufted titmice disappear entirely from around the house while they are raising their broods. Once, when a crow passed us carrying a stick to add to its nest, it saw that we were looking up. It realized it was observed. Immediately it dropped the stick and veered away in another direction. Similarly, toward evening during the first week of July, a red-eyed vireo, near my writing cabin among the juniper and aspen on the other side of the pond, sought in a transparent ruse to deceive me and conceal the fact it was carrying food to nestlings. When I caught sight of it—and it caught sight of me—it was carrying a small white butterfly to its nest. It abruptly changed its course, alighted on a twig, peered at me intently for some time. When I remained standing, watching it, the vireo swallowed the butterfly and then flew away, apparently convinced I had been misled.

This secretiveness extends to the careful elimination of all clues that might call attention to the presence of the nest, such as eggshells and the fecal sacs of the young. We see tree swallows dropping such sacs while flying over the pond and song sparrows transporting them to trees where they leave them attached to twigs. I recall one pair of chipping sparrows that nested on the lowest branch of an apple tree. The parent birds carried away the sacs in quick, furtive flight. They always left them in the same place, deposited on the top strand of a barbed-wire fence.

I believe the most secretive bird I have ever known at Trail Wood was a female bluebird that nested here in 1964. That was the year of our great Bluebird Summer, the year when, for a few months, hope revived for this tragically depleted species. To a friend, in the season when his father died, Henry David Thoreau wrote: "The bluebirds come again, as does the spring, but it does not find the same mortals to greet it. Perhaps there will be a time when the bluebirds themselves will not return any more." During recent decades, the loss of this favorite songbird, once so abundant in New England, this bird so soft of voice, so companionable, so ethereally blue in color, so gentle and appealing in its ways, has become more and more a possibility.

But during that nesting season of 1964, our Hampton bluebirds forged ahead. I know of more than twenty broods that were successfully hatched and reared that year in and close to the village. And at Trail Wood, a single pair produced an unprecedented three broods, one with five young, one with four, and one with two—a total of eleven new bluebirds that our farm added to the Hampton list. I have no doubt that part of this success resulted from the excessive secretiveness of this shyest of females. She was always on guard, al-way stealthy in her movements, slipping swiftly from the nesting box and disappearing, waiting until all was clear before returning again. The male bluebird would fly directly in with food for the young. But the female took no chances. Even when I was at a distance, if she saw I was looking in that direction, she would avoid the nest. She would perch on a twig, or on the top wire of a fence, holding food in her bill, waiting for me to go away. Only then would she make a quick visit to the place where her young were hidden.

The voices of certain birds seem to mark epochs of the year: the drawl of the pewee in hot summer woods, the clamor of Canada geese flying south in autumn, the bell-like trilling of the juncos on the snowfields of winter, the soft, melodious warble of bluebirds in the melting days of early spring. When we first hear that gentle sound, some of the hardness of winter softens within us. We are always surprised at how far it carries. Standing in the spring sunshine on the slope of Juniper Hill, beyond the pond, we often catch this strain, so simple, so rich, coming from the apple trees on the other side of the house.

Vastly different in quality, the voice of another bird clad in blue carries much farther, probably the farthest of any bird of its size we have. Loud, harsh, strident, it cuts through the air, a voice of authority. Countless creatures pay special attention when the blue jay screams a warning. In northern Maine, one summer day, I was observing with my field glasses six loons as they floated far out on a forest lake. A jay called loudly from the shore. On the instant, I saw the heads of all six loons turned in its direction. Beside our own pond at Trail Wood, Nellie and I were watching a muskrat swimming out from shore in the July dusk when a jay, passing above the water, uttered its screech of alarm. As though in synchronization, the muskrat plunged and disappeared. We have noticed how rabbits crouch down in the grass and gray squirrels sit up and look around when a blue jay calls. Its warnings, although frequently false alarms, are not ignored.

I think the most dramatic instance of the kind occurred early one spring when more than a hundred returning male redwings were filling the treetops along Hampton Brook with the tumult of their calling. The uproar was deafening. Yet when blue jays began to scream, the trees instantly fell silent. Not a redwing called. A minute or two passed before the excited chorus rose in volume once more.

One June day I awoke early, a little after four o'clock in the morning. As I lay listening to the indefatigable repetition of the phoebe's song outside the middle shed, I began to count the calls. Between four-thirty and five o'clock, the bird repeated its loud, emphatic *phoebe* 958 times—an average of one call every two seconds for 30 minutes. In emphasis, phrasing, rapidity of repetition, tonal quality, how varied are the voices of the Trail Wood birds!

We hear the spring song of the white-breasted nuthatch—a sort *whit-whit-whit* like calling up a dog; the goldfinches tuning up their little violins among the thistleheads; the tree sparrows tinkling like a chime of tiny icicles before a winter storm; the broad-winged hawks with their high, thin, whistled calls that bring to mind "piping the Admiral aboard." There is the *tink! tink!*—like tapping on metal—of young hairy woodpeckers just out of the nest; the incessant chittering sound of baby downy woodpeckers; and the low buzzing that suggests electric wires on a wet night that is the sound of small tree swallows on the nest.

In the eighteenth century, when he wrote *Rasselas*, Samuel Johnson commented on how birds endlessly repeat the same unvarying songs. These old, old songs—as freshly sung as though never sung before—are, in general, repeated year after year. But they are not, as Johnson supposed, unvaryingly the same. Modern electronic recording methods have revealed that, even more than the sharpest ears can detect, birdsong varies with conditions and individuals. More than a hundred variations of the familiar song sparrow's song have been recorded on tape. Included is the soft little autumn song of these sparrows that we begin to hear when September comes.

Perhaps the variations of individuals, both avian and human, account for the many different descriptions of the song of so common a bird as the robin. To John Muir it appeared to be saying: "Fear not! Fear not!" To many, at the end of a rainy day, it calls: "Clear up! Clear up!" An 80-year-old woman in Massachusetts once wrote to me that what the robin really says is: "Jonathan Gillett shine your skillet, shine it nice and clean." In the sunset of April days, it seems to Nellie, the robin sings: "Cheerio! Cherrio! Spring is here-eo!"

In our latitude, the birdsong of spring and the migration of fall meet in August. The scarlet tanagers are still singing in the woods when the bobolinks start for South America. Then the autumn tide sets in and the familiar companions of our summer days are swept away. Where are the towhees then? Who hears their bright *chewink?*

Rarely does anyone observe the exact moment of a songbird's departure on migration. Yet at Trail Wood we once witnessed just such a moment of drama. It came in the spring of 1962. All that winter we had been visited daily by a flock of more than 50 flashing black-and-yellow-and-white evening grosbeaks. All of them except two pairs left us for their northern breeding grounds early in May. These four birds stayed on and on, trilling in the apple trees, feeding on our sunflower seeds. They were still with us when the trees began to bloom—strikingly colored birds moving among the white clouds of the apple blossoms.

We were watching them on May 17th—the latest we have ever seen these birds—when, after feeding heavily, all four rose together from the tree. Usually they flew from tree to tree. This time they ascended higher and higher. Their flight seemed more definite and purposeful. They headed directly away into the southeast. We watched them as long as we could keep them in sight. They faded from view, and we saw them no more that season.

Living as we do among the birds, making our "field trips" by stepping outside the door, here at Trail Wood we feel a closer relationship with them. "The birds of the naturalist," John Burroughs wrote in his first book, "can never interest us like the thrush the farm-boy heard singing in the cedars at twilight as he drove the cows to pasture or like the swallow that flew gleefully in the air above him as he picked stones from the early May meadows." Something of this dawn freshness, this nearer companionship, is one of the finest features of having the birds of this old farm part of our daily lives.

THE APARTMENT, BY LOUISE DE KIRILINE LAWRENCE

For many species of birds, a tree becomes a coveted home site only when it is dying or dead. This is the story of one ancient aspen in a northern forest and its succession of tenants who, like their counterparts in man-made high-rises, are sometimes neighborly and other times quarrelsome.

What first attracted the pileated woodpeckers to the quaking aspen is not easy to say. Perhaps it was the tree's splendid sixty-foot height and its girth, where a man could measure it, of no less than fourteen inches. Or the small round hole on the trunk's northeast side, where a pair of yellow-bellied sapsuckers had nested a few years ago. Or the dry sticks that stood out naked against the sky above the aspen's still voluminous crown foliage. An aspen grows only so tall in so many years before reaching its prime. And then begins the decline—dry sticks at the top, rot starting at the core, and the wood becoming soft enough deep inside for a woodpecker to carve out its gourdlike cavity.

The male pileated woodpecker alighted forty-two feet up on the tree's exposed south side. He clung there for a while, then his measured peckings resounded loudly through the forest. His resplendent scarlet crest shook lightly with the effort of each mighty strike. And the sun played upon the great bird's shiny black featherdress with faint multicolored reflections.

Presently the woodpecker stopped pecking and gave a loud call: *cuk . . . cuk . . . cuk.* It sounded almost like a burst of big loud laughter. Far away from the west came an answering call. The male listened. He waited, sat, and waited. But before the caller was even in sight, off he dashed on mighty wingbeats, crest flat over the crown of his head, the neck with its white stripe stretched full-length.

The two birds met on a tall stub of another aspen long dead. The male drummed, at first slow big pecks, then faster like a drill, intense, sharp taps. The sound excited the female and she dashed off. Both vanished.

This engaging reciprocal play of drumming and dashing around, back and forth to the nest hole to peck there a bit, went on for several days. The birds' silver-lined black wings beat the air with a swishing sound; their claws, as they alighted *plunk* on a treetrunk, scraped and scratched upon the rough bark; and call answered call, loudly, emphatically.

But as the hole in the aspen became larger and a little deeper, gradually the birds' interest in it increased and, in like measure, their vehemence and excitement about each other abated. By the time the male slipped inside the hole for the first time and turned around, the two birds had reached a stage where they came and went, worked and relieved each other at the nest in a well-balanced rhythmic routine. Soon they had the cavity gouged out into its final shape, ready to receive the clutch of white eggs.

On a day in the beginning of May when the new light-green leaves of the aspen rustled for the first time in the soft spring breeze, the woodpecker pair settled down to their regular sessions of warming the eggs. All night the male slept on them and soon after the break of dawn the female flew in to relieve him for her longest session of the day, as if to make up for the time lost during the night. After that there was no haste or hurry in their alternate comings and goings, no noise, except the air swishing through their feathers as they flew in and out at the shifts.

And only on these occasions did excitement grip them briefly. The mate's loud call from a distance alerted the bird inside. By the time grasping claws scratched the bark of the trunk, it was on its feet with the shadow of its head playing faintly on the wall of the corridor between cavity and doorway. Quickly, once or twice, the arriving bird's head swept across the oval opening like the shutter of a camera. This was the signal. Out shot the bird inside, past its sidestepping mate. And by the time it was flapping its way to distant feeding grounds, the relieving bird had already popped inside and was covering the eggs as if no break had occurred.

In this benign season nothing untoward happened to prevent the success of the pileated woodpeckers' nesting. By the end of June the whole family was out and coursing the forest. Lest they miss the provisioned meal, the fledglings gave loud calls that echoed amongst the trees to inform the parents of their whereabouts. With soft notes and its gullet full of food, a parent approached to fill the gaping mouth of each impatient beggar about once every hour. In another week the whole family was off and away in search of other feeding grounds. And the quaking aspen stood alone with the large oval hole gaping on the south side of its trunk.

As winter approached the male pileated woodpecker returned, and on the aspen's west side about ten feet below the level of the south hole excavated a snug winter dormitory for himself. The waning light provided the cue for his goodnight ritual. From distant feeding areas he came flying soon after sundown—about ten to twenty minutes earlier on dull and very cold days—and slipped inside so quickly and unobtrusively that he was seldom seen.

Then in March, without any reference to his mate, the male pileated woodpecker decided on the site for the new nest hole. He tapped the first chisel mark of the doorway-to-be at a place about nine feet above and slightly more west of the first hole in the south side. And surprisingly, for it is not often so among woodpeckers, his initial decision proved to be irrevocable.

So far so good. But when the male attempted to transmit the important message to the female, her unwillingness—whatever was her motivation—to accept his decision almost wrecked his scheme. He resorted to every means of persuasion. He drummed at the site, spaced taps, alternating with strumming, short, fast taps. When in response to this signal the female arrived, he went into an elaborate tapping ritual at the edge of the would-be doorway, *tap . . . tap . . . tap,* his bill tapping stiffly under his breast, his scarlet crest erect, trembling, and his wings opened ever so slightly. The female promptly copied every move to the last detail.

But no, this was not the place *she* fancied for the nest! And off she flew, leaving him to tap and to strum and to bore his hole alone. For days he chased after the female. For days he drummed and he strummed. But still she would not listen.

Meanwhile, the male had the hollow well-started. Presently he was able to disappear inside to the tip of his spiked tail. And only then did the female begin to show sings of interest. She came, she looked, she watched, she answered his calls. And once she reached this stage, it did not take her long finally to accept the situation, to go in, and to start working upon the cavity herself.

The pileated woodpeckers were incubating their full clutch of eggs when a pair of sapsuckers, after a great deal of fuss and ceremony, decided to nest in a hole which the male had already started in the adjacent aspen. The dry, give-away top branches of this tree also advised of advanced core rot and, shortly after, a belated spring wind broke off the top and left it dangling down the side of the trunk. Soon, with red crest on end and red throat patch fluffed, the male sapsucker could be seen scattering billfuls of brownish chips upon the air with quick shakes of the head. A week or so later his female deposited her eggs, one a day, on a small collection of fragrant sawdust left on the bottom of the cavity.

About the same time, in the woods across the clearing by a small noisy creek, a pair of yellow-shafted flickers laid their eggs in a hole they had nested in the year before, near the top of a rotting birch stub. Five days they had been sitting on the eggs when a red squirrel discovered the doorway and smelled the eggs. Eagerly the squirrel tore at the rotten wood just at the place where the eggs lay inside the wall on the bottom of the cavity. But the wood held. Frustrated, he ran up to the doorway—where a mighty jab from the flicker's beak sent him sprawling to the ground.

For two days the flickers fought a brave fight for nest and eggs, but it was a losing battle. The red squirrel, never inclined to give up easily, by sheer chance hit upon the rare moment when both flickers were absent. He slipped in, naturally, and ate all the eggs but one that crashed to the ground.

In their search for a new place to nest the flickers came to the quaking aspen. They saw the doorway of the pileated woodpecker's winter dormitory. They inspected the cavity, found it suitable and in need of little fixing. To them this was important, because the season was already far advanced.

The sapsuckers at first met the intrusion of the flickers with hostility. By this time their young had hatched and this created a sensitive situation, for as the parents began bringing food and their movements gave the site of the nest away, the risk of its being detected by predators increased. And with that, naturally, the birds' nervous tension and their intolerance of intruders.

But the flickers were in a hurry and sought no quarrels. With the laying of the first egg they became secretive and avoided all brash behavior. Moreover, the sapsuckers operated on a lower level than the flickers. And with their respective doorways facing in opposite directions, occasions for clashes became practically nonexistent.

The maintenance of peace between the pileated woodpeckers on the third floor and the flickers never became a problem because of the slow rhythm observed by both pairs, a well-timed shuttle service at both nests that effectively kept the tenants out of each others' feathers. Nor did the loud chatter of the pileated youngsters at the top, transmitted to the flickers by treetrunk radio, disturb them. Only occasionally, when the adult pileated woodpeckers were absent, might a flicker be seen hopping up to the large oval doorway to look in.

By June 30th the two young ones in the pileated woodpeckers' nest were ready for their preemergence rites. The black-and-white stripes running along their undulating necks and their slim heads with their light gray bills wide open, calling or begging or just panting, gave them a distinctly reptile look. Each time a parent arrived to feed them and then departed, their excitement knew no bounds. Eagerly, roughly, they pushed each other from the coveted advance position at the edge of the doorway, often just missing a fall into space. But in spite of all near-misses the final tumbling-out did not take place until the cool of the next morning.

A few days afterward, the sapsuckers' nestlings fledged. With that the flickers had the premises to themselves and three weeks later, in the early morning of July 27th, they finally brought their second nesting attempt to a successful conclusion.

The following winter the male pileated woodpecker again took up nightly residence in the quaking aspen, this time in nest hole number one which he had excavated two years ago, while the female took over his westside sleeping hole where the flickers had nested.

In the spring, as early as March 12th, the male was already busy excavating a new hole facing southeast, twenty-five feet from the ground, his fourth in the quaking aspen. The weather was sunny and soft, and the snow, never very deep that winter, was fast disappearing, giving promise of an early spring.

Two weeks later a pair of starlings arrived and began casting covetous eyes on the holes in the aspen.

Starlings have an artful way of expropriating the cavities drilled by the native hole-dwellers, characterized by a kind of pseudotimid but tenacious obstructiveness. They arrive and they sit and they watch. No aggressive behavior, no contentiousness. These maneuvers first arouse in the rightful owners an uneasiness that gradually changes to irritation, then to fear mingled with anger, and these reactions increase in intensity as the season advances. But the starlings are not in any hurry. With admirable patience they wait for their chance. Gradually they become more daring. They inspect the cavity when nobody is looking, enter it and begin throwing out whatever is in it. The bird in the hole is almost invincible.

The pileated woodpeckers stood the strain of the passive menace for a while. But when two other starlings turned up to join the first pair, they abandoned the fourth hole and began excavating another in a tree thirty feet north of the aspen. To this tree the starlings also came to sit and look and wait. Enough of this! The woodpeckers quit and flew half a mile away to an old stub where they hurriedly began enlarging a hole once inhabited by a pair of hairy woodpeckers.

Had the fierce windstorm a week or so later not toppled this old stub, the pileated woodpeckers probably would never have returned to the aspen grove. But when once again homeless they arrived at the place, it seemed to be abandoned. The starling visitors had left, and the first pair—*hush, hush*—were sitting on newlaid eggs in the west hole, the flickers' ex-nest. The pileated woodpeckers' earlier-started hole in the aspen's sister tree gaped at them invitingly. Not there, but seven feet above it, they began boring another hole.

In this one the female eventually laid her eggs, and in due time the pair successfully fledged from it a family of three.

Meanwhile, the flickers returned from migration and so did the sapsuckers. The latter had little difficulty settling upon a nest site. Everything was there to attract them, familiar surroundings, their old hole from last year, and they bored their new hole just two feet above it.

But the flickers, having two previous home localities to choose from, one in the aspen and the other in the woods across the clearing, spent some time hesitating, flying from one place to the other—long enough, in fact, for the starlings to usurp their ex-hole in the aspen. That forced the decision upon the flickers and they nested in a tree across the clearing. But as in the previous year, this nesting also ended in disaster.

Now where would the flickers go? How strong is not the attraction of the tree once used! How enticing is not the familiar locality and the gaping hole beckoning!

All was quiet at the aspen when the flickers, hesitating several times, finally looked into the west hole. Except for some soiled nesting materials it was empty. The starlings were gone. But as if their occupation had attached to the hole some kind of miasma, the flickers would not go into it. Gingerly one of them hopped up to the pileated woodpeckers' empty hole at the top and looked in. But the flicker did not enter that one either. Then they discovered the hole the pileated woodpeckers had started on the southeast side of the trunk early in March. Forthwith they set about finishing it and there they laid their eggs.

About a week before the flickers had come to nest in the aspen again, a slender brown duck came flying surreptitiously and quickly from across the lake on rapid wings, neck outstretched and a little tuft of a reddish crest showing at the back of her head. It was a hooded merganser. For some reason of her own she abruptly altered course and sped in a circle out over the lake again, and then flew straight to the aspen. She rounded the stout broken-off branch by the pileated woodpeckers' first nest hole—and the hole literally swallowed her.

For four long weeks the little brown duck performed her rapid sorties and fly-ins directly and unhesitatingly to mark her infrequent recesses from incubating her collection of eggs at the bottom of the cavity. She appeared and she vanished like an arrow, and the hole forty-two feet up on the aspen's south side gaped seemingly empty. Who would see her? Who would know she was there? Not the flickers low down on the east side of the tree, absorbed as they were in their slow-rhythm attendance upon their eggs, and then upon their young ones.

On July 7th a wisp of dark downy feathers fluttered in the doorway of the duck's secret residence. And that was all, all that remained to tell of the ducklings' dramatic descent on spread but unpinioned wings and extended webbed feet into the thistles below. And two weeks later the flickers brought out another late brood from their second successful nesting in the grand old aspen.

Thus, aptly, by the simple means of cycles, rhythm, and timing, nature fits its jigsaw patterns of individual lives together into an interlocking harmonious whole. And the one life appropriately and unwittingly serves the other.

THE COMING OF THE IBIS, BY FRANKLIN RUSSELL

Tens of thousands of tourists pass through the Florida Everglades each year, gaping at alligators from fenced-in boardwalks and buying up tons of mass-produced curios. Few are aware, or would even care, that as they rush for their air-conditioned motels, one of nature's greatest spectacles is occurring far out in the mangrove maze bordering the Gulf of Mexico.

The boat turned toward the sunset, silhouetting clumsy pelicans perched in mangroves. The screams and wails of hungry young egrets and pelicans in nests that clung to the thick greenery punctured the soft air. There was something of the mood of a city in the middle of this southern Florida waterway. On all sides great birds hurried past us on their way home before the coming of darkness.

Joe Bird, the boatman, weathered as old barn siding, moved the craft west of the mangrove city, turned it diagonally, and cut the motor. "They'll be coming soon," he said, "and it will be a sight you'll not forget too easily."

We were waiting for the arrival of the white ibis, one of the most graceful and beautiful water birds in the Everglades. It is a slender, sailplane of a bird with broad, black-tipped wings, and its extraordinary beauty in the air is enhanced by its exquisitely curved and slender red beak, which looks as though it had been carved by a master artist, and by its long crimson legs, which trail far behind its short tail.

Like all the birds now before us in the mangroves, the ibis are survivors of the indiscriminate bird massacres of the late nineteenth and early twentieth centuries when American and European women proudly wore bird plumes, and when hundreds of thousands of ibis, and other water birds, went into cooking pots. They are survivors of bitter battles between men who wanted to kill them and other men who wanted to save them. Their preservation, and that of their fellow plume birds, sparked the formation of the National Audubon Society and was the motive for the murder of one of the first Audubon wardens to be stationed in Florida.

For me, the ibis has a special, almost mystical quality that is difficult to explain, but many others share the feeling. The Egyptians understood its power; they used its image to portray one of their gods. But even without the ibis, the scene before us was extraordinary enough—with pelicans and egrets feeding their young, the black bodies of cormorants skimming the water like dark arrows, and a lone vulture stumbling over mangrove roots as he filled his stomach with food dropped from the nests above.

It was an utterly primeval scene; the boat quiet, leaping mullet breaking the smooth, steel-blue water all around, an occasional fin showing, and the sun plunging behind us into a sky that changed its colors every few seconds.

But the ibis had generated an almost theatrical tension by *not* being present. Their mangrove islands stretched away from us in a long, curving line, all empty. Unlike the pelicans, egrets, and cormorants who regularly find food in waterways that slip through this world of the mangrove, or along shores built up by the mangroves' broad-grasping roots, the ibis cover hundreds of square miles in their hunting. Thus, every evening their mangrove home provides the spectacle of their return.

"And each night is different," said Bird, who has spent all his life in the

Everglades. "Why, I've brought some people out here a hundred times just to watch these birds coming home. Yes, each night it's different. Even surprises me."

It was not merely the anticipation of the arrival of these exotic and beautiful creatures that gripped the imagination. It was the atmosphere of the mangroves themselves. Without mangroves, the sea would sweep unimpeded inshore until it reached solid land to create a beach shoreline. But the mangroves have conquered the sea. Their twisted, intertwined roots rising starkly from the mud look like interlocked groups of men contorted by suffering.

The mangroves have mastered their self-made shores, and they are colonists that send seeds drifting in perpetual search for new living places. Here, they had formed a dozen tiny islands in the middle of a channel that plunged deeper into mangrove country. They provided an almost perfect refuge for the water birds, beyond the grasping fingers of raccoons, the jaws of foxes, bobcats, cougars, skunks, and other creatures who relished their eggs and nestlings.

Even more miraculously, the mangroves not only sheltered the birds before us, they also helped to feed them. Every year, each acre of mangroves dropped three tons of leaves to the water and mud below, leaves so nutritious they fed billions of shrimp, tiny crabs, insects, and small fish.

We were watching a self-sustaining world in which the mangroves were the genesis of practically all the life visible to us, the sole creators of an original American environment.

Meanwhile, as we waited, the sky went through a bizarre series of transformations. At first it was a brilliant pink, flanked by red-rimmed clouds. Homeward-bound pelicans were flying so low they looked as if they were about to crash. Then a great towering skyscraper of clouds caught an angry flush of sun and burst into flames. The ibis knew exactly the most dramatic moment to show themselves. Two hundred of them crossed the flaming cloud and passed out of sight into a purple backdrop.

That tantalizing glimpse of the ibis set Bird to reminiscing. "There was a young feller here once," he said. "A real smart young feller. Could have been with the Park Service, he knew so much about the country round here. But he wouldn't obey regulations. Why, he used to *feed* his family on young ibis —we call 'em Chokoloskee chickens, and they're supposed to be good eating. Well, this young feller, he'd hunt anything he could catch, just like them old folks used to, so he could stay independent. And he always had his boat just a bit more powerful than us park men. But one night when we was chasing him, he wrecked his boat on a rock. Just about broke his heart, they say, and he moved to Louisiana where he'd been told there weren't so many people protectin' the wildlife."

Bird was describing one of the last of America's frontiersmen, and somehow, this primitive place seemed a perfectly natural refuge for him. But in this world, either he or the ibis had to go. I felt sorry for the young man with his pioneer notions of independence, but I would have felt a lot sorrier if he had been allowed to kill off the ibis. It was his kind who had destroyed the magnificent green turtle, which had once swarmed in millions throughout these Florida waters. It was his kind who had brought the alligator to the edge of extinction and wiped out the Carolina parakeet and the ivory-billed woodpecker, and who had come close to destroying the entire Everglades wonderland.

We had chased him away, but he had been replaced, I reflected, by more educated destroyers—the roadbuilders, the housebuilders, the airport constructors, and vacation-resort developers who wanted to turn the world of the ibis into a playground for water-skiers and powerboat enthusiasts.

"There they are!" Bird shouted.

The ibis did not come directly to their sleeping places. It was as though they relished their freedom and would fly until the last possible moment before coming in to land. All the other birds were now in place, studding the mangroves so thickly that the plants themselves were hidden. Only the ibis islands remained unoccupied.

Thin skeins of ibis flew out of the roseate west, hundreds of them, but so distant they looked more like tiny butterflies than birds. They disappeared. Another skein appeared, brilliant white against the gray east, and moved before us in a graceful straight line until they, too, disappeared in the mauve gloom of the north. The birds tantalized us with the suggestion of their appearance, but gave us no clear view of who they really were. Perhaps of all these mangrove-loving creatures, the ibis best remembered the time of the hunters and had learned to risk nothing in their dealings with men.

Now we were surrounded by fleeting images of ibis. They flew high and white across the dying red sun, fluidly changing their formations. One moment, the flew in Vs, like geese, then the formation changed in seconds to a W-shape, returned to V, then snaked to an S, each so gracefully performed, it was pure ballet.

Still distant, they flew low on all sides so that the fluttering of their wings seemed like the twirling of countless handkerchiefs in the hands of a multitude. Etched against the changing colors of the southern sky, some low-flying birds abruptly rose a hundred feet, then dropped back to rejoin their comrades.

"Oh, oh," Joe Bird said, rubbing his hands. "This is going to be a good one, all right."

The light was fading fast now, and still no ibis had come close enough for us to see their forms or colors. Then abruptly—to this day I cannot understand how it was accomplished—one clump of mangroves was quietly covered with tall white forms. My field glasses, searching every horizon, had missed their arrival completely. And yet, there they were, not one hundred feet away, perfectly displayed and utterly composed before us.

They remained regally separate from the other birds. No sound or movement rippled through their congregation. The sun had gone, but the glowing reds of their beautifully curved beaks and slender legs showed in exquisite distinction to their white bodies and graceful necks.

"More, more!" Bird whispered, pointing.

With the light going, the ibis made their move en masse. A hundred of them came directly at the drifting boat from out of the west, their leaders rising just enough to clear us by a prudent height as they passed overhead. The broad wings beat rapidly, then they glided, beat again, glided once more, the ease of their flying belying their speed, which was probably more than twenty miles an hour.

The ibis poured inward through a world consisting entirely of the softest pink of sky and water, a perfect match for their own colors and movements. Mangrove clump after clump flowered with slender white blossoms as hundreds of birds simultaneously made their landings. It was an excitement of haste and rush, made eerie by its total silence. No cry disturbed the stillness, and the only sound was a soft and distant hiss of wings, like a small stream running over stones in thick woods.

With a final flourish, a hundred birds passed near our boat, showing a dozen brown-plumaged birds among them—the immatures who would not be breeding for another year or two—and then there was a long clear stillness. The ibis were home and safe, the mangroves loaded with their massed bodies as far as we could see in the pink gloom.

On the way back to the mainland neither of us spoke as we let the ibis fly again through our minds. The mullet were still jumping. The dark shores of the mangroves closed in as we neared land. As we coasted in to dock, an automobile horn sounded out of the darkness.

Its alien blare made me realize how completely we had briefly escaped from our "civilized" world, and the thought brought me an image of happy men fishing in these waters, of great hotels rising from the land that the mangroves had reclaimed from the sea, of tanned vacationers sprawled on manmade beaches. Only two of us had gone out to see the ibis homecoming; there were countless millions of other people out there in the darkness who had never heard of ibis and who probably would never see one.

I wondered, with a touch of foreboding, whether the ibis must face a final struggle to continue making their quiet evening spectacle among the mangroves of Florida's Gulf Coast.

Audubon's Photographers

Portfolio One

To capture small fish and shrimp, the black skimmer
plows the surface of a pond in the Florida Everglades
at a velocity of twenty feet per second.
(Photograph by Frederick Kent Truslow)

*On a prairie pond in Nebraska, an American avocet
cocks its head to follow the flight of a marsh hawk.
(Photograph by Mary M. Tremaine)*

*In a meadow clearing bordering a marsh in Denmark,
a ruff postures and displays its lavish breeding
plumage for the benefit of onlooking reeves.
(Photograph by Arthur Christiansen)*

A Hudsonian godwit shelters its newly hatched brood
of four chicks on its nest near Hudson Bay, in Manitoba.
(Photograph by Glenn D. Chambers)

A common loon assumes a low profile on its nest
of sticks and grasses alongside a lake in Maine,
ready to slip into the water if danger threatens.
(Photograph by Fred L. Knapp, Jr.)

A California gull soars over the Pacific surf beneath the cliffs of Vancouver Island, British Columbia. (Photograph by Douglas Faulkner)

*A red-footed booby stretches its wings on a jutting
chunk of lava high above the ocean on Necker Island,
a precipitous seabird refuge in Hawaii's Leeward Islands.
(Photograph by Warren R. Roll)*

An emperor penguin, largest of all penguins, surveys
its domain—the sea ice rimming the antarctic continent.
(Photograph by Roger Tory Peterson)

NORTH GOES THE MOCKER, BY JEAN CRAIGHEAD GEORGE

The song of the mockingbird is as much a part of Southern heritage as magnolias, catfish, and black-eyed peas. But the mocker's ever-varied and always imitative verse is being heard increasingly far north of the Mason-Dixon line, and even beyond the Canadian border, as the symbol of plantations extends its range into ski country.

The rusty gate, the courting nuthatch, screeching tires, whispering redpolls, dogs barking, the verbal grosbeak, a migrating whip-poor-will—all the sounds of a Northern spring were composed into a lengthy musicale by a ten-inch bird on a chimney outside Montreal, Quebec. A librarian on her way to work, hearing the wonderous singer and awed by a cascade of familiar sounds, stopped the first passerby and held him from his destination. "That bird," she said. "Please, listen." The man at first was tolerantly polite, then as the medley of calls, shrieks, songs, and bike bells said "Canada" to him, his politeness gave way to fascination. "What miracle records us?" he asked.

The miracle in Canada was explained in this brief statement in *Audubon Field Notes*, detailing the previous winter season and the winter bird population study for the National Audubon Society and the U.S. Fish and Wildlife Service:

"The mockingbird is still increasing in the North. In Ontario the planting of many *Rosa multiflora* hedges has provided winter food. Christmas Count records included three in Halifax, Nova Scotia, two in Maine, one in Montreal, nine in New Hampshire, 76 in Massachusetts, four in Michigan, one in Nebraska, and one in Saskatchewan."

Where only 40 years ago the mockingbird's northernmost range was listed in Forbush and May as southern Illinois, Ohio, and Maryland, it is now, like the cardinal, Carolina wren, and tufted titmouse, extending its range into the ski belt. The reasons given are many—warming climate, changing land use, internal dynamics, winter feeders. None and perhaps all explain the spirit of a species that gets up and blazes new frontiers in a century in which 31 American birds are extinct and more than 50 are on the U.S. Fish and Wildlife Service list of endangered species.

Whatever its reason for expansion, the mockingbird—symbol of plantations, magnolias, and the rocking chair on the porch—has reached the snowy yards and fields of New England, southern Canada, and the Maritime Provinces. The voice so familiar to the Southerner now sends the Northern birdwatcher to his field guide to check the white-flashing tail and wing patches, the incredible song. If the book is even as recent as the 1973 and 45th impression of Peterson, the researcher will be thrown off by the range, "from Maryland . . . to the Gulf of Mexico. A few north to Massachusetts and Great Lakes."

The voice, however, is the hallmark of the mockingbird and will give him away. A song sparrow's ditty, for instance, followed by a wren's, a blackbird's, chickadee's, mourning dove's, all repeated three to six times, with perhaps a few bars of Bach learned from the neighbor's fiddling child, is none other than the repertoire of the prince of song himself. Although the mocker is less fluent in the North, the rapid succession of repeated song phrases is easily distinguishable even beyond the Canadian border.

This flood of soul music is just one of the mocker's songs. He has some seven or eight less spectacular *cluks, chas,* and whispers given in the privacy of the leafy bushes and trees to his mate and young. These are of such significance as to be a language.

The vocabulary starts when the male mocker is 24 to 28 days old, the female 73. It would seem that such a mighty singer would be precocious, but the mockingbird is one of the last songbirds to find its voice. Song sparrows begin to sing at 13 days, thrushes 15, redstarts 18 and 19, robins 21. When the mocker does speak up he is a fledgling, a wobbly thing perched on a twig. First he warbles, then he improvises a nonsense melody of jerky notes that covers a wide range and pitch.

From this moment on he makes up for lost time. While most male juveniles are singing only incomplete songs in fall, the young mocker is in full swing, setting up his territory and protecting his food supply with a cascade of music professional enough to be given by an adult. This concert runs through November. December is a silent time for the mocker, but for a few nonconformists who can't repress themselves.

The full choir tunes up in February and March and the countryside by day and night is a flood of wonderous music. Most glorious is the night song that begins with the moonrise and lasts until dawn. Rising in the lonely darkness, this voice touches the spirit of man like none other. Called the "advertising song," the endless purling is announcement of the male's sex and a request to other mockers, brown thrashers, robins, and cardinals to identify themselves. It is also an outlet for energy and self-expression.

Since the males tend to be residents and the females migrants, the advertising song becomes ecstatic as the mating season approaches and the females arrive. Song trips over into dance than back to song again as the male tries to "hold" the female, a fickle creature who may remain but one hour, or one day, and then move on. At the sight of her the mocker will rise singing into the air, flutter, fall through limbs, strike the ground. He will glide from telephone pole to tree-top to chimney in an unparalleled bird effort to establish a bond with an elusive partner.

Should one stop, the male speaks with a strange new voice. Meeting her near the ground, he calls a rasping *cha.* She answers. He greets her again, then pursues her singing yet another song, a soft whisper of old familiar ditties. He picks up twigs and runs toward possible nest sites, head down, tail and wings spread. If she has not departed, his vocabulary changes once more and he sings the "binding song," an urgent *cluk, cluk, cluk,* pressing her to stay.

When he wins the female the whole world knows, not by loud proclamation but soft. His singing decreases as if the moment were hallowed. Most American songbirds sing louder with the taking of a mate, but the mockingbird and white-crowned sparrow lower their voices and sing sweetly, gently.

A mate to woo, the mockingbird no longer finds singing sufficient. The male now speaks in dance. On fence and tree limb, wall and log, he faces her. He steps forward, she back, then he back and she forward. They dance to the side and end with a sudden turn and flight as he establishes in her mind the borders of his some five acres of territory.

Harold and Josephine Michener, who studied the mockingbird in California, called this dance a "ceremony marking territorial lines." Anyone who has witnessed the stylized minuet, the well-timed steps, the astounding coordination, cannot doubt its deep significance.

Borders learned, the female will sing, an unusual occurrence in songbirds. She speaks only in territorial situations, however—the approach of another mocker or of a new neighbor settling in.

When she starts nest-building, the male helps by bringing grass and shredded plant fibers to one of many low bushes. Often the male works on in some distant bush when the permanent nest is complete. Bulky and rather sloppy, it is from three to twelve feet off the ground.

Egg laying begins and the voice of the male rings loudly again. It is lowered once more during the incubation of the three to five buffy eggs blotched with brown.

Upon fighting out of their shells after about twelve days, the babies are fed by both parents for approximately eleven days. Energetic and eager, they often come off the nest before they can fly; fluttering to the ground, many fall victim to the house cat, the mocker's worst predator.

Once upon their wings, however, the young mockingbirds follow their parents to feeders and berrybushes, gradually shifting their diet from ants, bees, wasps, and grasshoppers to fruits, seeds, and nuts. The song of the male from this time until the following spring becomes a "defense of food" aria. The holly berries, greenbrier, pokeweed, red cedar, black gum, sumac, dogwood, and poison ivy fruits are protected in this lilting song of summer and fall.

Like all birds, the mocker has an alarm cry, a short frantic *que-ah* that warns of cats, owls, and men. However, as might be expected of this oral bird, it has refined the call.

Mrs. Amelia R. Laskey, the Tennessee mockingbird expert, discovered that her hand-raised bird had a "spot alarm," or memory call. One of her juveniles *que-ahed* at the sight of a stuffed screech owl she placed near its cage. Many nights later she heard the mocker cry again, and turning on the light was amazed to see him staring at the spot where the owl skin had been!

Artist that he is, the mockingbird is not a gentle soul. Aggressive, dynamic, he chases songbirds from berrybush and feeding tray and even attacks the powerful flicker and blue jay. Mrs. Laskey has seen mockers strike flickers on the back, knock them from their perches, then turn and dive upon them. Song sparrows, chickadees, juncos, cardinals, all scatter at the pugnacious approach of the mockingbird.

As Northerners trill to this enchanting immigrant, Southerners warn, "Beware the charming mocker." No more proof is needed than the story of Mrs. Laskey's banded bird "Y" who nested in the honeysuckle vine near her garage and before the season was done, dominated house, lawn, walk, and people. "He resented our sitting in the garden or working in it," she writes. "His harsh *chucks* evidenced his displeasure and he frequently attacked me. He would pounce on my head or back, striking with both feet, scolding loudly. He would follow me from front to rear of the 300-foot lot, sometimes flying ahead with strident *que-ah* scolding notes, striking repeatedly."

69

As formidable as this sounds, it is Mrs. Laskey herself who eases the mind. The mockingbird, she writes in *The Auk*, "is not only noted for its colorful personality but individuals display distinctive characteristics; behavior and reactions in two individuals may coincide in some ways but in other situations are entirely different."

With this in mind, the Northerner may relax. Who knows, the mockingbird who owns your house and yard may be a saint and if not, at least in every way he is a prince of song.

SUCH GLORIOUS SPORT,
BY LOUIS J. HALLE *Airplanes can*
fly higher and faster than any bird, but there the superiority
of man's machines stops. Nowhere is this fact more evident
than on an ocean island colonized by seabirds. Come stand
on a cliff high above the North Atlantic and watch the spec-
tacular aerial maneuvers of the fulmar.

It is only in our time that we men have acquired, by artifice, locomotive abilities that the birds have always had by nature. Today we can move through the air faster and farther than any bird. To be carried in a flying machine, however, is not to fly as the birds do. The engine that takes to the air by roaring power lacks the grace of a bird's levitation.

Outside my window is a blizzard of small gulls. They are milling over the lawn, sweeping in a maze of arcs that intersect one another, each bird tilting and swerving through the swarm of others. These are black-headed gulls come together for a fly-catching party over our lawn. Every individual weaves swiftly in and out among all the others doing the same, with never a collision. What would the traffic-controller at any airport say to this?

The principal difference between the wing of an airplane and the wing of a bird is that the latter is changeable in its shape. The "variable geometry" wings on some airplanes today have two fixed shapes, one for low speed and one for high, but the wings of a bird are flexible over a wide range, their entire shape changing continuously to meet changes in the environment or in the bird's own purpose. What aircraft designer could match this?

The fulmar of northern seas is not as graceful as the gulls over the lawn, but it provides unique opportunities of observation for anyone fascinated by the virtuosity of a bird's flight. A fast, stiff-winged flyer, like its relatives the albatrosses and shearwaters, it is better adapted than gulls to driving itself forward by wings that beat swiftly. In the open ocean, low over the waves, it alternates such power-flight with intervals of gliding on wings held out rigid like an airplane's.

The fulmar is a northern representative of the great order of seabirds that includes the wandering albatross, among the largest of flying creatures, as well as storm petrels the size of swallows, an order that is dominant in the cold waters of the southern hemisphere, where it presumably originated. Until the last century the fulmar of the North Atlantic (there is another population in the North Pacific) still bred only in Iceland, except for an isolated colony on the Hebridean island of St. Kilda. Then it began to undergo an explosive expansion of its population that may still be continuing. Today it breeds all around the British coastline and has crossed the Channel to Brittany. It also breeds within 570 miles of the North Pole, in Franz Josef Land, and has been recorded farther north than any other bird, only 236 miles from the Pole. At high latitudes, over the heaving waters of the North Atlantic, it has become spectacular in the density of its numbers.

I first met the fulmar in 1968 on a visit to the Shetland Islands, far north of mainland Scotland. During a second visit to Shetland in the spring of 1970, I spent many hours, day after day, observing the tricks of its flight along the Shetland cliffs. What follows is an account of these observations.

Unlike the various species of gulls, the fulmar is designed for fast flight and high winds. This is shown by the fact that, in its narrower wings and shorter tail, it has less supporting surface than a gull of the same size. The more wind or the more speed, the less surface is needed to catch the wind, and the less surface, the less the flyer is held back by the drag of the air. Moreover, because they are narrow, it can beat its wings faster than if they were broad sails.

A fulmar's body is relatively shorter than a gull's, thereby also presenting less surface to the wind. The head is simply its forward end, not separated by a length of neck. The body also differs from a gull's in being wedge-shaped, broader at the front end, a characteristic that is most conspicuous when one sees the bird swimming. On the water it appears short and exceptionally bluff in the bows. A fulmar needs bigger pectoral muscles for its power-flight than the more leisurely gulls, and this, I take it, accounts for its girth across the breast.

The ease with which all the tricks of the fulmar's flight may be observed, albeit under specialized conditions, comes from its habit of patrolling the cliffs on top of which the observer may take his stand. He can watch its aerial maneuvers at the closest range, noting the action of every feather, for a fulmar may pass within three feet of his face as if he were not there at all. (I have, on occasion, tried to gain recognition for my existence by waving my arms and shouting, but without success. At last I am left feeling as if I must be realizing the dream in which one moves under the cloak of invisibility to observe the ways of this world's inhabitants.)

When there is little wind, or where the cliffs are sheltered from it, the fulmars follow their contours in relatively mechanical flight, beating and gliding. However, where a massive wind from across the ocean strikes the cliffs and is deflected upward, they ride its gusty support as if it were a mustang. Or they hang upon it like kites at the ends of strings, adjusting to its buffets by automatic changes in the shape and angle of wings and body.

Great black-backed gulls, herring gulls, and common gulls also hang in the updraft, but lacking the deft control of the fulmars, or their capacity for quick maneuver, they stay well away from the cliff walls, remaining either high above or some distance out. They do not risk themselves in the turbulence where the wind breaks like surf against the cliff. They take no chance of being flung against the rock. A fulmar, however, may allow itself to be carried backward and sideways on the turbulence toward the cliff, its landing gear lowered, to settle at last on some slight ledge, gently—then fold its wings away.

In order to keep its place in the updraft, a fulmar may draw its wings in, half-furled, or hold them up at a steep angle to spill the wind, but it must constantly be changing their set, generally with rapid and abrupt movements. In fact, since the wind bears against its whole body, its whole body is the sail to be constantly trimmed. When the fulmar hangs suspended in the wind, its legs dangle, its tail is bent upward, and its head, too, may be drawn back on its shoulders to the position assumed by the sitting bird. Or the flyer may hold its place by tilting forward into a dive, more or less steep, plummeting into the updraft at the same rate as the updraft would otherwise carry it aloft. Usually, however, it does not hang in one place. It uses all the devices I have described to control its drifting movement along the contour of the cliffs, to speed up or slow down, to rise or sink, to go forward or backward. Often its wings quiver in the wind.

Sometimes a fulmar, its back to the cliff, will swing slowly from side to side as if at the end of a string, like an inverted pendulum, moving up and down a bit at the same time, or forward and back.

In earlier published observations I confessed my inability to explain why the fulmars spend so much energy patrolling the cliffs back and forth, apparently without purpose. I assumed that this habit had some particular utility. On calm evenings, however, gulls will circle aimlessly far up in the sky for no utilitarian purpose one can imagine. I end this second set of observations, then, by quoting a note on the patrolling fulmars, more enthusiastic than scientific, that I made March 28th. "At Eshaness, watching their spectacular maneuvers at such close hand, I could hardly doubt that the explanation for their incessant patrol of the cliffs is nothing abstruse but, rather, the simple fact that it is such glorious sport."

VULTURE VIGILS, BY ROGER TORY PETERSON

Because of their carrion-eating habits and grotesque appearances, vultures are the most repulsive of all birds to prejudiced human observers. But to the artist and naturalist who is most responsible for the vast popular interest in birds, they are not only magnificent subjects for his brush and canvas but the occasion for ornithological adventures across several continents.

Vultures have always fascinated me, and I have spent not a few days of my life in their company. Call me a "vulture lover" if you will; I refuse to admit that there is anything macabre about it.

Years ago, when I lived a bachelor's life in a tiny apartment in Greenwich Village, I decorated my walls with that brilliant series of vulture portraits painted in Abyssinia by Louis Agassiz Fuertes. A friend looked them over and quipped that "A vulture has no culture—and its food habits are simply offal." When another visitor, appraising the decor, commented that I seemed to have a rather unhealthy outlook, I took down this rogues' gallery and substituted some Liljefors reproductions.

Later, when I went to Africa, my companion Bayard Read took an equally dim view of these "degenerate predators," as he called them. Whenever I would unlimber my Cine-Special to document the vulturine convocation around a lion kill, he would argue, "Why waste good film on those awful birds?"

But as an artist I must point out that vultures are not only magnificent in the air, as anyone will admit, but they are also very portrayable. Passerines lend themselves to delicate delineation, as do many other birds, but vultures— with their strong masses, form, and textures—are more truly paintable.

Taxonomists put the fifteen vultures of the Old World in the same family as the hawks and the eagles, *Accipitridae*. But the seven New World vultures, so much like them in appearance, are placed in a family of their own, *Cathartidae*. Curiously, the oldest fossils of what seem to be New World vultures have come from England, France, and Germany, from Eocene deposits laid down 50 million years ago, indicating that the family may actually have originated in the Old World.

That strange vulturine eagle, the palm-nut vulture of tropical Africa, I have seen but a few times, mostly along the Nile near Murchison Falls. At first glance it suggests an Egyptian vulture except for its white primaries and square tail. Addicted to eating the oily husks of palm nuts, it is neither quite fish eagle nor quite vulture, but something in between, a puzzle to systematists.

As for the bearded lammergeyer, the other aberrant vulture, I finally caught up with it in Crete within sight of Zeus' cave on the slopes of Mount Ida. Like an immense falcon with a nine-foot wingspread, the "bone-crusher" flew directly over us with the leg bones of a lamb dangling from its talons.

I have kept many a vulture vigil over the years—one day, two days, even three days at a time—but none more vivid in my memory than the three days I spent with three dead dogs while attempting to photograph Andean condors.

In January of 1958 I undertook a Yale University-sponsored, *Life*-financed expedition to the high Andes to find and photograph the James' flamingo, the mysterious little flamingo that had dropped from sight for 50 years. The editors had also asked me to get some pictures of condors if I could. During a month of field work in the high cordillera on the borders of northern Chile and western Bolivia I saw but one condor and that at a distance of at least a mile, soaring over one of the volcanic peaks—too far for any picture.

Actually, in the extremely arid country of northern Chile, condors are more frequent along the coast, where they feed on dead things cast up by the sea. Although some also live in the Andes, they seem to be absent from the 150-mile-wide belt of dead desert between the Andes and the sea—there is nothing there for them to eat.

I had seen condors patrolling the sea cliffs north of Antofagasta, so on my return from the flamingo lakes I elected to give them a try. But where would I get a carcass? A goat, perhaps? My Chilean guide and companion, Luis Peña of Santiago, informed me that goats were nonexistent in this rainless region of no bushes, no grass.

"What about a dog?" I asked.

"I think I know where we might get a dead dog . . . I'll get one," he promised. So while I photographed a tame whimbrel on the beach in front of the hotel, he scouted the municipal dump, returning at noon.

"I have met the king of the garbage dump," he announced. "A horrible man . . . you will meet him."

"What about the carcass?" I asked, getting to the point.

"No problem. The man has one; he told me to come back later."

That afternoon I met the "king of the garbage dump," and he was truly something to behold—in tatters, unwashed and black with filth. He lived in an igloo of garbage and apparently survived by scavenging the dump. He presented us not one dog, but three, all mongrels recently deceased. Two were red, one was gray. Gingerly we lifted them by their tails, while several half-starved pariah dogs (their friends?) gathered around. We put them in the back of the Dodge Power Wagon and drove to a headland 30 miles up the coast where previously we had seen condors.

The sun was splashing into a fiery sea where we made camp. The dogs were too odorous to leave in the truck so we buried them for the night in a shallow trench and covered them with boards to foil foraging foxes. I spread my sleeping bag on the sand 50 feet away on the other side of the truck, but apparently every flea harbored by those three dogs found my exposed arms before morning. For a month thereafter I was scratching their miserable bites.

That morning, early, we picked our site for photography—an open spot with a photogenic cluster of boulders on which we hoped the condors would sit, and another pile of rocks on a nearby slope where we constructed a natural blind. We stacked the loose rocks to form a circular wall and closed the top with a piece of canvas weighted at the edges with sand and stone. Just before we finished this tidy little fortress three turkey vultures rocked lazily past and then, straight toward us, sailed a condor, a juvenile. It passed overhead, circled to study the situation, then glided on. This was a bad sign. That bird, at least, would probably avoid the blind.

It was late in the morning before we put the dogs out and I entered the blind, my 400-mm telephoto lens at the ready. Turkey vultures arrived within twenty minutes, but either the dogs were not ripe enough for their taste or they were suspicious of the setup. They sat about in silence a hundred yards away while I stewed and sweated all afternoon in my cramped cell. Once in a while an incoming bird swooped low to inspect the dogs, now buzzing with flies, then joined the silently waiting company. The breeze off the sea blew directly from the fetid dogs to me.

I wondered whether the vultures, with their extraordinary eyesight, could actually see me through the chinks between the rocks; I could see out with no difficulty. Once, as I peeked through a crack to the ocean, I saw a great flock of guanay cormorants, an endless black ribbon of birds beating low over the waves.

The vultures were exasperatingly cautious. I spread my heavy jacket and my black focusing cloth against the walls and fastened them in place with small stones to conceal me further. That first day in the blind was a tedious failure.

The next morning, after I entered the blind at dawn, three or four turkey vultures approached within six feet of the bait and I got several frame-filling portraits. But I could, after all, have accomplished as much in Florida or even in New Jersey. And it was not until the third morning that a venturesome vulture tentatively nibbled at one of the dogs. As though on signal, vultures swarmed in from all sides. From my peephole I counted 50 on the sand. Then as suddenly as they had gathered they dispersed; a panic reaction spread through the mob. What triggered it? It was about that time, 11:30 A.M., Luis Peña told me later, that two adult condors circled over the blind two or three times, then flew down the coast.

That evening, with little to show for our efforts, we packed up to go. I had to catch a plane the next day for New York. One more day, Luis felt sure, would have done the trick, but I had a lecture engagement, and lectures are irrevocable. *Life* eventually ran a close-up of a condor, but it was taken in the Santiago zoo.

The Andean condor, with a maximum wingspan of about ten feet, is only slightly larger than *Gymnogyps,* the California condor, which might reach nine and one-half feet, and it is not much larger than the largest of the Old World vultures. Nevertheless, this giant among the world's birds of prey is so dwarfed by the immensity of the Andean landscape that I usually find it necessary to check a distant condor with binoculars to make sure it is not just another turkey vulture. I have seen condors as far south as the Beagle Channel in Tierra del Fuego, where they share the sky with albatrosses, and I have ticked off as many as eighteen in one day on the road to Paine National Park in southern Chile. Although the Andean condor has become scarce in the northern Andes, it is still a relatively common bird further south, and we pray that it may remain so, never to reach the tenuous status of its California relative.

The California condor, the second rarest bird in the United States (assuming that the ivory-billed woodpecker is still with us) is tenaciously holding on in the chapparal-covered hills north of Los Angeles and has become the focus of almost as much national attention as the whooping crane. In 1936, when I stopped in Los Angeles with six hours between trains, five young members of the Junior Audubon Club of Eagle Rock High School discovered I was in town, took me to Sespe Creek Canyon, showed me my first condors, tiny specks in the blue, and hustled me back to the railroad station with four minutes to spare.

Four years later I saw condors to better advantage by abandoning the canyon floor and climbing to the ridges where they glide on the deflected air currents. As they floated past, with primary feathers spread like fingers, they seemed prehistoric.

Alexander Sprunt, Jr., less lucky on his first condor quest, was discovered by a group of birders, I was told, lying beside the road at Sespe, trying to look like a cadaver. But the wily cathartids are not so easily duped.

James Fisher, my British colleague, and I nearly missed the condor on our tour around the perimeter of the continent in 1953. The morning fog blotted out the Sespe ridges. There was no sun to warm the canyon basins and release columns of hot, light air to buoy the vultures. Only when we were about to leave did the clouds lift and the thermals start. A condor came right over—a ponderous flat-winged bomber of a bird, quite unlike the slighter turkey vultures with their glider-dihedral. There was no mistaking its broad band of white on the underwing. As it soared away to become a tiny speck in the southeast, James ticked it off on his checklist. He agreed it was well worth seeing—in fact, worth traveling 10,000 miles to see.

The black vulture probably has a larger population than any other bird of prey in the Western Hemisphere. Having seen the vast numbers around the dumps and slaughterhouses of every tropical and subtropical town, I can well believe it. From Patagonia to Washington, D.C., it is commensal with man, somewhat more so than the turkey vulture. When we lived in the Washington area during the war years there was a large roost of both species near the towpath of the Chesapeake and Ohio Canal. The black vultures, more alert and aggressive, enforced segregation. The turkey vultures sat about amongst the dead Fords and Chevrolets in an auto graveyard and even tore the red inner tubes to bits—because, I suppose, of their resemblance to edible intestines.

I have the distinct impression that we don't see as many vultures in the eastern United States as we did 20 or 30 years ago. Pesticides in the food chain? Possibly. Or are they being struck by cars on the new superhighways when they come down for the road kills?

In Africa, the larger vultures are definitely declining, but for a different reason—the dwindling of the big-game herds.

Of the half-dozen kinds of vultures that come to carcasses in East Africa, the Egyptian vulture is the least common. If I were called upon to give a capsule description of the bird—a field-guide description—I would say it is a smallish vulture with the look (and size) of a gannet in flight, white with blackish flight feathers and a pointed tail. There the resemblance ends, for it has a shaggy neck surmounted by a bare orange-yellow face.

This scruffy fowl has been called "Pharaoh's chicken," a rather appropriate nickname, for it not only looks a bit like a slightly soiled white hen as it walks about the North African villages, but it also can claim ancestry from scavengers that once actually looked down on Pharaohs. Graceless though it may be as it shuffles about, it is transformed into an elegant gliding machine the moment it takes off into the blue African sky.

The Egyptian vulture once lived throughout most of the drier parts of the African continent, especially in the deserts north of the equator, where it still outnumbers all other vultures. But south of Tanzania it is rare. It is still commonplace in southern Spain, where I have seen a thermal wheel of two score or more on a hot day in the Marismas. From the Iberian peninsula, its Eurasian range extends eastward through the arid Mediterranean belt to India.

I saw my first Egyptian vulture in 1950 in southern France, where it is not at all common. The locale was Les Baux, a rocky jumble of hills not far from the Camargue. Later that same day my friends Robert Etchécopar and François Huë, the distinguished French ornithologists, showed me a nest on a low cliff, the first actual nest on record, they said, for France. We approached cautiously from above, but the bird slipped off so quickly that I got only a blurry shot with my Leica. By means of a fifteen-foot pole and a mirror we were able to look into the stick nest, which held two stained, rust-colored eggs.

In 1968 the Egyptian vulture made ornithological news. Jane Van Lawick-Goodall, of chimpanzee fame, and her photographer husband, the Baron Hugo Van Lawick, chanced upon a most extraordinary sight in Ngorongoro Crater in northern Tanzania. A nesting ostrich, routed by a grass fire, had abandoned its eggs. A crowd of vultures of five species had assembled, but only one of the birds, an Egyptian, seemed to hold the key to success. It picked up a rock and—holding it high—bashed it down against an egg. It did this several times until the egg broke; then the larger, stronger birds rushed in to gobble up the spoils.

This was an authentic case of a bird using a "tool" (which might be defined as any object manipulated as an extension of a hand, paw, beak, or claw). Up to that time the only true example of tool-using by a bird involved the Galápagos woodpecker finch, which grasps a twig or thorn in its beak and probes under the bark for grubs. Some purists insist that the satin bowerbird of Australia must be included in this category because it uses a wad of bark as a sort of "paintbrush" to paint the inside of its bower.

I had heard about the Van Lawick discovery long before the story broke in the pages of the *National Geographic*. Ornithological news such as this travels fast and quickly leaps oceans. A few months later, when I was in Tanzania with John Livingston, William W. H. Gunn, and a Canadian Broadcasting Corporation television crew, we made a special effort to film this extraordinary behavior. In Nairobi, we were presented with a freshly blown ostrich egg (after eating a tasty omelet made from its contents). We carried this egg about with us for two weeks before we had a chance to use it.

Then, late one afternoon as we crossed the flat floor of Ngorongoro Crater in our Land Rover, an Egyptian vulture flew over. We jammed on the brakes, set out the egg, and scattered a few stones that we had gathered in the event that none were handy near the scene of action. The vulture wheeled, obviously interested, while I readied the Arriflex to shoot from the front hatch. Meanwhile a second bird joined the first.

Scaling straight in, vulture No. 1 landed within three feet of the egg, directly picked up a rock about four inches long as if to test its heft, then dropped it. Picking it up again it walked over to the egg and with head held high projected it downward. It missed. Vulture No. 2 walked in with a rock, threw it and narrowly missed the bald yellow head of its mate. With further effort their aim improved, but the extremely tough eggshell, one-sixteenth of an inch thick, withstood a dozen hits. All this I recorded with a zoom lens that gave me frame-filling close-ups. Just as the egg broke the film ran out. Frantically we reloaded the 400-foot reel, but before I could resume shooting, a hyena, low-rumped and sneaky, rushed in, grabbed the broken eggshell, and ran off.

Where could we get another egg? Naturally we could not appropriate one in a national park. We put out feelers and finally acquired an egg several weeks old and undoubtedly very rotten that had been picked up after a grass fire. We carried it about in a cardboard box for a week or more without spotting another Egyptian vulture. There was no alternative but to return to Ngorongoro, where we could always find at least a pair or two. The best place in the crater was around one of the Masai *manyattas*, or villages, for these "foulest of scavengers," as Colonel Richard Meinertzhagen called the Egyptian vultures, eat human excrement.

Inside one of the abandoned compounds, with its ring of huts made of thornbrush and dried cowdung, we located two birds. Our crew set out the egg and after waiting an hour sent in the native driver to flush the bird. The first bird flew in the wrong direction and did not spot the egg. The second came right over, zeroed in on the egg, and we were able to shoot all the footage we needed.

Salvaging what was left of the empty egg (it still looked quite intact if one concealed a gaping hole) I planned further experiments. I would try it 170 miles to the north at Hell's Gate in Kenya. Was this rock-throwing a local habit, acquired by observation (as was the opening of milk bottles by blue tits and other birds in England), or was it innate or inborn? Hell's Gate, north of Nairobi, is famous for its lammergeyers and Ruppell's griffons. I had missed the lammergeyers, but on each of my earlier visits I had seen a pair of Egyptian vultures. There are also ostriches in the neighborhood, so the vultures should have had every opportunity to see and to know ostrich eggs.

I found the pair of Egyptians in the usual place. They soared along the face of the cliff wall, then perched side-by-side on the skyline. My egg, conspicuously placed in an open spot, gleamed large and white in the afternoon sunlight. For three hours I waited, but the exasperating birds took no apparent notice. They preened, sunned themselves, and finally flew off to their evening roost. The sight of the large glossy ovoid obviously did not trigger the rock-in-beak response. Perhaps they simply were not hungry. I must try the experiment a few more times on my next safari.

The hooded vulture is the common town vulture of most of tropical Africa, the vulture of the garbage dumps, comparable to the similarly sized turkey vulture in the southern United States. Driving into Nairobi, Kampala, Arusha, or any of the other East African cities, one invariably sees this species, and a wheel of black forms over the countryside usually means a settlement nearby. Basically a vulture of the cultivated districts, it has become commensal with man.

At Seronera Lodge in the Serengeti it prefers to scrounge dinner scraps around the dining tent rather than compete at the game kills. When excited its pale pinkish head, covered with thin gray down, blushes to a choleric red, just as a strutting turkey gobbler's head takes on transitory color.

There is a very definite peck order or order of dominance among vultures. The little hooded vulture is the one most likely to discover carrion through its own efforts and therefore it is likely to get first taste. It must give way to the larger white-backed vulture and Ruppell's griffon, which in turn defer to the white-headed vulture, the most beautiful vulture (if vultures can be beautiful). The largest and frequently the most dominant of the lot is the lappet-faced vulture. It often arrives half an hour late, toward the end of the feast, when the kill is reduced to bones and skin. Actually, the lappet-face seems to favor chunks of bone and big pieces of tough hide rather than messy viscera.

But at the lion kills even the largest vultures must wait until the King of Beasts and his retainer, the hyena, have had their fill. One dawn at Amboseli the lions were roaring within half a mile of our camp. William Gunn, who went out to tape-record the rumpus, returned to tell us that two lionesses had ambushed a wildebeest and, lacking support from the pride, had been driven off by hyenas.

We jumped into the Land Rover and were there in a jiffy. A huge circle of vultures, mostly white-backs, had already gathered but kept their distance while the hyenas crunched into the carcass with their bone-crushing jaws. Eventually, bellies sagging, the hyenas sauntered off while two black-backed jackals rushed in, tails wagging and jaws snapping.

For a quarter of an hour these little coyotelike animals kept the carcass to themselves while the vultures edged closer. If a vulture became too venturesome, a short run and a snap put the bird into the air. Finally the jackals had their fill, too, and with a good-natured wag of their tails trotted off. Immediately the vultures closed in, all 50 of them. They swarmed over the corpse like a writhing heap of maggots, jostling, squabbling, stepping on each other. One or two forced head and shoulders into the bloody body cavity of the wildebeest. In a matter of minutes little remained but the rib cage and the skull, with its curved horns and grinning white teeth.

As for the hungry lions, they had to make another kill that day, another wildebeest. This time they ate their sirloins in peace, unattended by hyenas, jackals, or vultures—but not ignored by photographers.

Why won't vultures kill a dying animal? Possibly those that try come to grief themselves. In one reported case, an Indian white-backed vulture attacked a calf not yet dead. The calf seized the vulture by the neck and strangled it before dying itself. Thus it might be argued that natural selection would eliminate mutant vultures with impatient tendencies.

Vultures will wait long hours until all life is extinguished before touching even the most helpless prey. John Livingston and I chanced upon an agonizing scene at Lake Manyara in Tanzania. We heard the coughing of a lion and later saw a half-grown cub emerge from the grass and walk across the lake plain. We thought nothing of it until vultures started to come in. Investigating, we found a small zebra, a very young foal, in desperate condition, alive but with its tongue nearly torn out. One leg was broken and in shreds. It lifted its head and tried to stand but fell back into the grass. We knew what had happened. The inexperienced young lion, a mere cub separated from the pride, had tried to make the kill alone. It made a mess of things and then walked away without finishing the job.

John was all for slitting the unfortunate foal's throat but then had second thoughts. The rules of the park forbid anyone to interfere in any way with the affairs of the animals. We parked the Land Rover at a little distance to see what the vultures would do and to film them. First on the scene were the hoodeds, then the larger white-backs and one or two Ruppell's griffons, distinguished by their pale, scaly feather edgings. Later a lappet-face joined the group, which was assembled in a pod about 100 feet from the dying zebra.

A school bus came down the track and, noticing the crowd of vultures, the driver stopped. Pressing their noses against the windows were about 20 Indian children from Arusha. Two of the older boys stepped out of the bus, hunkered down to examine the mangled foal, still alive, and I could almost read their thoughts on their faces. It is one thing to put predation into perspective intellectually, another to be confronted with it in all its reality. I regretted that the children should see this; they will probably always be anti-lion.

After the bus departed we waited and so did the vultures. They preened and some sunbathed with spread wings. Every now and then one of the hoodeds took off in a low glide over the foal to see if it still breathed. But so long as there was a flicker of life they waited.

My experiences with vultures both in the New World and in the Old indicate that they are more cautious or capricious about coming to bait put out for them than they are to a kill or to natural carrion. Do they sense the unnaturalness of the setup? Or does a carcass have to be at precisely the right stage of decomposition? Or if they have recently fed must they wait a while?

One August day near Bear Mountain on the Hudson River, I found a white-tailed deer that had been killed by a car. Hauling it to an open spot in the woods, I put up my burlap blind and camouflaged it with wild grapevines. For two days I waited in this airless sweatbox while the dead buck ripened and flies swarmed. About a dozen turkey vultures came, but they sat at a discreet distance in the dead hemlocks, like undertakers waiting out the proper period of time before burial. On the third day I dismantled my blind. Immediately after I left, the vultures did the job; when a friend passed by three hours later all that remained of the deer were a few scattered bones.

On my first trip to Queen Elizabeth National Park in western Uganda I made a blind of thornbrush while a native sergeant of the game guards kept a lookout for the local lions. My bait, a goat, soon attracted a swarm of white backed vultures, several hoodeds, a white-headed vulture, a marabou stork, two white-naped ravens, and a black kite, but only the kite and one of the hoodeds fed. The others simply sat it out until I went away.

Another goat, in an equally promising site at Lake Magadi in southern Kenya, lured no takers up to the second day. Not even a hyena had touched it during the night.

On another occasion, trying for griffon vultures in Spain, Guy Mountfort and I waited an entire day in two expertly concealed blinds. We placed the body of a deer in the bracken at the foot of a dead cork oak. Pictorially it was a perfect setting—one that Paul Gustave Doré would have devised for vultures. But not even a black kite came to investigate. The Spanish horsemen and *guardas* who had helped us construct the hide seemed disappointed in the *inglés* and the eccentric *americano* when we returned to the *palacio* at sundown and reported our failure.

Four years later, near the same spot in the Marismas, I tried a cow, deceased at least two or three days, and although one Egyptian vulture investigated the bloated animal briefly I again drew a blank with the griffons. Yet that same week, Guy Mountfort, setting up his blind near the completely stripped and sun-dried backbone of a fallow deer, within 20 minutes focused his lens on nine vultures of three species—griffon, Egyptian, and the rare cinereous or European black vulture. The latter is the largest bird in Europe, equal in size to a California condor.

Forty miles to the southeast of the Marismas, at Arcos de la Frontera, the griffon vultures of that part of Spain have one of their great roosts. It is quite likely that most of the birds that patrol the Marismas spend the night there in the safety of the cliffs along the Guadalete River, for they can easily cover the distance from the great marshes in an hour. It is estimated that a griffon may travel 200 to 300 air miles during the six or eight hours of the day when it is on the wing. Although its cruising speed is about 40 miles per hour, it may achieve speeds in excess of 100 miles per hour when zeroing in on a carcass.

By late afternoon as many as 200 griffons gather on the cliffs below the ancient walled town, and there is no better vantage point from which to film them. In 1956, Eric Hosking, the British bird photographer, and I were admitted to the balcony of an old castle 400 feet above the river. As the birds cruised past at eye level I shot them in 16-mm color with my Bolex cradled in a camera gun equipped with gunsight. At 64 frames per second, the slow-motion speed, film rushes through the camera at the rate of $10 or $12 a minute, and it is terrifying, simply terrifying, when one pulls the trigger and the bird does the wrong thing—veers off in the wrong direction—and spoils the shot.

I have never admitted to my wife how much footage I exposed in that one hour, but the sequences I have shown to lecture audiences here and abroad have been called my best. Still, I should like to try it again.

OF ART AND THE NEST,
BY ROBERT ARBIB

As there is incredible variety among kinds of birds, so too is there incredible variety in their nests. A nest may be simply a bare ledge on a precipitous sea cliff. Or it may be a marvel of architecture, construction, and beauty, skillfully fashioned with the bird's bill in a way no human hands could ever duplicate.

The Christmas tree, a full and shapely Scotch pine, the snow brushed from its boughs, secure in its stand, was carried from the yard and placed in its traditional corner by the fireplace. Upright, its pointed tip almost touched the ceiling. Perfect! Suddenly the room was flooded with the scent and memory of forested hillsides; submissive, the tree waited for the box of treasured-from-childhood ornaments and twinkling lights that would transform it from something wild and lovely and lost into something joyous and enchanted.

I climbed the stepladder to begin the transformation with the garlanding of lights. And then, as I looked down into the tree, an unexpected darkness, like a secret, caught my eye. A malformation of the trunk, a knot of dead needles? I parted the branches and peered into the heart of the tree. A bird's nest! With something small and pale cupped in it—a speckled little egg!

There is an old Scandinavian saying that has somehow made its way to America, that to find a bird's nest in the Christmas tree brings good luck the new year through. I cannot now recall what kind of luck that nest brought, but for that moment and that Christmas Eve, the beautifully fashioned thing brought a sense of discovery and a lingering delight. A Christmas gift from nature herself; a reminder that this tree sang sweet songs above the soft sighings of the wind; that a family of living creatures had been sheltered here—hatched and brooded and fed and fledged—that this now silent and sacrificial tree had only a few months earlier been alive, the glinting of its glaucous needles threaded, woven, and shot through with the dartings of flashing wings.

This, we resolved, would be our last living Christmas tree. Even the knowledge that it had been grown on a tree farm especially for this purpose did not, somehow, completely alleviate the burden of guilt that this living loveliness had been cut down to serve a week's house decoration, and would soon be a dead and desiccated skeleton, to be carted off in a garbage truck. The tree that is its substitute today is an attractive artifact, but it brings no scent or dream of frosty mountain slopes, no magic, and no secret birds' nests. It is a fake and a fraud, but it has already served to spare seven living trees.

The nest in the heart of the pine brought with it more than the sudden joy of surprise. There was an added bonus of mystery. What birds had built this nest? Who were the landlords of our Christmas tree, the tenants of this hidden home? The nest itself might provide the answer: surely it belonged to a small bird, for its inner cup was no more than two and a half inches in diameter. Too small for a pine grosbeak or even a pine siskin, but just about right for a brooding warbler. The outer shell was neat and tightly woven, of twigs and fibers and perhaps thin strips of bark. The inner lining of the cup was, as always, of softer materials, to cradle the eggs without piercing them, to protect the chicks from injury and from the elements. Grasses, moss, hair (deer, fox, rabbit?), and one or two feathers were now all matted into a soft felt by use, and by the weather. Firmly attached to a forked branch close to the trunk of the little pine, it was a compact work of utter artistry, invisible to any observer on the ground, and with clusters of dense foliage above it, to keep it from the eyes of predators aloft.

Surely this was a warbler's nest, as the egg itself—the other important clue—seemed to confirm. But only a few warblers nest in evergreens, and fewer still will nest so close to the ground. Assuming that the tree had been harvested somewhere in the northeastern United States or Canada, the list of possibilities could include only ten species: pine, parula, magnolia, Cape May, black-throated blue, myrtle, black-throated green, Backburnian, bay-breasted, and blackpoll —among them some of the loveliest of all warblers!

The bay-breasted was quickly eliminated; its nest would be loosely constructed, with unkempt tresses of grass trailing from it in all directions. Blackburnian and magnolia likewise would build a much less compact nest than this. The blackpoll was automatically ruled out because it nests almost exclusively in spruce—and this was a pine. The handsome black-throated blue was considered and then rejected; it rarely builds more than two or three feet above the ground. What about the tiger warbler, the boldly marked Cape May? No, its niche was at the other extreme: up near the tips of towering trees, far above the ground! And as for parula, its trademark would be festoons of gray-green beard moss, and here there were none.

The choice was narrowed now to three, all builders of compact nests, all frequenters of pines, all known to build on occasion within six feet of the ground. But of these, the pine warbler almost always chooses a site far out on a limb. And now there were two, and it was for the egg to decide. The tiny, ovate white egg, a faint gloss still burnishing its surface, was etched and decorated with the finest of lilac-rust flecks around the large end, in a perfect wreath. And here, in Frank Chapman's classic *Warblers of North America,* we find pictured an egg identical to ours—the egg of the black-throated green warbler! And suddenly, in that snowy winter season, with the nest's builders and occupants long since flown to more provident winter grounds in Mexico, Puerto Rico, Panama, or Costa Rica, the image of that golden-headed elf with the "delicious lazy little drawl" filled and blessed the room.

The nest was left in its secret place, the most treasured of the ornaments that year, its beauty all but invisible in the leaf-clad pine. But apart from evergreens, it is the winter season that reveals to us many of the secret nesting places of birds, both suspected and unknown. Works of astonishing craftsmanship and no little engineering skill when they are built, they are no less handsome when autumn's cold winds peel away, leaf by leaf, the sheaths of their concealment and leave them finally stripped and naked to the world. Forsaken now by the quick and living, they are still objects of surprising beauty and harmony.

For now the greens of the grasses with which they are woven have weathered to browns and ochers and grays; what began as a blend of rich greens and browns is now a more subtle palette: the grasses straw-gold and gray, the twigs and vinelets umber and black, the mosses bleached near white, the linings silver and rust and rose. Now, even more distinctly than when fresh, the components of the warp and weft are distinct and identifiable, each element having aged in its own way: texture and tone and shape interwoven in one fabric and blended and mellowed by the seasons. But the spider silk that has bound the framework together so cleverly has now all but disappeared.

And yet it is a fabric of ruin and decay. No bird will nest again in last year's crumbling wreckage. Only those birds with massive platforms built of sticks return again and again to their eyries, yearly freshened and repaired—the eagles, ospreys, some hawks and owls. Herons and ibis nest on stick platforms, but these are flimsy, one-season efforts. Most small tree nests serve for a single brood, or rarely, if that first brood fails, a second (usually a completely new nest is built for the second brood, if the first nest has been damaged or otherwise struck with misfortune). The following year the parent birds may return to the same area, to the same garden or field, or even to the same tree or thicket, and they (or other birds) may borrow materials from the abandoned nest, but the nest they will use for breeding will be new.

There is, of course, an infinite variety to the form and shape, the structure, and the favored site of birds' nests. Many species are virtually nestless, laying their eggs without site preparation on sand or mud or rooftop, although the patch of earth on which the eggs are deposited and incubated may be as carefully selected and stoutly defended as a most elaborately constructed nest. Thus the murres will lay their eggs on the bare rock of narrow ledges on towering cliffs that overhang the sea. The common nighthawk will lay its speckled eggs on barren gravel or the corner of a pebble-surfaced flat roof, while its relative, the whip-poor-will, deposits its more blotched eggs without ceremony among the leaves at the woodland edge. Many of the beach-nesting birds lay their eggs in shallow saucers or scrapes in the sand or mud without the slightest trace of nest lining or decoration; among them are the least, sooty, royal, and Caspian terns. Forster's and Sandwich terns often avoid even the bother of making a depression, laying their eggs on undisturbed sand. Perhaps most incredible of all nonbuilders is the fairy tern of the South Pacific, which chooses a tiny flat spot on a horizontal tree limb as a platform for its single white egg. But equally nestless is the emperor penguin, whose egg, raised less than an inch from the Antarctic snow, rests on its own two feet, enfolded in its abdominal skin. Here it incubates, for nine long weeks, while the fasting male parent bird shelters it from the icy elements.

Slightly more concerned for nesting decor, but scarcely to be called nest-builders, are those species that may line a body-molded scrape in the sand with shards of seashells, pebbles, fish bones, or other bright objects; among these are the American oystercatcher, common tern, black skimmer, piping and Wilson's plovers. Others, preferring grassy fields to beaches, may form a similar body-saucer in the grasses, with nest-building confined to a scanty lining of dead grasses. Upland plover, spotted sandpiper, and prairie chicken are among these.

Many other species of birds construct more substantial nests on the ground of preferred available materials. The double-crested cormorant will make a heap of seaweed and other sea wrack serve on treeless islands and sandbars, but where spruce trees are close to water in Maine and the Maritime Provinces, tree nests of stick platforms are preferred. Common loons will build a heap of weeds close to a lakeshore, as will many waterfowl; each with a firm notion of how high and wide the nest shall be, what materials shall be used, how it shall be concealed, and with what it shall be lined.

I once watched an American coot working on a nest in the middle of a pond on Long Island; it was doggedly trying to fit into a nest whose outside diameter was perhaps eighteen inches a section of *Phragmites* stalk about three feet long. Its method was to poke the stalk into the nest until the end in its beak was neatly flush with the nest. Then it would swim around to the opposite side, discover the protruding end, and push it back until it too was flush; whereupon it would race around to the other side, only to find that end protruding! The game continued until (and probably long after) I tired of watching it; I never discovered how it ended, but the completed nest had no projecting stalks. Perhaps the stalk itself gave in to the repeated pokings, and broke. It was interesting that although the errant stalk in no way lessened the practicality of the nest, it offended the esthetic sense of the coot: the nest, then, was not merely an object of utility, but in the eyes of its builder, a work of art.

Flamingoes build their raised platform nests of the available material, which is mud, an adaption no doubt both to the comfort of the sitting bird, with its beanstalk legs folded beneath it, and to the safety of the eggs. Mud is the basic or a component building material of many species; from cliff swallows to eastern phoebe to robin.

There are, of course, many birds' nests hidden in burrows underground or in sandy banks, such as those preferred by puffins and petrels and other seabirds, by kingfishers and bank swallows. Some species of swifts and the South American oilbird and a number of other unrelated species select caves for their nesting: chimneys and hollow trees make suitable substitutes, at least for our chimney swift. In somewhat the same category are the hole-nesting birds, which seek out natural or excavated cavities in trees, to find them ready-made and rented for a song by friendly mankind. The parrots, the woodpeckers, the tree swallow and purple martin, many owls, the wood duck, the sparrow hawk, prothonotary warbler, bluebirds, nuthatches, chickadees, creepers, and the great crested flycatcher are among the fraternity of hole-nesters.

More elaborate woven nests are the choice of a number of field, meadow, and marshland species, which build more "standard" bowl-shaped nests from conveniently available grasses, rushes, leaves, and other dried or living vegetation. Often these nests are sited close to or under a concealing shrub or bush or taller tuft of grass. Some, like the nests of the bobwhite, the meadowlarks, and the grasshopper sparrow, may be roofed over with a canopy of taller grasses. The meadowlark is particularly adept at concealing its nest; often it is at the end of an arched tunnel, with more than a single exit.

Fascinating as are all these myriad nest forms, it is the woven cup and the woven pendant sack that intrigue us most. Marvelously fashioned by the bill (and sometimes the feet) of one parent bird or both, it may be securely fitted into a fork or tree crotch, perilously attached to a swaying branch tip, or carefully saddled over a limb. Instinctively measured to closely confine the average clutch laid by the female, even when constructed by the male, it provides that each egg will be equitably warmed by contact with the incubating parent, yet allows for the ever-expanding volume of nestlings to come. The orioles are our master pendant nest-builders, but they are rank amateurs compared to the skill exhibited by their tropical relatives, the caciques and oropendolas. Perhaps the most masterful of all woven nests are those by members of the Ploceidae, or African weaver family: densely woven grass and fiber globes formed on a single woven and knotted ring of grass stems, their entrances often guarded by a maze of thorns. Our own adopted weavers, the European tree and house sparrows, are slovenly by comparison.

But if the books tell us that the nests of most species are as distinctive as the birds themselves, we must allow some latitude for variation. Some species are strict traditionalists; every aspect of nest and habitat must conform. Others are more adaptable, and we may discover the nest that should be thirty feet up in a hemlock sixty feet high in a fir. Those who feared that the Baltimore oriole might disappear with the vanishing of its favorite tree, the American elm, are pleased to find it adapting to oaks, maples, lindens, and other deciduous hardwoods.

But on the average, each species maintains its preferred nesting habitat. In a recent and most elegant exercise in biostatistics, zoologist Frances James measured the nest site requirements of forty-six Midwestern species for fifteen variables, ranging from canopy height and percent of canopy cover to number of tree species present and shrub density. When the means of these criteria were plotted on a three-dimensional chart, it was found that each species did indeed have a unique and discernible niche: that there was clear ordination of habitat relationship to the nest sites of these species. The prairie warbler, for example, requires the least variety in plant species for its habitat, the wood thrush the most. The Baltimore oriole and the hooded warbler are most closely associated with tall isolated trees, the ovenbird, the least. The prothonotary warbler most faithfully selects for density of medium-sized trees, and/or lowest shrub density, with the white-eyed vireo at the opposite end of this scale.

In the final location and composition of the nest, we can attribute some part to learning: the adult constructs a nest resembling in site, materials, and dimensions, the one in which it developed as a juvenile. But to what, other than heredity, can we attribute the actual skills of construction? The new builders, if they breed in the first year after hatching, as many species do, have never watched a nest being built, have never been given a lesson in how to buttress and anchor a foundation, how to gather and interweave the materials, and how to fashion and line the interior. What teaches the tailorbird of Asia and Africa to actually sew a large leaf together, with fiber, to make a cup for its nest; or the megapode of New Guinea to lay its eggs in warm sand or a compost heap it builds, and then leave them to hatch on their own? This knowledge, like so many other behavior patterns of birds and all animals, must surely come with the genes.

With what consummate skill birds' nests are fashioned can be witnessed, if one is patient and observant, by finding a pair at work. But this takes time, and persistence. Often, for obvious reasons, most nests are concealed to the best ability of the builders—deep in hedges or thickets, or in the densest foliage of the tree, often high above eye level. How often we watch a pair busily foraging for nesting material, purposefully making trip after trip to a presumed nesting site, only to disappear into the green, the nest never found until the leaves are down in autumn! I recall one spring in New Haven when ornithologist John Davis and I spent hours watching a Lawrence's warbler, mated to a female blue-winged, carrying nesting materials into an impenetrable thicket of catbrier and head-high poison ivy; later we watched them carrying food. But though we flailed our way through, over, and under that murderous patch, no nest could we ever find, nor even pinpoint the bush that held the nest. Birds enter and leave their nests by devious routes, we finally decided.

It is in late autumn, then, when the leaves fall and those hiding places are revealed, that one may more easily search for nests. Sometimes we are amazed to find a nest exactly where we thought it was, but could never see it in summer. It is then that we discover that the catbird did indeed nest in the privet as we suspected, and that the song sparrow's nest had been incredibly dead center in the viburnum. But there will be surprises: the mockingbird that we thought had been both unmated and nestless had somehow raised its brood unnoticed in the secret maze of foliage in the neighbor's euonymus; and there was, indeed, a tanager's nest near the top of the pin oak, where it could never be seen from the ground.

Should you take them, or leave them where they molder? Since these small birds' nests are now ownerless and forsaken, there is no harm, except possibly (and temporarily) to bush or tree, in taking possession of them. Close examination and even dissection will often reveal much about bird behavior: how the nest was braced, strung, attached, suspended, woven, insulated, and lined. You might, perhaps, even find an infertile or a cracked egg, now to be examined and admired without guilt. The work that goes into the nest construction is fully revealed. Nests have been carefully dismantled and their components sorted and counted. One such house sparrow nest, according to John K. Terres, was found to comprise no less than 1,282 separate items: 1,063 pieces of dead grass, 126 strips of grapevine bark, 15 pieces of paper, 10 pieces of cellophane, 13 pieces of Kleenex, and 16 pieces of blue cotton thread, plus 28 feathers of wild birds, from blue jays, cardinals, and catbirds, 9 pieces of cotton, 1 piece of twine, and 1 cotton bandage!

Other species are well known for appropriating castoff human largess: orioles will weave into their nests lengths of brightly colored knitting wools. Golden eagles also like nest decorations: daily the male parent will bring a fresh pine branch to grace the family domicile. One wonders, now that the pill has replaced the condom, whether great horned owls will go back to snakeskins for decoration, or find another substitute?

If you are interested in finding birds' nests in winter, and identifying them, there are a few helpful guides. *A Complete Field Guide to Nests in the United States* by Richard Headstrom is useful, but it leaves something to be desired, particularly since there is no mention anywhere of one of the most important clues to identification: what the eggs look like. New in 1975 is *A Field Guide to Birds' Nests in the United States East of the Mississippi River* by Hal H. Harrison, in the Peterson series, with full-color illustrations of the nests and eggs of 285 species. Perhaps the most comprehensive descriptions of American birds' nests (and the eggs that they hold) will be found in the 22-volume series on the

Life Histories of North American Birds, edited by Arthur Cleveland Bent. Many other regional works, and some field guides (such as the Audubon field guides by Richard H. Pough), have brief nest descriptions.

A book filled with tips on how to find nests, and how to see into them when they are overhead (mirrors on poles) and other fascinating lore, is Bruce Campbell's *Finding Nests,* published in London. In Britain, it appears, nest-finding is as competitive a sport as list-chasing in America. Campbell notes that the hawfinch was the 158th species on his nest list, and discussing the chiffchaff, quotes the eminent nester Arthur Whitaker as considering it among the most difficult of nests in Britain to find; he had a life total of only 26 nests (as against 343 willow warbler nests!). How many North American birders know exactly how many nests of each species they have found, or even how many species' nests they have ever found?

Much more about bird biology and bird behavior, however, can be learned from patient and persistent observation at the active nest. Which of the pair does the actual building? Is it the female working alone, as with the hummingbirds, the ovenbird, the red-eyed vireo? Or the male alone, as with some of the shrikes? Is it the female with materials brought by the male, as with the mourning dove? Or is it the other way around, as with the magnificent frigatebird? Is it the female with materials brought by both sexes, as with the raven? Is it built by both partners, as is the case with kingfishers, woodpeckers, swallows, the cedar waxwing, and many other species? Does the male build practice or display nests with which to lure and please the female, as with the long-billed marsh wren? Is there a "helper" at the nest, of a different generation from the parents?

Are nest-building and maintenance part of the courtship activities of the pair? How long does it take to construct the nest? Does it take two or three days, as with many small birds, or several weeks, as for the elaborate sack of the chestnut-headed oropendola? Is the second nest built faster than the first (usually it is—the breeding season is getting short)? Are nests in the Arctic built faster than those in temperate climates? How many gathering trips are there per nest (203 for one Kirtland's warbler's nest)? What are the various stages of construction, and how is each accomplished? Is there a special effort to camouflage the nest? Is there one special route to and another from the nest, by either parent, or do the routes vary in different stages of the breeding cycle? Is there a threshold perch that is used just prior to the final flight to the nest?

Is the nest territory defended before the nest is built, while it is in use, and even after the young have flown, as it is with some species? How is the nest defended against other members of the same species, the same family, against aerial enemies, against snakes, rats, and other predators? What is the defense against clutch parasites: the brown-headed cowbird, for example?

How is nest sanitation maintained? How is nest maintenance performed? Are materials added during the incubation of young, and is this a function of courtship, pair-bond, or utility? How does the nest serve as a feeding platform, a flight training platform, and finally, what becomes of it when finally deserted?

Although there are still many Middle American species whose nests have never been found (and one locally common North American bird, the marbled murrelet, whose nesting place was only recently discovered), no one has answers for all these questions, even for the most ubiquitous species. The next time you find a nest new or old, occupied or abandoned, remember that it is an object of esthetic pleasure and more—that every straw and twig and hair and feather can teach lessons in animal behavior, and that there are worlds of knowledge waiting to be discovered by the questing eye and the questioning intellect.

LITTLE AUK! LITTLE AUK!, BY JOHN HAY *Although millions of its kind nest in the Far North and spend the winter months in the stormy seas off the Atlantic shore, the dovekie is familiar to only the Eskimos who gather its eggs, feast on its flesh, and make coats of its skins. For the rest of us, our only contact with this tiny but so very important sea-bird will be accidental—and perhaps revealing.*

It was in December and a slight snow had started. Inland of Cape Cod waters there was very little wind, and the flakes were spaced far apart. They seemed to hover. They would lift and dip, then slant down and touch slowly to the ground. The day was gray and quiet, tempered by the even recital of falling flakes, with a dull sky and a strip of gray sea in the distance. I watched the snowflakes acting in the space around me, over and inside and by each other in slow periods, and then I drove down to the outer beach.

The surf there was roaring, and hard wet flakes of snow came in heavily, driven by a seaward wind, and made my eyes smart. The curled-over, breaking waves were glassy green in the gray day and pushed in soapy sheets of foam along the sands. The ocean itself seemed full of kingly mountains meeting or withholding, conflicting, pushing each other aside, part of a collective immensity that could express itself in the last little bursting spit of a salt bubble flung out of the foam that seethed into the beach, a kind of statement of articulated aim out of a great language still untamed.

Out on those cold looming and receding waters seabirds rode. There were flocks of dark brown and black-and-white eiders a few hundred yards beyond the shoreline. Gulls beat steadily along the troughs of the waves. Then I caught sight of thirty or forty dovekies, the chunky black-and-white "little auks" that come down from the Far North during the winter to feed off the coast. Their color showed clearly against the green water, white under black heads, black backs and wings, with little upturned tail feathers. They dipped continually into the water, so quickly as to escape my notice much of the time. They made fish flips into those tumultuous sea surfaces as easily as minnows in a gentle pond.

The dovekie, called the little auk in Europe, breeds by the millions in the high Arctic, principally in north Greenland, Spitsbergen, northern Novaya Zamlya, and Franz Josef Land, with scattered colonies in subarctic areas. Drift ice is their principal habitat. They like areas where the ice is not too densely packed, and they feed in openings or leads between the floes on small crustaceans in the plankton. They seem to avoid the warm waters of the Gulf Stream, following the Arctic currents instead. Especially during periods of great population growth, emigration flights of dovekies take them on long journeys which scatter them to many regions, and occasionally take them inland in dovekie "wrecks" where they may be killed or injured, and become vulnerable to many kinds of predators. Their short narrow wings make it difficult, though not impossible, for them to take off from inland areas. One winter I saw many dead dovekies scattered down the Cape Cod highway, little penguinlike birds unknown to most drivers.

These dovekies off Cape Cod were flying and diving, casting their bodies back and forth between air and water like so many balls. Their speed is not great, but when they fly off over the water their wingbeat is very quick, and their landing and diving is done with a dash and play that belies their stumpy appearance.

In fact a dovekie in flight, though it lacks the agility and swinging maneuverability of a swallow, is at the same time somewhat reminiscent of those birds, with its short wings alternately beating fast and gliding, like a swift. When they swim underwater these chunky little "pineknots" do so with a quick, supple, almost fishlike beat, making me think that fins after all are not so far removed from wings.

Unseen, though they brought it with them in some measure, these vast distances down to New England, was the grandeur of the Arctic, whose auroras, growling ice, and sunsets I could only imagine. Dovekies breed in bare heaps of rock that cover great screes—hillsides of stone sloping down to the sea. They arrive there in the spring when green begins to show through frozen ground and rivulets and waterfalls begin to sound and the dovekies themselves utter a watery, twittering, trilling call. There they dot the slopes in great numbers "like pepper and salt," it says in *The Birds of Greenland,* and fly about "in huge flocks which resemble at a distance swarms of mosquitoes or drifting smoke."

To the Eskimos these little birds are of primary importance. They capture them with long-handled nets as they fly over their breeding cliffs and store them in the frozen ground for winter food. Eskimo women gather their eggs, where their nests are found between the rocks and stones, beginning in June. They also use their skins for a birdskin coat called a *tinmiaq.* For one such coat about fifty skins are needed. Admiral Donald B. MacMillan, the Arctic explorer, has described in a passage quoted by Edward Howe Forbush how much the spring arrival of the dovekies has meant to the Eskimos: "But what is that great, pulsating, musical note which seems to fill all space? Now loud and clear, now diminishing to a low hum, the sound proclaims the arrival of the true representative of the birdlife of the Arctic . . . the dovekie, or little auk (*Plautus alle*). The long dark winter has at last passed away. The larder open to all is empty. The sun is mounting higher into the heavens day by day. Now and then a seal is seen sunning himself at his hole. The Eskimos are living from hand to mouth. And then that glad cry, relieving all anxiety for the future, bringing joy to every heart, *Ark-pood-e-ark-suit! Ark-pood-e-ark-suit!* (Little auks! Little auks!)."

Arctic foxes also depend on dovekies for food, as well as on their immaculately bluish-white eggs. Dovekies are preyed upon by ravens and gyrfalcons, too, but the big, persistent enemy of which they are in mortal fear is the glaucous or burgomaster gull.

The nitrogen-rich guano of the dovekies, filtering down through the massive hillsides of loose bare stone, fertilizes a deep growth of moss in brilliant green bands. This and other plant life supports hare and ptarmigan and is probably good pasturage for what was once an abundant population of caribou. And in the sea this little bird that makes for provision in depth, both good and cruel, is often eaten by white whales, large fish, and seals.

What a major burden for one so small! Millions of dovekies feed their young during the nesting season and a whole Arctic world depends that they be successful, on and on into the future. The little ones are constantly hungry and chirp in a shrill impatient way until "the old bird feeds them by disgorging into their bills the content of its well-filled pouch. The consoling, soothing murmur of the old bird to the young, and the satisfied chirping of the young shows how solicitous the one and how grateful the other." Sweet domesticity still keeps the terrible world in order. The little auk is also a tough, all-weather bird, capable of survival in extreme circumstances, and so far it has the room it needs and the isolation and a major range.

How can we predators dare count the bodies, human and other than human, of those on whom we prey! How dare we wipe out whole populations in the first place, either by pulling a trigger or by spreading our wastes and poisons by the ton. Still, *dare* may not be the right word for a brutal carelessness so widespread that many men do not dare do anything but trade on it. How many tons of waste go into the air every minute? How much sewage goes into the earth's once pure and flowing waters, or how much of oil's dirty devastations is spread on the seas? How much overkilling will it take for us to come face to face with what is left of the vital innocence that has upheld the world without us up to now, like the dovekie and its Arctic pyramid of needs?

As I watched the dovekies, I saw one come in out of the water, letting itself be washed ashore with the broad sheet of foam sent in ahead of the breakers. It staggered and flopped up the slope of sand beyond the water's reach and stood there. I walked up to the little bird and it made only a slight effort to get away. Its thick breast feathers were coated with oil. They were also stained with the red of its blood. Since oil fouling causes birds to lose the natural insulation of their feathers, and poisons them when they preen, I supposed that this one had been weakened and perhaps flung against a rock by the waves.

I picked it up, and what a trembling there was in it, what a whirring heart! I carried it back to my car, thinking to clean the oil off later and see if I could bring it back to health, always a precarious job. But after a few minutes in the heated car the bird's blood began to flow from its breast, to my great dismay, and there seemed to be little I could do about it. I began to feel like a terrible meddler and a coward.

With that I took it back to calmer waters, on the bay side of the Cape, and let it go without illusions about the cruel mother than might take care of it better than I, but I felt that my fruitless attempts to save it would be worse. I remember the little beak with its pink lining, open and threatening, as the dovekie protested my picking it up, the black eyes blinking and glistening, the feel of its heart.

It was more than a small bird in mortal trouble. It had in it the greatness of its Northern range. I had, I suppose, with no excuses for what I failed to do, given it back to its own latitude, to the spirit of choking, roaring waters, of skies with smoky clouds where the little auks themselves look like smoke in the distance, and of swinging winds and draws between the ice floes, and the rivulets of spring.

That bird, which had bloodied me and been so close and warm in my hand, left me on the beach to shake with human ignorance.

SHED FEW TEARS,
BY HAROLD MAYFIELD

We rue the loss to a neighbor's cat of the songbird nest in our garden. We are shocked by the death of thousands of migrating birds against some man-erected obstacle to their flight. But such losses, though they are conspicuous and seem tragic at the moment, become insignificant when the dynamics of populations and survival are viewed without emotion.

To note the fall of a sparrow is the traditional mark of great compassion. This kind of concern comes easily to those of us who love wild creatures. When we awaken one morning to find the robin's nest at our window destroyed, there is general dismay in the household, and dark threats are uttered against the unknown, but suspected, predator. When ten thousand migrating birds die against a television tower on a foggy night, our legislative halls may echo the news.

Such solicitude is understandable. It is also valuable. This reservoir of sentiment, readily released whenever need arises, is the formidable power behind most conservation movements.

Yet that very estimable emotion, often impelling people to act according to their hearts rather than their minds, may lead them to waste their sympathies and energies on the wrong causes. To fight the conservation battle wisely, we need to identify our problems and enemies accurately. Sometimes this calls for considerable insight into the complex patterns of nature.

No aspect of nature is so difficult to study unemotionally as death and destruction. Yet these are part of an ancient pattern of survival and adaptation. Moreover, many of the most conspicuous examples may be far less than serious when seen in broader perspective, while the truly ominous influences may often be silent and unseen.

To be more specific, I am suggesting that the bird tragedies you see with your own eyes may make you sad, but they usually need not alarm you. This distinction is important. And in view of the gloom that pervades many conservation articles, I hope to convey a wry ray of optimism: Things may not always be as bad as they seem.

Consider the loss of a nest. If it is a nest you have been watching, it is a sad event. But is it significant to the welfare of the species? Probably not.

For many small songbirds, odds are against the survival of a nest to the point where the young are fledged. That is, the loss of the nest is the most probable outcome. This may seem a melancholy fact, but it need not cause worry. Most pairs of parent birds promptly build again. Many would produce only one brood a year anyway, and they are prepared to try several times if necessary. For these, the loss of one nest means only delay, not total failure.

Generally, the destruction or failure of some nests is a normal part of avian economy. If the birds did not have resources to cope with losses that to us seem severe, they would not be here.

Even more difficult to appreciate is the likelihood that the loss of some nests may, in the long run, be beneficial to the species. This culling of nests here and there tends to remove those that are vulnerable—the poorly constructed, the poorly concealed—and keeps pressure on the species to build well. It also spreads serious risk by guaranteeing that not all nests and broods are in the same stage of development at the same time. If every pair started nesting at the same time, and nothing happened to any of the nests, all would have eggs and young simultaneously. And a storm or freak calamity could wipe out the entire nesting effort in a day. Without frequent accidents to individual nests, the species would lose its practiced habit of renesting, and the eventual disaster would then be truly catastrophic.

To be reasonably philosophic about bird mortality, we need to know a little about its magnitude and inevitability. In general, the only tolerable state is one in which a population neither increases nor decreases eternally, but fluctuates within permissible bounds. When we are cheering for a favorite species, it is easy to forget that only a limited success is desirable. If any species continued to increase year after year, it would become a scourge to other forms of life, including our own, and ultimately become its own worst enemy through intra-species competition and vulnerability to plagues.

We have had just a hint of what constitutes "too many"—to us—in our experiences with the starlings, or indeed with the whole blackbird clan, of which 500 million are estimated to be found in roosts each winter in the United States.

To achieve a roughly level population, each pair of birds must on the average produce enough young to counter-balance the mortality between one nesting season and the next. That is, for each adult pair this year, there should be one adult pair surviving next year. Suppose a pair brings three young birds from its nest; of this total of five, only two will be alive at the beginning of the next summer. Three will perish one way or another. This fact is elementary.

Consequently, most songbirds—which produce an annual average of somewhat more than two fledglings per pair—will sustain losses during the year greater than the total adult population at the start of the nesting season. Since the spring bird population in the United States has been roundly estimated at about six billion, the deaths for the year must be of this same magnitude, perhaps rather more than less, since many birds produce more than two young per pair. For the sake of simplicity, I have not attempted to sort out the widely divergent mortality rates for different kinds of birds, nor have I considered the numbers of Canadian birds that migrate through the United States.

Against these startling totals, even those seeming disasters that occasionally come to our attention shrink toward insignificance.

Most bird deaths probably occur as isolated events, affecting only one bird or a small number of birds at one time and place. Scavengers promptly remove the evidence. Observers often marvel that we find so few carcasses in comparison to the great mortality we know occurs. Large numbers of dead birds come to our attention only in unusual circumstances, and man-made conditions often make the results conspicuous.

High visibility can likewise give a predator an undeserved bad name. A hawk or owl will be attracted occasionally to the abnormal concentration of birds at a feeding station or game farm. Here, in plain sight, it pecks away at an unusually vulnerable group—bunched, exposed, perhaps including individuals unable to survive without artificial help—and thus may seem a great menace to wild populations.

So when one bird dies in front of us, we grieve. And when a thousand birds fall at our feet, we are appalled. Indeed, this sometimes does occur at television towers, which often rise to heights of more than 1,000 feet, penetrating the lower altitudes used by night migrants.

Once, few man-made obstacles protruded hundreds of feet above the surrounding terrain. Today, nearly every city of consequence in America has one or more of these towers. Usually they are placed in the open country or on a hill top to increase their effectiveness, and are marked with lights at night to warn airplanes.

On nights when migration is heavy but visibility is poor, many birds are killed at these sites. They collide with the tower and its guy wires, and they collide with one another as they mill about in confusion, perhaps attracted by the lights, or the partial illumination of the steelwork, or the calls of the birds already gathered there. The casualties are often seen on closely mowed grass at the base of a tower.

A very thorough study of birds killed at a television tower was made near Tallahassee in northwestern Florida. Herbert L. Stoddard, Sr., and his associates attempted with meticulous care and diligence to retrieve the bodies of all birds that fell there. The toll averaged 2,500 per year.

The Committee on Bird Protection of the American Ornithologists' Union, under the chairmanship of Victor H. Cahalane, has calculated that, if the Tallahassee results are typical, the annual death toll from this cause is more than one million birds. Such destruction, of course, is highly variable from night to night, year to year, and location to location. In Wisconsin, in one instance, perhaps 15,000 birds were killed in a single night.

Considered by themselves, these figures overwhelm us. But when placed into perspective against all bird losses for the year, they are not quite so frightening.

If one million birds are killed each year at television towers, this cause of mortality takes one in about 6,000 of the year's bird casualties in the United States. Proportionately, 16/1000ths of one percent is not a significant number of deaths from a single cause.

Indeed, the chances that a human being will eventually die in an automobile wreck are more than 100 times as great as the odds that a bird will end its life against a television tower. Deplorable as these highway fatalities are, no one has suggested that autos are endangering the human species. Deaths of birds at television towers would need to be sixty times as great to account for one percent of the year's losses.

This, then, reminds us of the enormous toll of birdlife that nature takes, and prompts us to think about how the other 99.984 percent of deaths occur. In detail, we do not know. That is my point. We tend to become alarmed by a comparatively small loss that we *see* and thus have little concern left for vastly larger losses that are not obvious.

How many birds are killed by collisions with trees, mountains and other natural objects? How many are hit by airplanes or autos? How many fly against wires? How many are lost at sea? How many are dashed by storms? How many migrate to unsuitable areas where they cannot survive? How many are killed by natural enemies or disease? The very hopelessness of these other hazards tends to quell our curiosity about them.

Some may feel that I take undue comfort from my sweeping totals. They may point out that television towers, for example, might be particularly dangerous to certain species. Indeed, some kinds of birds are particularly numerous in the lists of those killed at television towers. Among the most frequent are the red-eyed vireo, ovenbird, Tennessee warbler, magnolia warbler, palm warbler, yellow-throat, catbird, and the thrushes. It is reassuring to note, however, that these are common and widespread birds, and their prominence on these mortality lists may be merely a confirmation of their large continental populations.

This is not to say that you should not feel concern about an identifiable cause of death to thousands of birds. The loss may not be significant to the continental population, but it may include the wood thrush that sings in your yard.

Many of us recall Thomas S. Roberts' unforgettable account of a disaster to Lapland longspurs, described in his *Birds of Minnesota*. During a wet and heavy March snowstorm, flocks of longspurs milled about in confusion, and many of them died from collisions with obstructions, the ground or each other. He estimated there were 750,000 carcasses on just two snow-covered lakes, and he believed the total loss may have amounted to millions of birds in an area of 1,500 square miles. Yet he noticed no appreciable diminution of longspurs during the next and succeeding years.

Evidently the species was able to sustain these losses without lasting damage, although it is possible there may have been an appreciable decline in the nesting population in one part of the widespread Arctic range of this bird. If it were not so, the longspur would not be with us, for spring snowstorms of this kind must have occurred many times in the past.

One might view with equanimity even heavy losses of an abundant species, but still feel a tremor of alarm about the possibility that some very rare bird, like the Kirtland's warbler or Bachman's warbler, might be endangered by one bad night at a television tower. In fact, in recent years one Kirtland's warbler was picked up at the base of a 300-foot lighted monument on an island in Lake Erie, and as far back as 1886 one was found in Cleveland "under the electric light mast," a newfangled obstruction of that day.

But I think experience argues against the likelihood that the Kirtland's warbler population might be decimated at a television tower. The migration of this species is spread over several weeks in both spring and fall, and it is unlikely that many of these birds would be in the air at one time and one place. Generally, it is reassuring that the species killed at towers seem to reflect the relative abundance of birds passing through at the time; that is, rare migrants are rare on these mortality lists.

As for more abundant species, we take their resilience for granted. In a ten-year study of a local population of purple martins, I found that the number of nests—and presumably the number of adults—declined as much as 41 percent one year and increased as much as 82 percent the next season. Curiously, these fluctuations were similar to those summarized for gamebirds by Dr. Joseph J. Hickey at the University of Wisconsin. Probably the numbers of nearly all wild creatures fluctuate rather widely from year to year, and most of these changes go unnoticed.

In trying to understand the ability of birds to withstand heavy losses, we must realize that losses from different causes are not simply additive. They are interrelated in complex ways. The loss of a thousand birds in the nest in June or at a television tower in September usually does not mean a thousand birds fewer the following June. When birds are lost, the chances of survival are improved for those that remain. Competition is reduced, and the pressure from enemies usually relents.

Most predation is density dependent. That is, predators are opportunists, tending to seek the prey that is easiest to catch and specializing momentarily in the kind that is particularly accessible. The forces generated within a group when it is crowded constitute one of the factors which makes a creature more vulnerable to its enemies than it would be ordinarily. Conversely, when a species becomes less abundant and harder to catch, it is more successful in evading its enemies, partly because the predator often turns its attention to other sources of food.

So, the dead birds we see are not likely to represent a significant loss to the species. Nearly every wild creature has the ability to sustain heavy annual losses and produce a surplus every year against the inevitable attrition of natural agencies.

But these remarkable survival powers operate only as long as the bird has suitable habitat. It is adapted to surviving in a particular environment, one which provides food and shelter and meets the psychological requirements of the species. If the habitat is disturbed or destroyed, the bird is affected at the roots of its existence and may not be able to live and reproduce.

When this happens, the species wastes silently away. Thus the worst of all disasters does not present itself dramatically as a pile of carcasses.

Our heroic efforts to save the whooping crane would not be necessary if the lands formerly inhabited by many hundreds of cranes were not now used for growing wheat, and if the tiny remnant population were not pushed off into a remote nesting area of borderline suitability.

It is sometimes true that deaths caused by either the hand or works of man are the limiting factor on a population, but these instances are not numerous. Obvious examples are the large mammals that man can hunt to the point of extinction. However, the most serious impact of man usually is indirect. Even in the instance of the passenger pigeon, where man wrought the extinction of perhaps the most abundant bird on earth, the breaking up of successive nestings was more important than any imaginable slaughter of the birds.

Therefore, our conservation efforts show insight when they are directed mainly to the preservation and restoration of natural conditions. This is the fundamental requirement for keeping bird populations in a healthy state and fully able to sustain the high losses that inevitably occur from one cause or another.

THE POWER OF THE OWL, BY ANGUS CAMERON

People who are not otherwise interested in birds are often entranced by owls and collect their images in art and figurines. Indeed, since the Stone Age, these hunters of the night skies, with their silent wings and eerie cries, have cast a spell over primitive and civilized man.

The contemporary and perennial interest in owls is very ancient in human culture and stands at the end of a very ancient artistic tradition. The first representation of any bird that can be identified by species was that of an owl, and since the day that Old Stone Age engraving so easily identifiable as a snowy owl was scratched on the wall of the cave in France called Les Trois Frères, men have been continuously preoccupied by owls. Owls have served as totem animals; they have been the companions of gods and goddesses in the pantheons of deities; they have figured and still figure prominently in human folklore and literature. Today the owl's continued appeal is evidenced by the thousands of collectors of owl statues and figurines. Indeed, the universal appeal of owls was recently demonstrated by the fact that a prominent New York City department store devoted a full-page advertisement at Christmastime to the numerous porcelain, glass, and wooden owl figures that could be had at the store's sales counters.

Undoubtedly the fascination owls have had for men predates the Cro-Magnon who made the cave painting; the eerie hoots and near-human screams and gobblings of owls, which even in our relatively unsuperstitious times can produce a tiny shiver of fear on a dark night, more powerfully affected men in millennia more ancient than the times of the cave painters.

A bird that flies by night, when the mysteries and terrors of life have always been most rampant in men's minds, was certain to have an awesome place in men's imaginations. In times when every inanimate object and living creature was thought to be possessed by spirits, the owl must have seemed dire and fearsome indeed. His very appearance is unlike that of other birds; his eyes, set in the front of his face where they can stare in manlike fashion at his observer, add a strong touch of the human to his aspect. His weird hoots, screams, demoniac laughter, and gobblings and chucklings lend a devilish character that draws him compulsively into the human (or superhuman) world. His solemn mien, his level, two-eyed glare, his dignity of stance, and upright perch give him a quality of reserve that seems to spell wisdom and self-contained insight. The phrase "wise old owl" must reflect a judgment about the bird that is very old in man's lore.

The Greeks associated the owl with their patroness, Athena, the goddess of knowledge and wisdom. The big-eyed judgment of the wise bird looked out from the obverse side of Athenian coins at generations of Greeks who thought of the little owl (*Athene noctua*) as a symbol of their own superior qualities. Although the overt association of the owl with wisdom comes to us most directly from the Greeks, long before their time the owl figured in human folklore as a bird of power and portent. In fact, Athena herself seems to have been a goddess derived from an Anatolian female deity, an Earth goddess of fertility. The owl may have been associated with this earlier figure, or its association with Athena may have come more mundanely from the fact that it nested amongst the buildings of the Acropolis.

It is natural that the owl should be associated with darkness, and therefore with the underworld. Indeed, Lilith herself, Sumerian goddess of the underworld, whose name is translated in the Authorized Version of the Bible as "screech owl," is represented on an ancient cult plaque as winged, taloned, and flanked by two owls. The goddess holds in her hands measuring ropes, symbols of judgment. It is interesting in this connection that the famous "owl cups" so common in Greek ceramics may also have been used as measures, and thus as standards or as symbols of judgment. Owls appear as mummies among the grave furniture in Egypt and commonly on tomb paintings. In China the owl was the symbol of thunder and lightning, and was portrayed in ornaments called "owl corners," which were built into the corners of roofs to protect dwellings from fire.

The owl's configuration in folklore is early, worldwide, and universal, and for this reason folklorists have been intrigued by man's preoccupation with the bird. In many parts of Europe and Asia, merely seeing an owl called for countersigns and propitiatory rites. The owl, however, was not only an early portent of evil and even a common harbinger of death, but like all associates of shamans, sorcerers, and necromancers, it became a symbol that in the proper hands could avert evil. This conversion of a symbol of evil into a thing endowed with beneficent powers is common in man's history, and the process is well described by the British ornithologist E. A. Armstrong in his book *The Folklore of Birds:*

"So the owl which terrifies folk by gazing at them with its two great eyes or by wailing or shrieking like a soul in torment may be enlisted against the many powers of evil with which it is associated. The visible object of fear may be employed to inspire fear in the invisible powers which are feared. Thus the evil thing can be transformed into an ally by enlisting it against evil. But for the exploitation of this principle in the vaccines of modern medicine many of us would not be alive today."

The cave painter of Les Trois Frères was probably a shaman himself, working his magic in the depths of darkness in the grottoes, rendering his creatures for magical purposes. It seems most likely that the snowy owls may have had the apotropaic function described so well by Armstrong.

From the British Isles to China the owl has been associated with evil deeds. Where Shakespeare has Macbeth cry, "I have done the deed; didst thou not hear a noise?" and his lady says, "It was the owl that shriek'd, the fatal bellman/ Which gives the stern'st good-night," she is making an association most ancient in human lore. And the witches had anticipated her, for when the cauldron boiled they added an owlet's wing to that infernal brew. Both Jeremiah and Isaiah in leveling curses predicted that "owls shall dwell therein," and many cultures have formulas in their magic for pacifying the forces of evil when an owl alights on a dwelling place. Although Pliny himself was skeptical about the matter, he reports the superstition that death follows the owl that perches atop a private house and national disaster occurs when the same bird roosts in a public building. When Casca says, in *Julius Caesar,* "And yesterday the bird of night did sit / Even at noonday upon the market-place / Hooting and shrieking," he is following Plutarch, who in turn must have followed Pliny's sources, which were not from literature but from lore.

Thus "the bird that snatches the soul," as the Chinese put it, was almost universally an omen of death and doom. And lest we get the notion that these superstitions are a thing of the distant past, it may be useful to quote Armstrong further: "W. J. Brown, writing in 1934, mentions that when he commented to an old man on the death of a mutual acquaintance, he remarked: 'It weren't no more nor I expected. I come past his house one night, and there were a scret [screech] owl on his roof, scretting something horrible. I always reckon to take note of them things.'"

Whether or not the old man had an antidote for the evil of owls, other men have had.

Just as the hex sign painted on the side of a barn is meant to avert evil, so the owl and owl wings, nailed on the side or door of a barn, are evidence of a continuation of the ancient belief that the owl is "strong medicine" that can turn aside bad luck. Owl broth turns up regularly in folk pharmacopeia as a remedy for children's diseases, and parts of the owl, such as its foot or heart, were thought to be cures for ailments as diverse as madness, bad eyesight, and heart disease. The Romans used an owlish design to counteract the evil eye, and the Altaic people in far-off central Asia kept the bird itself near a child's bed to fend off evil spirits. In Japan the Ainu nailed representations of owls to their houses in times of epidemics or famine. Alcoholism, epilepsy, and gout have variously been treated by the eggs and flesh of owls.

To some, the owl's powers could far transcend their use in private ministrations. In *The Wasps,* written in 422 B.C., Aristophanes attributed the victory at Marathon to the fact that "Pallas sent her night bird." And Agathocles, Tyrant of Syracuse, claimed that his stunning victory over the Carthaginians in 310 B.C. resulted from his release of owls over his army.

The appearance of owls in the folklore and art of pre-Columbian America may have stemmed from ancient lore carried across the Bering Strait by the forebears of the American Indian and Eskimo, or it may have arisen afresh here because people made the same association between owls and the supernatural that the Europeans and Asiatics made. The owl turns up as a canny creature in Eskimo lore and as a worthy antagonist to the sly coyote in the lore of the Zuñi and other southwestern American Indians. The Mixtecs and Zapotecs have fine owl tales to tell, often memorialized on their ceramics. The Mayans associated the owl with childbearing and indicated this by the use of the bird as part of a headdress on female figurines.

The Mayans put the owl in a classic position that harks back to Lilith herself, for the screech owl was the symbol of Ah Puch, the god of death, who ruled the lowest level in the underworld. It was left to the Aztecs, however, to make the ultimate association of the owl with death. As Faith Medlin reports in her interesting book *Centuries of Owls,* "During the rites of human sacrifice, stone containers such as the *cuauhxicalli* with the owl motif were used by priests to hold the hearts that were torn from the prisoners and offered to the gods. *Teponaztli* (drums), carved from a hollowed-out log and adorned with an owl face, beat dramatic tempos during the gory ceremonies. The Aztecs associated the owl with the god of the dead. Even today many descendants of those Aztec warriors believe the owl's night cry is fatal to anyone who hears its portentous call." And many descendants of other warriors from other cultures still half believe it today.

Thus, the owl figurine that sits on your occasional table or whatnot shelf is an ancient and universal symbol of power and portent.

A FREE MARGIN FOR BIRDS, BY HAL BORLAND

The science of ornithology has by no means explained all the ways of birds. The methods of migration, for example, still baffle the experts. Perhaps it is best that some of these mysteries remain unsolved. Then, like the ancients who invented marvelous legends about birds real and preposterous, we may continue to be inspired by the song of a thrush or the plunge of an eagle.

"You must not know too much," Walt Whitman once wrote, "or be too precise or scientific about birds and trees and flowers. A certain free margin . . . helps your enjoyment of these things."

Whitman's "free margin" is responsible for the most enduring legends and fables about birds, some of which go back to the early Greeks, some of them common in American Indian lore, and some actually embedded in scientific ornithology. Take the kingfisher, for instance.

The kingfisher's generic name is *Alcyon*, directly out of Greek mythology. Aeolus, Greek god of the winds, had a daughter, Halcyone, who married Ceyx. Ceyx was drowned in a shipwreck, and Halcyone was so distraught she plunged into the sea and drowned herself. But the compassionate gods revived both Ceyx and Halcyone and changed them into kingfishers, who built a floating nest at the edge of the sea. It was about the time of the winter solstice and the stormy waves threatened to destroy both nest and eggs, so again the gods intervened. They calmed the weather for a week or so, till the eggs hatched, then calmed it another week for the nestlings to get a start. Hence the halcyon days, a spell of calm, quiet weather around the time of the winter solstice. Hence the kingfisher's scientific name.

It doesn't matter that our kingfishers mate and nest in the spring and the nest is in a hole they dig in a cliff or a steep riverbank. Those were Greek kingfishers. And to Saint Ambrose and others who told the story, the kingfisher really was a princess, not a mere bird.

Another of the legends that reach over into the scientific names is that about the whippoorwill. The ornithological name for the genus is *Caprimulgus*, literally "goatsucker." Its origin reaches far back, to rural Greek life, where superstitious goatherds, seeing how the whippoorwills hovered about their goats in the evening, seeing the birds' open mouths and knowing next to nothing about them, said they sucked milk from the teats of their goats. Actually, the birds were catching the insects the goats stirred up from the grass, seining them from the air with their open mouths. But goatsuckers they were called, and goatsuckers they still are, by scientific name.

American Indians have other whippoorwill stories to tell. The Omahas believed the whippoorwill calls, "Hoia, hohin?" and if a man hears he replies, "No!" If the birds at once fall silent, the one who answered will soon die, but if the birds keep on calling, the one who answered will live for a long time. The Utes consider the whippoorwill the god of the night. They say it created the moon out of a big frog. Among the Iroquois the common orchid we call lady's-slipper was known as the whippoorwill moccasin.

Various birds were regarded as sacred among the Indians. To the Omahas the red-bellied woodpecker was a guardian and special god of children because it kept its own children in a safe place. To the Pawnees the wren was a god of happiness. They called it "the laughing bird" because it sang so exuberantly. To the

109

various Plains tribes, the crow was sacred as the bird of the ghost dance. The Navajos held the mountain bluebird sacred because the blue of its back was the same blue that in their religion was the color of the South. It was the herald of the rising sun, their supreme god.

Among primitive people the "sacred" birds almost always had practical as well as mystical virtues in their favor. The ibis and the hawk in Egypt are minor gods, but they also are scavengers, eating young crocodiles, poisonous snakes, mice, and other pests and vermin. The stork in Europe represents filial piety, but it also is a persistent street-cleaner and eater of carrion. In Australia the aborigines deify the native kingfisher—which the whites call "the laughing jackass"—and appreciate the fact that it kills snakes as well as fish.

Geese have inspired many tales and legends. Who hasn't heard of the goose that laid golden eggs? The myth probably goes all the way back to India. He who was to become the Buddha was born a Brahmin, grew up, married, and fathered three daughters. He died and was born again as a golden mallard or a golden goose—the legend is a little misty on this point. Anyway, he had golden feathers and gave them up, one by one, for the support of his former family. One day the mother decided to pluck the bird clean, and despite the protest of the daughters, did so. But as she plucked the golden feathers they turned to plain white feathers, worthless. And when the bird grew new feathers they, too, were common white feathers.

But what of the barnacle goose? That probably goes back to hungry monks in eleventh-century monasteries. As a result of their limited, meatless diet during Lent, a group of monks in Ireland insisted that certain geese could be eaten because they were born on fruit trees. The fruit of these trees, if left to decay, produced worms which became hairy, then feathered, then winged—which did, in fact, become geese. The monks were reproved, but came up with various explanations of the origin of these geese, the most ingenious, perhaps, being the one repeated by a monkish traveler of the late twelfth century, Giraldus Cambrensis, who said: "In this area [Ireland] there are many birds which nature produces in a miraculous manner. They resemble marsh geese but are somewhat smaller. They originate from pine wood which drifts upon the seas. The small birds hang from the wood, protected by clamshells, by their beaks. After their plumage has grown they drop off and fly away."

Hence the barnacle goose, actually hatched by Irish monks who wanted a good meal of roast goose during Lent. But still called the barnacle goose.

For some reason, possibly because birds could fly and man could not, the birds were long believed to possess esoteric knowledge and the power of prophecy. Clever men who declared they could understand what birds had to say or interpret what their actions meant became prophets, or augurers, or *auspices*. There was even an *auspex*, who examined bird entrails for omens and answers. So a whole volume of bird lore accumulated. Some of it persists even today.

It was of special importance in which direction the birds were flying. If an eagle, for instance, flew past from right to left it was one of the best omens the gods could give. Vultures were both good and bad omens. Aristotle and Pliny considered them unlucky birds. Swallows were unlucky birds under any circumstance. They appeared in the tent of Pyrrhus before his defeat and on the ship of Mark Antony before his navy was overwhelmed by Octavian. Owls were considered bad omens in Greece, except in Athens, where, being sacred to Athena, the owl was believed to be a bringer of success and victory. Mariners considered swans good omens, bringers of favorable wind and good weather.

There is a Greek legend—several of them, in fact—about swans that persists till this day. It is embedded in the language in the term "swan-song," and it simply means that the swan, not a musical bird by any means, does achieve a sweet voice and something like a melody as it nears death. Its origin is wholly clouded over, but possibly the legend is related to the story of Apollo and the swans in Greek mythology.

Zeus, though married to Hera, was in love with Leto, and they had an affair. Leto, pregnant, looked for a place to bear her child, but Hera, jealous, issued an order that no land on Earth should be host to the expectant Leto. Wandering in search of a refuge, Leto at last found a floating speck of Earth. It was not a "land," so it was exempt from Hera's command. Miraculously, it fastened itself to the bottom of the sea and became the island of Delos. Apollo was born there and, according to the poet Callimachus, "The swans . . . circled seven times around Delos and sang over the bed of childbirth, swans, the most musical of all birds that fly." And in celebration of that event, Apollo later strung his lyre with seven strings, honoring the swans that circled his birthplace seven times.

Some believe that Hera cursed the swans after this episode and decreed that henceforth they should never sing until the moment of death. If so, I find no record of such a curse in Greek mythology.

Ravens and crows have long been powerful omens. Ravens croaking on the right hand were a good omen, but on the left were a bad sign. If a crow appeared with its mate at a wedding, it meant a long and happy life for the bride and her husband; but one crow alone meant sorrow and separation. In parts of New England today it is said that two crows flying together to the left is a bad omen. This seems to have been borrowed originally from magpie lore in England, where the same belief persists. In the South it is believed, in some rural areas, that if two quail fly up in front of a man on his way to close a deal he had better go home and forget the deal.

Swallows have baffled observers for a long time because they seemed simply to vanish at the end of summer. Apparently nobody saw them go south, so it was believed they did not migrate. As early as Aristotle's day the explanation was that swallows, swifts, and nightingales spent the winter hibernating, like frogs, in the muddy bottom of ponds. This fantastic notion persisted for centuries. Even Gilbert White, the English cleric whose *Natural History and Antiquities of Selborne* was published in 1789, was inclined to believe English swallows hibernated. And Alexander Wilson, America's first ornithologist, thought it necessary to insist, in 1808, that swallows did not hibernate in the mud. Even then many people still believed that old story.

An Eskimo tale says that cliff swallows are changelings from happy Eskimo children who were shaping "playhouse" mud igloos on the top of a cliff. That is why the swallows come back every summer and build their own mud "igloos" on the cliff. Another swallow story said that two miraculous stones were hidden inside every swallow. One was red and cured an invalid instantly. The other was black and brought good fortune. It also was believed that by some kind of magic or inspiration swallows found a special kind of stone on the seashore that would restore sight to the blind. Longfellow talks of this legend in *Evangeline* when he says, "Seeking with eager eyes that wondrous stone, which the swallow/Brings from the shore of the sea to restore the sight of its fledglings."

Two of the old myths, both deeply embedded in the language, concern a wholly mythical bird and another bird as real as a robin. The first is the phoenix, age-old symbol of resurrection after death or destruction by flames. The first known account of this fabulous bird was by Herodotus, some 400 years before Cleopatra, when he told his fellow Greeks about wonders he had seen on a trip to Egypt:

"There is another sacred bird, called the 'phoenix,' which I myself never saw except in a picture, for it seldom makes its appearance among the Egyptians —only every five hundred years, according to the people of Heliopolis. They state that he comes on the death of his sire. If at all like his picture, this bird may be thus described in size and shape. Some of his feathers are the color of gold; others are red. In outline he is exceedingly similar to the eagle, and in size also . . . He is represented as coming out of Arabia, and bringing with him his father to the temple of the Sun, embalmed in myrrh, and there burying him."

But Herodotus missed the whole point of the legend—or the legend was later amplified. Either way, the phoenix legend says that after its allotted five hundred years, the bird flew into the sun and was burned to ashes, from which the new, young phoenix arose. In another version, the legend says the old phoenix burned itself on a pyre, and out of its ashes arose the new, young bird. Somewhere along the way the bird and the legend gained a place in Egyptian religion, the phoenix being an Egyptian god symbolizing the sun, which burns itself to death each evening and is resurrected every morning.

The second of these birds that have become a byword is the ostrich. Who has not heard about "the ostrich sticking its head in the sand"? The idea, of course, is that the bird stupidly thinks it is invisible that way. Probably the oldest reference to this is by Diodorus Siculus, in the first century B.C. In his *Historical Library*, he wrote about a creature that has "the shape both of a camel and an ostrich, so that this creature seems both terrestrial and volatile, a land-beast and a bird. But being not able to fly by reason of the bulk of her body, she runs upon the ground as swift as if she flew in the air; and when she is pursued by horsemen with her feet she hurls the stones that are under her, and many times kills the pursuers with the blows and strokes they receive. When she is near being taken, she thrusts her head under a shrub or some like cover; not (as some suppose) through folly or blockishness, as if she would not see or be seen by them, but because her head is the tenderest part of her body."

Even then, apparently, it was thought that the ostrich hid its head thinking it thereby hid its whole self. So the origin of the tale is lost completely. However, it is said that when brooding an egg the ostrich actually does stretch its neck along the ground and keeps this position as long as it is being watched by anything it fears.

One of the grimmest of all legends is the one about the pelicans. Oddly, the pelican is ubiquitous—in art, religion, even in heraldry. But this particular legend goes back to the ninth or tenth century, perhaps even farther. In substance, it says that when young pelicans are hatched in the nest, they soon grow rebellious. At a certain point, when the mother bird is away from the nest, the father bird is so provoked by the nestlings, who gang up and give him quite a trouncing, that he kills them, leaves them in the nest, and goes his way. The mother pelican returns, is heartbroken to find her youngsters all dead, gashes her own breast with her beak and draws blood, with which she revives the dead children.

This probably comes from the mistakes of early observers who saw a mother pelican return to her nest, open her capacious beak, and allow her nestlings to reach in and pluck from her pouch the predigested fish she had gulped up for them. The interior of the pelican's mouth is almost as red as blood, so some offhand watcher thought he saw a bleeding breast and the young pelicans eagerly taking the blood, rather than the fish that revived them from their normal between-feedings somnolence.

The whole idea of resurrection engendered by blood, of course, fitted into early religious dogma, so the notion persisted. And the pelican for a long time was one of the common religious symbols.

Among primitive peoples, birds were believed to have notable powers of prophecy, which they expressed by actions, by singing, by not singing, or merely by looking or moving in a certain way. Typical is the legend of the *Charadrius*, a plover with unusual prophetic gifts. If anyone were seriously sick, the *Charadrius* came and looked at him. If the sickness was critical and would soon end in death, the plover looked away, indicating that the case was hopeless. But if the situation was not to be fatal, the plover looked intently at the patient and the patient looked at the bird, and all those gathered to mourn their friend's death could celebrate instead, certain of his recovery.

Among the American Indians, particularly those of the Plains tribes of the West, the eagle, the magpie, and the sage hen were revered. The eagle was the thunderbird and superior to all others, maker of winds, creator of storms, source of lightning and thunder. (On the West Coast the condor was the thunderbird.) The magpie was considered wiser than most birds because it talked so much, but was not wholly trusted because it was a gossip. The sage hen was a bird of the morning, the start of the day. But in virtually all Indian bird lore the central figure was the crow, in part because its color was a reminder of death and the shadowland beyond, in part because it was a messenger from the spirit world.

In many Indian stories, the raven, the crow, and most of the other birds were originally white. Their eventual colorful plumage was accounted for in various ways, involving flowers and sunset colors and various pigments the Indians used to paint themselves. There are several accounts of how the raven became black. Among the Tlingits of the coast of southern Alaska, it was said that the raven, in a house with the petrel, played a trick that angered the petrel. The raven tried to escape by flying up through the smokehole but got stuck there, and the petrel built a smoky fire under him. Ever since then the raven has been smoke-black. In another story, told among Greenland Eskimos, the raven and the snowy owl, close friends, quarreled over a new black-and-white dress; the snowy owl threw a dish of sooty lamp oil at the raven, and the raven has been soot-black ever since.

Neither the Tlingits nor the Eskimos who told these tales ever heard of the early Greeks, but they, too, had their white ravens who were changed to black. Ovid tells of the snow-white raven who was a protégé of Apollo. One day the raven told Apollo that Coronis, a Thessalian nymph and Apollo's mistress, was being unfaithful to him. Apollo killed the nymph, then turned on the raven because he hated tale-bearers. He spared the raven's life, but he turned him black, every feather, and took away his ability to speak a language men could understand.

Men have admired birds and envied them ever since men came down out of the trees and realized that they could not flap their arms and fly. They have invented tales about birds ever since they had words to express their thoughts. Birds still inspire us with awe and wonder. Who can listen to a wood thrush at evening without half remembering an untold myth? Who can watch an eagle soaring and not know deeply, inwardly, what the Indians knew when they called the eagle the thunderbird? Who can hear the wild goose, high overhead, coming north in spring, going south in autumn, and not hear the voice of freedom and adventure? The great goose, like the thrush and the eagle, is more than bird. He is yearning and dream, search and wonder, the very epitome of myth and legend. Even with Whitman's "free margin," we all know that.

THE ROBIN *SEES* THE WORM, BY FRANK HEPPNER

The pursuit of graduate degrees in ornithology leads to some pretty esoteric research projects—like counting the bumps on sparrow legs and speculating on what profound effect the number of bumps has on the birds' lives. Occasionally a student's thesis may produce data of lasting interest to science. And in the rarest instances, as in the author's investigation, a question asked by thousands of birdwatchers may be answered.

As I released the football player from the folds of my mist net, I explained that I was collecting robins, and that robins landed on the football field during his scrimmage hours. He made a rude and profane remark. I shrugged, picked up my paraphernalia, then trundled back to a little patch of ground behind the handball courts at San Francisco State College, where I was to spend the next year and a half trying to discover how robins find worms.

I was a graduate student at the time, and I think my boss, Dr. Robert I. Bowman, kept me around for comic relief. For as reports about a man crawling on all fours on campus lawns, and of subway train roars coming from the handball courts in late afternoon, began to filter in to the biology department, the word was that something highly irregular was going on.

Everyone who watches robins foraging on a lawn sooner or later begins to wonder what the bird is doing when it runs across the turf, stops, cocks its head, then suddenly pounces forward and tugs back an instant later with a worm in its bill. One's first impression is that the bird is listening for worms when it cocks its head—just as people do when they try to hear faint sounds. This observation can be misleading, because the external opening of the robin's ear is located right next to its eye, and from a distance it is almost impossible to tell whether the eye or the ear is pointed toward the worm hole.

A few frustrating field observations convinced me that some sort of experimentation was necessary to determine just how robins *do* find worms. The problem was to find a set of experiments which would yield the needed information.

What senses *could* the robin use to find worms? The kiwi of New Zealand can smell worms underground, but the kiwi probes its slender bill into the earth to perform this feat. Most other birds have a poorly developed olfactory sense, and the behavior of the foraging robin is not typical of animals which locate prey by smell. Olfaction was a possibility to be investigated, but not a promising one.

It might be possible that the robin feels vibrations from moving earthworms through its feet. But robins easily find worms when streetcars and heavy trucks rumble past. And the bird would also have the problem of distinguishing the vibrations of one earthworm from the movements of hundreds of other worms in the immediate vicinity. A robin's foot, moreover, is a hard, horny structure, not the delicate sensory organ needed for such a precision task. Furthermore, why would the robin cock its head instead of making rapid foot movements?

Hearing *was* a distinct possibility. Robins do cock their heads so that the ear is close to the ground, and worms do move. So I needed to answer two questions: Do worms make noise? If so, does the robin use this noise to locate the worm?

Vision did seem to present the strongest case. Most passerine birds have good visual acuity and, even more important for worm finding, have the ability to resolve objects which are moving rapidly. If we were to scan our eyes quickly over a table with many different objects on it, we would have difficulty singling out individual items. Birds seem to be much better adapted to do this, and such an attribute would be invaluable for spotting worm signs while running across a lawn.

I attacked the question of smell on two fronts. First, to test whether a robin could be affected by any smell, I soaked pieces of paper with the vilest smelling liquids known to man. These repulsive bits were placed in the food dishes of captive wild robins at feeding time to see if their appetites would be adversely influenced. While I choked and gagged twenty-five feet away, the birds nonchalantly ate foods smelling like rotten eggs, decaying meats, rancid butter, and the absolute worst of all bad smells, mercaptoacetic acid, which has been described as a cross between sewer gas, rotten cabbage, a skunk and a stinkbug. The stench had no effect on the bird's eating habits.

The next step was to see if a robin would respond to something that smelled like a worm, but in no other way resembled one. Earthworms were variously rubbed upon, ground up and spread on, and otherwise applied to pieces of paper which were put in the birds' feeding dishes on days when they had not been fed. The birds weren't interested. As a control experiment, plain pieces of paper were placed in the dishes, and again the birds displayed no interest. Earthworms do have a very distinctive odor to humans—somewhat sharp but not unpleasant.

Sound and hearing were tough to eliminate. The most logical step was to obtain some robins, deafen them, and then determine if the birds could still find worms. Dr. Mark Konishi, then a graduate student at the University of California at Berkeley, had succeeded in surgically deafening robins, but the operation required extreme care and sometimes damaged the bird's inner ear. I tried making earplugs out of liquid silicone rubber, but the birds dug them out with their claws. And anyway I had no way of knowing whether they worked or not.

It then occurred to me that if I couldn't deafen the bird, I might be able to use the Boiler Factory Effect to prevent the robin from hearing earthworm sounds. This is the phenomenon noted, appropriately enough, in boiler factories where there are very loud and constant noises. A person who can hear a normal conversation in a quiet room can't perceive voices in a boiler factory, because the noise of the machinery includes the same sound frequencies as the human voice, only much louder.

If I could discover the frequency characteristics and intensity of worm noises, I could build an electronic noisemaking device which would mask worm sounds. Thus there would be no concern about whether the bird could hear such sounds in the wild. I could assume the bird had that ability, and then ask, "Does the bird *use* the sounds to locate worms?"

Dr. Bowman had the sound analysis apparatus I needed to dissect the earthworm's rumblings. I simply placed a box of worms in a soundproof chamber, then made a tape recording of the worms' activities. The tape was processed through a sound spectrograph to determine its frequency characteristics. When greatly amplified, the worm sounds resembled the noise of stale potato chips being crumbled. The intensity of the sound was very low, and the frequency ranged from one to seven kilocycles.

Armed with this information, I obtained a noise generator to mask earthworm sounds. The noise produced resembled a jetliner at full throttle flying one hundred feet overhead. The actual experiment was simple. A captive robin was released in a large flight cage with a grass bottom, and the number of worms it discovered in a short time period was counted. The worm supply in the lawn was then replenished, and the next day the procedure was repeated—with the noise generator turned on. The result? The masking sound had no effect on the bird's worm-finding ability. The bird cocked its head in the usual way, even though it could not hear worm sounds.

Further studies showed that a light breeze blowing through the grass, or even distant city noises, were sufficient to mask worm sounds.

So I was left with vision. It would have been possible to put eye masks on the birds and turn them loose on a lawn to see if sight were essential to worm finding, but preliminary experiments were unsatisfactory. The birds panicked at first, then fell asleep.

The next best thing was to contrive a situation in which sound, smell or vibrations could provide no clues to the worm's location, but where visual ones could. Phony worms and dummy worm burrows did the trick.

A baking pan was covered with worm-free dirt, and holes were punched in the dirt with nails to simulate worm burrows. These were quite realistic, since dirt was piled up around the rims of the holes like worm castings.

Fresh worms were then cut into one-quarter-inch pieces and the ends inserted into the holes, giving the appearance of worms which had partially retreated into their tunnels. A few of the "worm holes" were left empty. The pan, worm pieces and all, was placed on the grass in the flight cage, and a robin was released in the enclosure to see what would happen.

The bird at first paid little attention to the pan, but as it ran over the dirt in its explorations, it screeched to a halt, cocked its head, pounced, and *voilà*, fell backwards with a worm end in its bill. On two occasions the bird cocked its head toward an empty hole but did not peck at it. I also had several worms that had been preserved in alcohol, and when these were sliced up and placed in the holes, the robin had no trouble finding them—even though they were soundless, odorless, and vibrationless. On two of the trials, the noise generator was cranked up to maximum intensity, but the bird's worm-finding behavior was not adversely affected.

The clincher came when I asked myself, "Well, if the *robin* finds worms by looking for them, why can't *I* do the same thing?" So one wet morning I ventured forth on the campus lawn with my eyes as close to the ground as focusing would permit. Sure enough, it was possible to see the worms in their burrows.

You might try this yourself. But when the policeman asks, tell him you lost your contact lenses.

A HERONRY IN THE HOUSE, BY GEORGE B. SCHALLER

A lifetime of relative ob-scurity—in the laboratory, in teaching, or at some remote research outpost—awaits most students who choose a career in the natural sciences. Only a few will gain worldwide renown for their fieldwork and their writings. Those readers who immediately recognize the author for his famous studies of gorillas and big cats may be surprised to find him raising a nestling heron on a college campus.

Students of animal behavior have in recent years become greatly interested in tracing the development of behavior patterns in young animals, especially birds. Scientists try to determine, among other things, to what extent various actions are inborn, and how learning affects them in the course of the animal's growth.

When on one May 10th, at 4:20 P.M., a great blue heron wriggled from his egg onto the wire tray of my incubator at the University of Wisconsin, he was far removed from the influences that would have shaped his behavior in the wild. As Siegfried, which I later called him although I never knew his sex, struggled and kicked in an attempt to raise his rubbery neck, he saw not a nest of sticks high in the crown of an elm—which was his natural home in a rookery in south-eastern Wisconsin—but only the confining walls of a room; he saw no adult herons landing with rushing wings at the edge of the swaying nest, but only a man standing by his nest box.

However, Siegfried had no visions of the proper state of affairs. His only concern was for food—a voracious concern which changed him from a two-ounce weakling at birth to a two-pound fighter at three weeks.

Immediately after emerging from the egg, his gray down plastered wetly to his plump body and his scrawny neck lacking the strength to hold up his head, Siegfried emitted his food call, a rasping *kek-kek*. By the following morning he could raise his head and feebly lunge with open beak at pieces of liver I dangled in front of him. After grasping a piece between the mandibles, he threw back his head as would an adult heron and swallowed.

His grabbing for food was inaccurate, and he missed as often as not. But when something stimulated the lining of his bill, he showed a curious behavior. As if someone had flipped the switch of his internal motor, he lunged and lunged, five to ten times, at nothing in particular. If a leaf or branch inadvertently landed in his bill, he tried to swallow that too, and I had to be careful to eliminate all small objects from the nest. This chain reaction of swallowing is undoubtedly useful when the helpless youngster is fed a mass of regurgitated food by his parent in the wild.

After a meal Siegfried rested, stretched out, looking like a fuzzy, long-necked gourd.

By the age of five days he had changed to an alert youngster. He sat on his haunches for the first time, though somewhat wobbly and barely balanced on his rounded belly. He watched avidly as I prepared his food, and he pecked at spots and shiny objects within reach. Interestingly, now that he could peck with precision, his automatic lunging for food had all but disappeared.

I had also been raising one of Siegfried's nest mates, a female as it later turned out, in the same room but out of his sight. I put the two herons together for the first time on May 18th, anticipating an amicable meeting. But both sat rigidly upright, facing one another with wings spread and with neck and bill stretched skyward. The pinfeathers on their necks stood erect like quills, and the long tufts of down on cheeks and crown flared outward, giving the young herons the appearance of angry old men with side whiskers.

After briefly holding this adultlike threat posture, they emitted some loud, sharp *cau-cau* calls, indicating annoyance; then they jabbed at each other's head with rapierlike thrusts of their bills. Siegfried grabbed the bill of his sister and twisted it sideways until she fell on her side. He then aimed a few more jabs at his downed victim, handling his bill like a sword. It was for this flashing bill that I named him Siegfried, a hero of German legend who had a magic sword.

Like many other birds, herons apparently have no inherited means by which they can recognize others of their own species. By the age of eight days Siegfried had learned that I was his parent. Once recognition was established, he accepted no other animals, whether dogs, chickens or other members of his species.

On May 24th I again attempted to put the two herons together. They immediately assumed their threatening posture, and Siegfried started to jab at his sister. But he only clapped his bill and, when his sister responded in similar fashion, he bowed down, touching the ground with the tip of his bill as if in submissiveness. However, as before, the meeting ended with the herons hammering away at each other.

One project occupied Siegfried for the next few weeks: learning to stand up. At the age of two weeks he rose from his haunches for the first time, but his bottom was so heavy that it pulled him back down. Thereafter, until he could stand like an adult, he maintained his upright position in two ways: he either leaned far forward and, like a tripod, balanced himself by touching the tip of his bill to the ground, or he stood bolt upright, resembling an animated wine bottle.

Siegfried's voracious hunger never abated. When I came into the room he danced up and down, beat his wings while throwing his snakelike neck back and forth, and roared in a most ferocious manner. Feeding was now an easy matter: I simply dropped a whole perch or rat down his gullet and watched it slowly slide down the distended neck. Bones and skin were later regurgitated in a pellet.

Satiated, Siegfried huddled close to me, emitting soft, musical *ka-kas*. He sometimes preened my bare arms with a rapid sideways movement of the head and, when I picked him up, he rested his neck over my shoulder. Yet, unlike a duckling, he never followed when I moved away from him. The tendency to follow would be fatal to a flightless heron in a treetop. Not until June 17th, when he was well feathered out, did Siegfried step from his nest box onto the table on which it sat.

Although he usually tolerated other persons, Siegfried seemed ill at ease with them—and they with him—for he lashed out at their faces on occasion. When I took him out-of-doors, he stood motionless, like a post, his gray-blue plumage blending into the surroundings. If a stranger inadvertently wandered close to him, he suddenly turned into a feathered fury, roaring and running at the intruder with clapping bill, spread wings, and ruffled feathers. It was a stout soul who stood his ground.

On July 28th, after a heavy rainstorm, I carried him to a large puddle, the first he had seen. He stared into the water as if remembering his heritage. In a flash he jabbed at a pebble below the surface of the water, held it to the ground, and "killed" it by shaking his head rapidly. The heron's method of obtaining prey had appeared in its full form without previous experience.

In mid-July, Siegfried felt independence coming upon him and began to break the social bonds that linked him to me. Previously, he had enjoyed being scratched, but now he drew away from me; instead of permitting me to feed him by hand, he preferred to pick up his own food; rather than welcoming the chance to be carried, he scolded me. Perched at the edge of his nest, he beat his powerful wings in practice and occasionally leaped five feet to another part of the room. On July 28th, he flew for the first time, low over the ground, but in typical adult fashion with stately wingbeats and folded neck.

The time had come for Siegfried to gain his freedom. I had learned much from him. He had shown me that many of his actions, even complex ones like threat displays and prey-killing movements, were largely inherited, but that learning may play an important role, as in species recognition.

On August 11th, when he was three months old, I took him to a marsh where reeds grew densely and open leads of water would provide good fishing for a heron. He stood in the shallows, neck poised for a strike. watching minnows scurry away, as if he had done this all his life. His inscrutable face betrayed in no way that he was in a strange place. As always, his mind was on food. I felt that he could survive on his own. When I walked away, he flew up and circled above me before landing at my feet. Again I carried him into the marsh, then hurried away.

Little did I know Siegfried's restless soul. The following day he landed on a house about twenty miles to the northwest of the marsh and was identified by the number of the band on his leg. And on the same day he was reported forty miles to the west—a fine flight for a bird which had never before flown farther than a few hundred feet.

I never heard of him again.

THE SNIPE
REDISCOVERED, BY
AUSTIN L. RAND *Birdwatchers*

seldom accord more than a glance to those species they see regularly and recognize immediately, even though their knowledge of a bird's habits is limited to the sketchy information they have read in a field guide. Their loss is the insight that can be earned with a few hours or a few days of attentive observation.

You may see a bird casually many times over the years and still know no more about it than is in your bird books. It is just another species to check off on your daily list. Then comes a happy set of circumstances that focuses your interest on the species. The birds, going about their daily activities in front of you, emerge as distinct personalities with quirks and traits that surprise and intrigue you.

So it was for me with the Wilson's snipe, now called the common snipe (*Capella gallinago*). I had known the snipe for many years as well as most bird students, I suppose. I had come to think of it as a shy, secretive bird, hiding in the grass of boggy meadows and marshes. It would flush ahead of me and dart away with swift, twisting flight and hoarse *scape* calls.

I had listened, too, to the "winnowing" of the snipe's nuptial flight high over wet meadows where the birds later made their nests and laid their four spotted eggs. I had also been scolded by a nesting pair perched on dead stubs—the most improbable perching birds—giving froglike croaks. Rarely had I seen the bird on the ground probing for earthworms and, presumably, for the many other invertebrates it is said to eat.

This is the picture of an unusual bird. But an equally unusual portrait, though a different one, emerged one autumn in northern Indiana. It was during the snipe's southward migration that I had the chance each weekend to watch a dozen or more of the birds on the mud flats of a small, drying pond.

Much, of course, has been written of the snipe as a gamebird, of its "winnowing," and of recent censuses on its breeding grounds. But few people seem to have been fortunate enough to observe snipe on their daily rounds as I was able to do.

These snipe were not the shy, secretive birds of my earlier impressions. Despite their dead-grass-patterned plumage, there was nothing cryptic about them; their dark backs and white bellies made them even more conspicuous than the killdeers that were also feeding on the mud flats.

The snipe fed, bathed, preened, rested and slept in the open like sandpipers, and paid no attention to me while I stayed in the car that served as a blind. But when anyone walked along the road by the pond, their behavior reminded me of their more usual habits. Then the birds crouched and froze, belly to earth, bill parallel and close to the ground, quite unlike a sandpiper. At a casual glance, they looked like clods of earth.

Disturbed further, the birds flew to a distant part of the pond or circled the marsh before returning to alight.

I was surprised how sandpiper-like the snipe *were* most of the time, however. They belong in the sandpiper family, along with the yellowlegs, willet, curlews, godwits, tattler, knots, dunlin, woodcock, dowitchers and sanderling. But in my mind I'd grouped them with woodcock as quite different—long-billed, short-legged probing birds of dense cover. Now, out in the open, the snipe's behavior emphasized its sandpiper relationships.

The feeding snipe walked over the mud and in shallow water up to their bellies, probing as they moved, intent on processing the mud for the animals in it. Sometimes only half of the bill or less was immersed, sometimes it went in to the level of the eye, making a probe or two at each step and reminding me strongly of the way a sandpiper's bill is dabbed in the water as the bird walks.

But the walk or trot of the snipe lacked the twinkling speed of the sandpiper. The snipe sometimes had a waddle in their walk, as if they were having a little trouble with their long toes, and the bill was sometimes held in the mud for a moment as if the bird were waiting for tactile impressions from an unseen prey against its touch-sensitive bill tip.

The water and mud of the pond, as I found by sieving, swarmed with small crustaceans a few millimeters long. There were also many nymphs of damselflies, some small leeches, tiny reddish water mites, red threadworms, small snails, and beetles.

Apparently these were the snipe's food, and evidently they were much more common some places than others, for every now and then instead of making a probe or two each step, a snipe would stop and probe a dozen times or more in one small area before continuing its walking search. If such small items were its prey, as seemed probable, no wonder that I could rarely see the snipe swallow anything, or that it barely paused in its probing. Never did these birds appear to use their eyes; never did they run ahead to pick up something on the surface.

But occasionally one would find bigger prey, a blackish, wriggling animal an inch or two long. It was easy to tell when this happened, for then the snipe drove its bill deeper and deeper until it was probing up to its shoulders in the water. Finally it brought up the prey and processed it to quiet its struggles.

A songbird would "bite" such a catch and hammer it on the ground. But the snipe seemed to push it back and forth in the mud. When the water was too deep, the bird sought a firmer mudbank to continue the process.

Eventually, smoothly and quickly, the prey moved up the snipe's bill and through the gape with little or no jerking of the head to toss it along.

No wonder some of the earlier literature says the snipe sucks up its food. A more reasonable explanation, however, is its use of backward-projecting serrations inside the bill. These run lengthwise along the lower two-thirds of the central part of the upper mandible. The tongue—short though it is considering the length of the bill—could, by working back and forth, move prey along until the spines that arm the base of the tongue can catch and pull it into the gullet.

Once, in the spring, I saw a few snipe probing in a flooded winter wheat field for angleworms. Several times when a snipe swallowed a big worm the bird was apparently satiated, trotted to nearby grass, nestled down and slept. How different were these autumn birds. Perhaps it was because of the small size of their prey, but they seemed to be feeding intensively in certain areas.

A contributing factor may have been their arrival at the end of the first long leg of their journey from the subarctic, with their fat, their accumulated supply of food, used up. Here in Indiana they were refueling before embarking on the second leg of their southward flight, as dowitchers do on the New Jersey coast.

When a snipe did stop feeding, it sometimes bathed much as many birds do, by squatting, fluttering its wings in the water and then ducking its head to let the water run down its back. The preening that followed included nibbling at the base of the tail with the long bill; rubbing the head against that spot, presumably to utilize the secretion from the oil gland; running the bill through the flight feathers; and raising the head as high as possible to preen the upper breast feathers.

Then the bird might rest with head between its shoulders, and bill pointed forward; or sleep with bill turned over the back among the feathers, standing on one leg like any sandpiper.

My first day's observations yielded data on the activities of individual birds. To my surprise, on the second day I found there was considerable social activity I had overlooked. The first day I had concentrated on the details of the things that I knew the birds did. The second day, with these basic patterns in mind, I was receptive to activities that I didn't know about and didn't expect.

Snipe are known to move in flocks, but otherwise seem mostly solitary. On the mud flats of the pond where there was room to be solitary, they tended to keep a few feet or yards apart. But some of the birds did seem to be loosely grouped. Often I had six to nine birds in the field of my binoculars at 20 to 30 yards' distance.

Occasionally two birds seemed to be feeding near each other, and two or three sometimes slept in a group. But one bird occasionally ran at another and, with or without raising and spreading its tail, drove the other away. The attacking bird did not point its bill at the opponent's body but kept the tip much lower. Perhaps snipe bills are too sensitive to be used in fighting.

Two birds in an actual encounter met breast to breast with russet tail raised to the vertical and widely spread, wings drooping, heads high and breast feathers puffed out. They flew into the air a foot or so, but I could see no details of the contest.

Another time, one bird, perhaps a male from its small size, repeatedly approached and displayed to a larger feeding bird, presumably a female. The female displayed and repulsed the smaller bird by rushing at it, then turned its back, tail still in display, and continued feeding. The smaller bird retreated a few feet, crouched belly to earth but with the tail still displayed, and periodically returned to the attack.

Presumably these activities are similar to snipe mating behavior in the spring when the birds are said to display like fighting cocks. Another display resembled a formalized dance. One bird was feeding alone; another came up to it, and each spread its tail and tipped it sideways. Then the two birds, side by side and a few inches apart but headed in different directions, tried to walk around each other for a dozen or so revolutions before they broke off and went their own ways.

These activities can be considered remnants of mating behavior carried over into autumn, like the singing of white-throated sparrows on fall migration.

Despite these social activities, when the birds flushed they behaved as solitary individuals, circling and alighting alone. Presumably they *do* migrate as a flock.

The conspicuous display of the russet tail that is part of the spring mating display was here not only used in intra-species aggression but also in inter-species squabbles with blackbirds. For scores of redwings and grackles came to this pond in the evening on their way to roost.

The blackbirds did not confine their quarreling to their own species. Frequently one perched near a snipe and flew at it. The snipe sometimes crouched, sometimes did not, but usually the tail was erected and displayed. The snipe often displayed to a blackbird flying by, and while the snipe usually stood its ground, sometimes one flew and was chased around the pond by a blackbird. On one occasion, indeed, blackbirds routed all the snipe off the pond—even those wading where no blackbird could perch.

The intolerance of birds for each other varies greatly from species to species. The eastern kingbird (*Tyrannus tyrannus*) reflects in both its scientific and its vernacular name the bird's well-known pugnacity. Besides defending its territory with such vigor as to drive both hummingbirds and crows away, it will knock feathers from such inoffensive species as the upland plover and, in fall migration, attacks green herons.

The red-winged blackbirds of the marshes seem equally endowed with an excess of pugnacity, chasing ducks, herons and killdeers as well as snipe. One can well ask, "Is all this activity necessary?"

For the most part, however, the snipe fed undisturbed, ignored by and ignoring pectoral sandpipers, yellowlegs, killdeers, teal and wood ducks.

The main southern migration of snipe here is usually from early September to mid-October. I first found them on the pond in late September, when early autumn colors were painting sumac red, sassafras orange, and grape and hickory yellow.

The ranks of snipe I watched were presumably changing from day to day. Sometimes there would be as few as a dozen, sometimes as many as 30, but usually I counted two dozen. This lasted throughout October, when the early color of woodlot and hedgerow was at its height and cattails were just turning brown. The temperatures were unusually high, often in the 80's, and there was an unusually small amount of rain and no frost.

Then came showers that half filled the pond, and colder weather. By the first weekend in November there were no more snipe. Pebbles flung on the pond skipped and rang over the new, thin ice.

A few snipe may linger all winter in open spring holes, but my snipe season had ended.

Audubon's Photographers

Portfolio Two

Deep in the boreal forest of an island in Maine,
the winter wren has skillfully concealed its nest
of pine twigs within a curling sheet of birch bark.
(Photograph by Eliot Porter)

Tail cocked, white throat feathers puffed out,
a great horned owl hoots into the spring night.
(Photograph by G. Ronald Austing)

A screech owl brings a June beetle, a favorite food, to its nest hollow in an Ohio woodland. (Photograph by G. Ronald Austing)

A bald eagle backpedals with its great broad wings
—their spread is seven feet—to maintain its balance
as it lands on the dead stub of a Florida mangrove.
(Photograph by Frederick Kent Truslow)

An osprey feasts on a sea trout caught
in the shallow waters of Florida Bay.
(Photograph by Frederick Kent Truslow)

On their whitewashed stick-nest platform on a mangrove island in Florida Bay, naked two-week-old brown pelican nestlings wait for their parent to regurgitate food. (Photograph by Caulion Singletary)

A bright-yellow eye identifies the female of a pair of black-necked storks on their nest at a sanctuary in India. These storks stand nearly five feet tall. (Photograph by M. Philip Kahl)

THE FOOTPRINT THIEVES, BY GEORGE MIKSCH SUTTON

Bird study can be adventurous, even dangerous—like losing one's way on the almost featureless snow-covered tundra of an arctic island, with the temperature far below zero. But in this instance, discovering the reason for one's bewilderment was worth a moment of panic.

When a man from a temperate region winters for the first time in the Far North he knows he is out of his element, but he is reluctant to admit it. He dreads the thought of freezing to death. He has heard such fearful tales of snow blindness and the phenomenon called "all white" that he is half afraid to look at a snowflake.

He rubs the muzzles of the huskies and pulls their ears playfully but wonders when the great brutes will suddenly cease being just dogs and revert to being wolves. He enjoys the companionship of the Eskimos, thrills to their strange and beautiful language, but remembers that according to their code of ethics a white man whose presence threatens them with a serious food shortage must, in fairness to all concerned, be put out of the way.

Some years ago I wintered on Southampton Island, a 39,000-square-mile heap of rock just north of Hudson Bay. My daily companions were the chief trader of the recently established Hudson's Bay Company post at Coral Harbour, the trader's son, two Roman Catholic priests, and an Eskimo family employed by "the Company."

The company supply ship had left me at Coral Harbour in mid-August. Throughout the fall I had been traveling to various parts of the island, gathering data on its birdlife and collecting museum specimens. Now that winter had set in and most birds had long since left for the South, I was concentrating on a study of Southampton's land mammals.

My friends had taught me how to set fox traps, and by early November I had established my own trap line. I needed a few Arctic foxes in prime winter pelage for my scientific collection. I also planned to preserve the weasels, hares, and snowy owls that were occasionally caught. Extra fox skins could be traded with Eskimos who came from time to time with unusual bird specimens.

On a particularly fine day in midwinter, I was making the rounds of my fifteen or so traps. At high noon the full sun was above the horizon. As usual I was walking, partly because I was not very good at driving the dogs and partly because I could see and hear more when I had no team and sledge to manage.

By now I knew what really cold weather could be like. The air temperature had ranged from 20 to 50 degrees below zero for what had seemed weeks on end. I had frozen the end of my nose, the rims of my ears, and areas on my cheeks, chin and forehead, so I had learned how to dress warmly. The first two pairs of sealskin boots the Eskimos had made me had been too short, but the pair I now wore was perfect.

Despite the cold I rejoiced in the vastness of the tundra, the low-hanging sun with its bright rays, and the long, incredibly colorful shadows. It was exciting to consider the creatures of this frozen world—lemmings literally by the thousand, not curled up in hibernation but racing about under the snow through a network of tunnels whose total length was beyond reckoning; seals moving from breathing hole to breathing hole in their dim netherworld below the thick ocean ice; great white bears, the pregnant females asleep in dens awaiting the arrival of tiny cubs, the males at the floe edge hunting seals.

These creatures and their problems of existence occupied my mind as I trudged through the snow. I had visited the last of my traps and was on my way back to the trading post. The weather was perfect. The day had been windless. Some of the brightest stars would soon be out, and I chuckled as I recalled arguments we had had at the post as to whether these were visible in broad daylight to keen-eyed persons.

Then as the sinking sun touched the horizon I realized that the nine- or ten-mile return trip would require two full hours unless I pushed on as rapidly as possible.

Anyone who walks a great deal in the Far North learns to choose his route with care, especially if he uses neither skis nor snowshoes. Deep drifts are to be avoided unless they have a very firm crust. Low-lying areas with scattered clumps of knee-high willows are likely to be troublesome. Ridges are ideal for travel in calm weather, for their windswept crests remain free of snow all winter.

I reached the end of one of these long, gravelly, snow-clear ridgetops. Here the tracks I had made an hour or so earlier, as I ascended, should have been easy to find in the snow. I could not, however, seem to remember exactly which part of the bare area I had reached first. Although I searched the entire end of the ridge thoroughly, I could not find my footprints.

Merely bewildered at first, I checked my surroundings, noting first the brilliance of the sunset, then, one by one, the ridgetops to the right and left. I knew that even if I were standing on the wrong ridge, I must surely have walked along one of these crests earlier in the day. There had been no fresh snowfall; there had been no wind; there was no reason why my footprints should not be clearly visible.

True, I admitted to myself, tracks usually do not show distinctly on such a gradual approach to the end of a ridge, because the crust there is often firm. But I clearly remembered breaking through time after time on this particular slope. I recalled even wondering whether the going might have been easier had the sun been less bright and warm.

Then, with the swiftness of a gyrfalcon's stoop, the first panic seized me. What if I were really lost! What if I had been traveling in the wrong direction for some time! What if the weather were suddenly to change! What if I were to wander hour after hour in the darkness, walking in circles as lost persons invariably do, afraid to rest for fear of falling asleep and freezing!

My misgivings centered next on a new, major dread. My friends at the trading post would at last have to harness the dogs and go after that greenhorn, that newcomer, that *outsider*—just as they had been anticipating they would have to do.

Panic, however, must be put in its place. I decided, sanely enough, that I should first determine if my directions were straight. I was thankful for clear skies; had even a light snow been falling I could not have seen distant landmarks.

Returning to the highest point on the ridge, I looked for a cliff the Eskimos called Itiuachuk. It was exactly where I had expected it to be—thirty miles away, a long line of black rock on which snow never gathered.

That direction was east. It had never been anything but east. It had to be east now. Then to the south—not very distinct, to be sure, but reassuring—was the *sheenah,* a vapor cloud that gathered over the open floe in the bay.

I was not wholly lost. I might have been following the wrong ridge, but I had been heading in the right direction. My footprints were obviously either somewhere at the far end of this ridge or on a similar rise with the same bearings.

Yet fear remained. The weather could change with freakish swiftness. I was a long way from the post. Fumbling home along the coast would be a dubious alternative since the shoreline was obscured by ice and snow.

I walked back to the end of the snowless stretch, and again I failed to find my footprints. Boldly I decided to plunge on in what I knew must be the right direction. As long as the bare ridgetop was visible, I could return to it, and, if worst came to worst, I could go to the last of my traps and try backtracking from there.

I could not seem to regain confidence. Something was wrong with everything that had been happening. Time after time, I remembered, I had followed a certain ridge in visiting my traps. How could this be anything but that ridge? The only proof I needed was missing. There were no footprints.

I turned to look at the barren crest, now dead black in the waning light. Itiuachuk was out of sight behind the ridge. From where I stood I could not see the *sheenah.* My concern was hardly relieved when I wondered whether, after visiting the last trap, I had reached this ridge by dead reckoning rather than by following a trail or watching landmarks. A man could become overconfident in this country—especially in fine weather.

It was at precisely this moment of uncertainty that I glimpsed something dark on, or just above, the snow and not far from my feet. Instinctively I removed my snow glasses for a better look—a mistake. The sudden glare made me blink. I replaced the glasses. No, it had not been an illusion. There *was* something black and glittering in the snow—the black of a beetle, or a button, or a bead.

The black dot did not move, but it seemed to change shape ever so slightly, and something did shift a bit: something bright, something almost as bright as the sky, something that changed position with every move I made.

Then, around that tiny spot of black, I gradually discerned the shape of a bird's head. In front of the shining black dot of the bird's eye was the dull black of a blunt beak. Under that beak, very clear by this time, was the curved toe of a man's footprint.

Found: a snow-white willow ptarmigan crouched within an authentic man's footprint—all in all just about the best-looking footprint I had ever seen!

During this split second of recognition I felt an odd mixture of profound gratitude, scientific exultation—if there is such a thing—and warm affection for the lovely little thief which had found my track such an acceptable resting place.

I knew a good deal about these partridges of the snow. I had watched them kicking out their beds near almost-buried willows and filling their crops with willow buds and twigs before going to roost. But it had never entered my mind that a whole flock of ptarmigan might appropriate a man's footprints so completely as to obliterate a trail. The birds filled the tracks very neatly; scarcely a shadow was visible.

Peace of mind and confidence returned rapidly enough when I realized I had found my trail. I looked at the ptarmigan in the next footprint; its eyes were almost shut. Ahead of me, as far as I could make out detail, were ptarmigan ensconced in footprints. Not a single footprint was without its bird! Characteristically enough, the grouse had been moving as a flock. And when the time had come to roost, they had kept as close together as they could. My trail was made-to-order hostelry.

I quite agreed that bedtime had arrived. My own bed, however warm, was miles away. The comfortable, sleepy birds opened their eyes in acknowledgment of my presence but showed no alarm. These particular ptarmigan, for all I knew, may never have seen a human. They may have decided in their grousey, drowsy way that since I did not slink toward them in the manner of a fox or wolf I was not dangerous and not worth the worry.

As I beheld the tucked-in birds I could not help thinking of the tremendous difference between them and me. This was their home; they belonged here. This was no memorable experience for the ptarmigan. Their crops were full; a kind Providence had given them beds for the night; even this intruder upon their slumber meant no harm.

I stood in the snow in rapt admiration. Hung on my miserable frame were enough garments to outfit a small army—light underwear, heavy underwear, cotton socks, woolen socks, duffel socks, sealskin boots, ordinary trousers, caribou-skin outer trousers, woolen shirt, turtleneck sweater, caribou-skin parka (*kooletah*), inner mittens, outer mittens, the latter attached by thongs to prevent their being lost, and a "Nansen cap" of knitted wool designed to cover the whole head except for the eyes. Even wearing all this paraphernalia, I was not truly warm all of the time.

The body temperature of the birds at my feet was far higher than mine, so presumably it was harder for them to keep warm than for me. But so wonderfully complete was their feather garb, and so wonderfully efficient the tiny muscles which lifted this plumage to create a dead-air layer between skin and feather tips, that they were blissfully comfortable. "Not a scarf, not a galosh, not a zipper," I muttered, as I started the long tramp home.

It was a beautiful world, this land of blue-white snow and brightening stars, and pale green and gold aurora borealis shifting ever so slowly. More beautiful than the stars in its own way was the light that shone from the east window at the Hudson's Bay Company trading post.

What a time I would have telling my friends of the day's happenings! How it would amuse them to hear me pontificate on losing and finding Arctic trails! How could I describe the beauty, the very special beauty, of these ptarmigan?

Over and over these words came to me: ". . . yet I say unto you that even Solomon in all his glory was not arrayed like one of these."

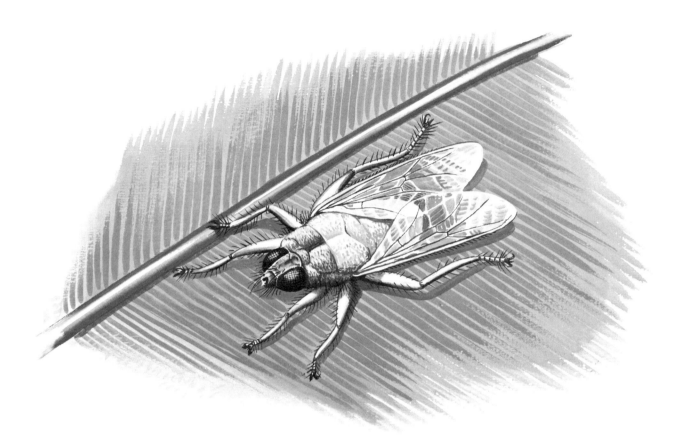

WAYS OF A PARASITE,
BY JOHN K. TERRES

Throughout their lives, on their nesting grounds and on their long migration flights, birds carry permanent passengers whose evolution, to an entomologically inclined observer, is every bit as fascinating as that of their hosts. Moreover, even the birds' guests carry hitchhikers.

One September morning, some years ago, I gathered up several hundred crippled and dead songbirds that had fallen the night before on the roof setbacks of the Empire State Building in New York City. They had been brought down in the darkness by flying into the tower of the building that rears 1,472 feet above the streets below. At the time I was interested in the numbers and kinds of birds killed there during each autumn migration. They were mostly small, colorful warblers, but I found among them that morning two white-breasted nuthatches, scarcely larger than the warblers themselves. As I picked up one of them, a strange, long-legged ghostlike fly appeared on the bird's outer feathers, then swiftly disappeared in its plumage. When it suddenly reappeared, I caught it. It was a hippoboscid (pronounced hip-po-BOS-sid) fly, *Ornithomyia fringillina*, the finch louse fly as it is called in England, one of the commonest parasitic bird-flies of the temperate zone of North America and of the Old World.

The hippoboscid flies have a highly developed sense of the body temperature of their hosts, and if the host is killed, they will leave the cooling body soon afterward. The problem then for the fly is to find a suitable new host before it dies for want of food and shelter—not an easy task. Even if a bird-fly should transfer from one bird to another, as when a hawk or owl captures a songbird, and thereby catches some of its parasites, the bird-fly may be so selective in its choice of a host as not to be able to live permanently on the predator. It is even more critical for the bird-fly that transfers from its dead bird host to a mammal, because bird-flies cannot live long on mammals, nor can mammal-flies live long on birds.

After the host dies, fully winged hippoboscid flies try to solve the problem by flying about at random toward any moving object. They are guided toward their prospective hosts by definite sensorial responses and tropisms. They are averse to light at times, move upward, and ordinarily seek the darkness within feathers or fur as a place in which to hide. Though their eyesight and sense of smell are poor—they perceive only differences in light intensities—they may be guided or orientated toward a bird or mammal by the shadow that it casts.

With such weak means of finding a new host, it is small wonder that many hippoboscids often transfer to the wrong hosts—to a hunter's dog, for instance, or even temporarily to the hunter himself. Many years ago, on picking up a freshly killed ruffed grouse, I saw hippoboscid flies suddenly appear on the surface of the bird's feathers as, like rats leaving a sinking ship, they sought a new refuge. One of them flew in a wide circle, returned, and alighted in my hair.

I remember to this day the squeamish feeling I had as the flattened, quick-moving fly crawled about briefly on my scalp. As in all insects, the hippoboscids have six legs, and each foot is armed with two clamps. In crawling and running about, the sharp, toothed claws can scratch the skin. A British scientist, M. Evans, quoted an informant from India who said that the dog-fly common there has claws "so sharp that the hair grasped by it is cut into shavings like wood by a carpenter's plane."

Even had my related bird-fly the doubtful "claw-power" of the dog-fly, I need have had no misgivings. It left my hair, with no damage to my scalp, and did not return. Had I been the right host, it would have flattened its belly and thorax tightly against my skin, for most hippoboscids are strongly stereotropic and press closely against their hosts.

The hippoboscid flies—the name derives from the Greek *hippos*, meaning horse, and *boskein*, to feed, in reference to an Old World species which sucks the blood of horses—are the most highly specialized, or host attendant, of all flies that parasitize birds. The adults live permanently on the bodies of birds and mammals, and both males and females suck blood from their hosts by using their highly specialized mouthparts.

What I find so wonder-stirring about these insects is the fact that the female gives birth to living young, one at a time, and apparently about a week apart. She is the only insect in the world, except for the related African tsetse fly and two families of small flies parasitic on bats, known to nurse her unborn young from "milk glands" inside her body. (Many insects lay up to hundreds or thousands of eggs from which young hatch and go about their feeding unattended.)

During their evolution, the hippoboscid flies developed an extremely efficient piercing and sucking beak and special anatomical and physiological arrangements that insure the free flow of blood from the host—and later, the blood's digestion and assimilation. With such perfect adaptations for feeding (the bite of a hippoboscid is no more annoying than the bite of a flea), and protection within the feathers of the bird host, what would prevent hippoboscids from overpopulating birds and causing illness or death from loss of blood—and the disappearance of a great many species?

Apparently birds are rarely, or never, decimated by the hippoboscid parasite because it is necessary, for the welfare of the parasite, not to endanger the survival of its host, or to reduce its numbers so much that future generations of the parasite would no longer have a reasonable chance of reaching a proper host. According to one authority, because of their low birth rate the hippoboscids have adapted "to the point of perfection" with the numbers of the birds and mammals whose blood they feed upon.

Years ago, when I was trapping wild birds in my garden and banding them for the U.S. Fish and Wildlife Service, I often found the finch louse fly in the feathers of song sparrows, white-throated sparrows, juncos, cowbirds, towhees, catbirds, and brown thrashers. This fly, which has been taken from 104 species of North American birds, has also been collected from pheasants, woodpeckers, and owls. A Canadian ornithologist took four from a young evening grosbeak being fed by its mother.

Like other bird-banders, I used to catch hippoboscids from my live-trapped birds by carrying them in the darkness of the collecting cage into my house for banding. When I searched their plumage for hippoboscids, while holding them near a window, the flies would dart toward the glass to escape. There I easily caught them for later identification by an expert. In all the birds I examined, I rarely found more than two to four hippoboscids on each. Other bird-banders have had similar experiences; but some have found up to 10 or 20 or more bird-flies on cowbirds and red-winged blackbirds, species which the finch louse fly seems to favor.

Large birds with their greater blood supply often have more bird-flies than smaller birds. Birds with long feathers or dense plumage, and even more, those with a short neck and a broad, short, hooked bill, which prevents them from preening effectively, are likely to have more hippoboscids than other species. This explains why hawks and owls, nighthawks, and swallows and swifts frequently have greater numbers of bird-flies than the smaller, more agile songbirds. Some time ago, when I was living near Ithaca, New York, a great horned owl was shot from which Dr. C. E. Palm collected 61 bird-flies of the species *Lynchia americana*. This hippoboscid is another common one that also parasitizes hawks, falcons, pheasants, and wild turkeys. Ruffed grouse are an important host for this bird-fly.

I recall, a few years ago, a bird-fly which suddenly left the plumage of a dead saw-whet owl that had flown against the side of my car in the April dusk near Chapel Hill, North Carolina. I had taken the bird home in a paper bag to examine it more closely. When I opened the bag in my kitchen and picked up the small owl, a bird-fly buzzed swiftly out of the owl's feathers, flew in a circle, and alighted on the back of my neck. Then it took off again and disappeared. I never recovered it, which disappointed me as I wanted to have it identified. It might have been *Lynchia fusca*, which is common on owls in our southern and western states. Amelia R. Laskey, a noted bird-bander of Nashville, reported one of these bird-flies from a saw-whet owl captured in Tennessee.

Anyone who has ever seen a bird-fly run must have marveled at their swiftness. Even fully winged hippoboscids rely mainly on running and hiding in the feathers or fur of their host to escape danger. With their long legs that grow out from the extreme sides of the flattened thorax, bird-flies can dart rapidly in every conceivable direction.

In Argentina, several Dutch scientists determined the running speed of the pigeon-fly, *Pseudolynchia canariensis,* by allowing these bird-flies of domestic pigeons to run in a glass tube 75 centimeters long. The fastest running speed of the flies was 540 centimeters a minute (about four inches a second) or about 1,053 feet in an hour. At this speed it would require about five hours for one of these bird-flies to run a mile. This is a swift pace compared with that of a lady-bird beetle I timed in my Long Island garden which would have required 17.5 hours to run a mile; but it is slow in comparison to an American cockroach, which can run at a top speed of almost three miles an hour.

It is the agility of the bird-flies, and their ability to turn and dart about rapidly in different directions, that gives the illusion that they move at a far greater speed than they really do.

Many of the bird-flies—the hippoboscids I have been especially interested in—void their pupae in the nests of their hosts. However, the zoologist C. W. Johnson reported a great horned owl from Massachusetts that had the puparia of one bird-fly, *Ornithoica vicina,* in its ears during September, and it is believed that because of their thick plumage, owls may act as winter hosts for some kinds of bird-flies which then spread to other hosts in the spring.

Generally, transformed adults, when newly emerged from the pupae, reach the host either by flight or by running, and most are in nests or near nesting sites where nestlings and juvenile birds are within easy reach.

Some of the known cases of the bird-flies straying to the wrong host are remarkable and unaccountable. In England, a bird-fly, *Ornithomyia aviculare*, as a rule parasitic on songbirds, has been found on a lamb, on herons, bitterns, and curlews. The finch louse fly has been found on curlews, plovers, oyster-catchers, and even on a white stork.

Rarely, two different species of bird-flies have been taken from the same bird. In North America, the finch louse fly and another very common hippoboscid, *Ornithoica vicina*, have been taken simultaneously from a blue jay, a tufted titmouse, and a rose-breasted grosbeak in New Jersey. A great horned owl in Massachusetts had 32 of *Ornithoica vicina* in its feathers, and at least 19 of *Lynchia americana*, which has a wide range of bird hosts.

Dr. Joseph C. Bequaert, a world authority on the hippoboscid flies, has pointed out a striking example of how highly specialized insect parasites may perish if the host bird strays too far from its "home." A man-o'-war bird, or frigatebird, of tropical seas wandered far north of its normal range and was shot in central France. On it were bird-flies, *Olfersia spinifera*, which live only on frigatebirds. Even though they might have escaped from their dead host, they could not have survived for want of other frigatebirds in that part of the world.

When a bird begins to extend its range into new territory, it may establish its parasites there by its own repeated and increasing presence. Since the 1920s, the turkey vulture has been extending its range northward in the eastern United States and is now a breeding bird in southern Michigan, southern Ontario, central New York, and parts of Massachusetts and Connecticut. Farther south, the bird-fly *Olfersia bisulcata* is a specific parasite of the American vultures. It will be interesting to see if this bird-fly will become established along with its host in its northern territory.

Besides sapping a bird of its blood, there are other consequences to a bird bitten by a hippoboscid fly. Although the bite itself is not especially painful or harmful, a concentration of blood-sucking bird-flies on the head of a mockingbird in California caused the bird to lose most of its head feathers. Far more serious may be the effect on a bird's health of certain blood parasites carried by the bird-flies. These are transmitted from the blood of one bird to that of another by the bites of bird-flies. According to Dr. Carlton M. Herman, a bird pathologist with the U.S. Fish and Wildlife Service, some of them, called *Haemoproteus*, cause a serious malarialike disease in domestic pigeons and in California quail. Herman writes that the hippoboscid flies may also be involved in transmitting other parasitic diseases from bird to bird.

In addition, bird-flies often carry on the outside of their own bodies other insect parasites, which feed on the feathers of birds. These hitchhikers are Mallophaga, the feather-lice of birds, and their method of getting transported by an insect to other bird hosts is called phoresy. Each bird-fly usually carries one or two of the bird feather-lice on its body; exceptionally, there may be a dozen or more.

In Wisconsin, an investigator, K. MacArthur, found a finch louse fly on a robin. When he examined the bird-fly closely he discovered that it had eight feather-lice on its abdomen, all arranged with their heads pointing toward the center of a circle. There are so many records now of feather-lice being carried by bird-flies to all parts of the world that it is no longer regarded as abnormal.

There is some evidence that the feather-lice, which cannot fly, attach themselves to the bird-flies soon after their mutual host dies. When a bird-fly seeks a new host, the feather-lice go with it. And if the bird-fly fails to find a new host, the hitchiking feather-lice die with it.

TWO HOURS ON AN AFRICAN ISLAND, BY ERWIN A. BAUER

In the few years since this story was written, the jackass penguin has become a victim of Middle East strife and the energy crisis. The closing of the Suez Canal, and the building of superships too big for the canal anyway, forced tanker traffic to round the Cape of Good Hope. Unending oil spills—both accidental and deliberate—have fouled the penguin's habitat, drastically reducing its numbers and threatening its very survival.

February 2, 1967, was a golden day I will remember as long as I live —even though high adventure is my business. It began just after daybreak in Cape Town harbor where the patrol boat *Wagter II* strained uneasily against her mooring lines.

Even at that early hour a wild southeast wind whistled in the rigging and the Republic of South Africa's tricolor flew flat out above the old Custom House nearby. On a normal summer morning in this corner of the world, the wind does not freshen until early afternoon. But now the weather was changing, and crew members were slightly apprehensive as they warmed the *Wagter*'s twin engines for departure.

"Today," one of them greeted me as I handed aboard a case of cameras, "is going to be a bloody rough one."

"I hope you have strong sea legs," Captain Ward Smith added. "And a strong stomach."

A few minutes later I knew what he meant. As soon as we passed the protection of the harbor breakwaters, we were plunged into a cold and heavy sea. From Table Mountain which loomed in the background, we set a north-northeast course roughly parallel to the Atlantic Ocean's coast.

The *Wagter*'s mission this morning was to watch for illegal fishermen. She belonged to the fleet of the Division of Fisheries of South Africa's Department of Commerce and Industry. Russian trawlers had been poaching in South African territorial waters, fishing for shoals of tunny and setting traps for rock lobsters. Only a week before, the 46-foot *Wagter II* (Afrikaans for "Sentinel") had been launched at Knysna and now was making its first attempt to intercept poachers. It was serious business.

My own status aboard was that of a hitchhiker. Since the day's scheduled patrolling would pass near Dasseneiland (Dassen Island), I had obtained permission to go along and, if possible, to visit that bleak and lonely bit of real estate 30 miles up the coast from Cape Town. That wasn't very easy. As an American, I had to sign a bewildering number of releases and waivers. I could be injured or killed, I was reminded. But I didn't give a second thought to getting involved in an international incident, since Dasseneiland happens to be the breeding home of some 55,000 jackass penguins, *Spheniscus demersus*, a species which only a handful of ornithologists has ever seen. Also called the black-footed penguin, it nests only on islets off South Africa's west coast, dispersing to Natal and Angola.

Even though we had a following wind, it was a damp and turbulent ride. We occasionally passed seals and schools of porpoises, but not many birds were flying. The Cape gannet was the only species I could positively identify.

Six miles from Cape Town we passed inside Robbeneiland (Robben Island), which is interesting for two very different reasons. It is an Alcatraz-type penal colony with a perfect record of no escapes (according to the crew), and the nesting site of a large colony of gannets. Beyond Robbeneiland (*rob* is Dutch for "seal") there is no landfall until Dasseneiland, which we reached in about two hours. No unfriendly fishing boats were sighted on the way.

Except for the peppermint-colored lighthouse at the island's west end, a boat could crash into Dasseneiland before the crew could see it above the towering waves. Nowhere does it rise more than a few feet above sea level. Except for rocky barrier shorelines, which are continually pounded by the surf, the island is absolutely flat and would seem in danger of being washed away. It has no harbor—nor even any sheltered bays—so that going ashore can be a considerable risk.

Two men and a woman live on the island—the lighthouse keeper, and a wildlife warden and his wife. A rickety wooden pier on the island's east end makes it possible for a small boat to dock only on the few calm days each year. This was not one of those days. In fact, many lobster boats had been driven to anchor just off the island to wait out the wind.

"Your only chance to get ashore," Captain Smith explained, "is if you will trust hitting the beach in a dinghy. Even then you will have to be ready to leave in two hours. If the wind continues, I might not be able to come close enough to pick you up at all. You could be stranded for weeks."

"I'll try the dinghy," I answered before I had time to use better judgment.

I have always regretted being born a generation too early to enjoy today's surfing boom. But after that wild ride onto a tiny sand beach, I now know the same thrill. Somehow the single boatman and I made it with cameras intact—and dry—and I waved as the *Wagter II* pulled away.

The warden, not a particularly friendly fellow, was waiting. "Stay," he insisted, "on the east and north shores. We don't want anybody anywhere else." He didn't explain, but greedy eggers once exploited the penguins of the Cape of Good Hope; 630,000 jackass penguin eggs were harvested in one single year, 1901.

The restriction didn't make much difference to me. A hundred feet from where we bounced ashore, troops of jackass penguins were waddling to and from the water. Beyond that, as far as I could see, the rocky, kelp-strewn shoreline was a seething mass of birds—most of them penguins.

What did I do with only two hours to spend in such a nature photographer's bonanza? The truth is that I can't remember—exactly. I only have impressions of hurrying around frantically, burning up film as fast as I could run it through my cameras.

I tried to portray the groups of penguins as they marched from nesting grounds to catch a meal in the sea. They did so with almost military precision. They seemed about as unsophisticated as wild birds could be. Penguins are swift swimmers in the ocean, but on land they are comparatively clumsy and helpless. The jackass penguins of Dasseneiland lumbered about as if intoxicated and seemed to stumble over even small pebbles. It is a shame I did not carry movie cameras.

Here and there, usually on patches of very sandy ground, were groups of nesting penguins. And to approach these birds was similar to walking through a pasture full of donkeys. They "brayed" at me exactly as would jackasses. The sound was hard to believe at first.

In a single nesting area, there were young birds of all ages, while some adults were still incubating or just now excavating nests. The youngest birds resembled balls of gray fluff in which it was difficult to distinguish either head or feet. Some nests were underground in sandy, cavelike burrows; others were simply sandy depressions beside or beneath rocks. Adults noisily defended the young birds and eggs; they pounced on any other penguins passing too close and they also charged after me.

Once, while photographing an adult with two young birds, I backed too close to a well-hidden nest. The next thing I knew, the occupant lurched out of it and struck me on the back of the leg just above the heel. The bite drew blood.

My main impression of Dasseneiland is of a constant loud din—a blending of birds, wind and surf. It becomes deafening. The surf smashes against the skeletons of a hundred wrecked ships which litter the shore, while the wind whines through twisted ribs and rigging. These derelicts range from small lobster boats to large whalers with rusting hulls. Cape cormorants have found the flat places in those broken hulls to be good nesting sites, and nearly every wreck contained a few cormorant eggs or young. Like the guanay of Peruvian islands, Cape cormorants and jackass penguins are a rich source of guano for fertilizer.

There were many other birds on the island, but I am not certain if they were nesting. Clouds of black-backed gulls and Hartlaub's gulls (a small species confined to the coast of the Cape Province and also called the king gull) would flush screaming from their community roosting places if I wandered too near. Many black-backed gulls were scouting for undefended or abandoned young penguins, and I saw a pair of gulls fall on a half-grown chick and pull it apart. I also identified a few black oystercatchers, Sandwich terns and a single Cape wagtail on a tiny sand beach.

Even on such a lonely and remote island, civilization has left several of its usual ruinous calling cards. European rabbits, introduced by mariners more than a century ago, are abundant (Dassen means "rock rabbit"). They were originally released to provide an easy supply of food for travelers en route around the Cape of Good Hope. Perhaps even more destructive is a herd of goats which keeps all vegetation cropped close to rock bottom. And countless house cats left behind by lighthouse keepers have supplied the island with a large and completely wild feline population. It is unfortunate that the South African government does not see fit to eliminate the three aliens.

All the while I walked about filming, the wind kept growing stronger. But except that it blew sand into my camera case whenever I left it on the ground, I paid little attention. There were so many things to see and photograph. Then suddenly I saw the *Wagter II* laying offshore, its blinker flashing shoreward. A moment later a dinghy was launched to pick me up.

There have been times when I have considered less hazardous professions, and the moments that followed were one of them. The boatman made it onto the Dassen beach easily enough—in fact he was swept in—but launching the small boat *into* the surf was another matter. We nearly capsized—twice—before getting beyond the first line of rollers. Then we had to row furiously with two sets of oars to reach the *Wagter*. There we were practically lifted aboard.

I can remember only one ride in a small craft rougher than that one back to Cape Town. Whereas our trip to Dassen had been with the wind at our backs, now we had to face directly into the sea. Although the boat was capable of better than 35 knots, we needed four hours for the trip. That means we averaged less than quarter-speed as waves broke completely over the boat. Even the crew members, all used to rough water in the South Atlantic, were happy to get home safely.

As I said, I will never forget that day in April—nor the braying penguins of that African island.

QUEST FOR THE QUETZAL, BY JAMES A. KERN

Birdwatching is a bloodless expression of man's primitive hunting instincts. We have substituted binoculars and cameras for the gun, but we still seek a trophy—a new species on our life list, or photographs of one of Earth's rarest and most exquisite creatures. Our search may take us no farther than a nearby meadow—or it can lead to the cloud forests of tropical mountains.

When I stepped off the plane at Coco Airport outside San José, Costa Rica, my single goal was to find and photograph the rare and exquisite quetzal, perhaps the most beautiful bird in the Western Hemisphere, if not the world. To my knowledge the quetzal had never been satisfactorily photographed in the wild; certainly not in color. In getting the first such pictures, however, I was caught up in a crisis about which Costa Rican people are largely ignorant—the destruction of their country's wildlife and its natural resources. It is a crisis which confronts other Central and South American countries as well. And the quetzal has become a symbol of this trouble.

Few sights in the world compare with the male quetzal; and few persons have had the privilege of seeing it. One of these is the noted ornithologist Alexander F. Skutch, who studied the quetzal from mid-1937 to mid-1938 and subsequently published the only comprehensive paper on the bird. Here is the description written in his journal on April 28, 1938, while he was living daily among the quetzals:

"The male is a supremely lovely bird; the most beautiful, all things considered, that I have ever seen. He owes his beauty to the intensity and arresting contrast of his coloration, the resplendent sheen and glitter of his plumage, the elegance of his ornamentation, the symmetry of his form, and the noble dignity of his carriage. His whole head and upper plumage, foreneck and chest are an intense and glittering green. His lower breast, belly and under tail coverts are of the richest crimson. The green of the chest meets the red of the breast in a line which is convex downward. The head is ornamented by upstanding bristly feathers which form a narrow, sharply ridged crest extending from the forehead to the hindhead. The bill is bright yellow and rather smaller than that of other trogons, even those of inferior size.

"The wing quills are concealed by long, golden green feathers of the coverts which stand out beautifully against the crimson that shows between them. The dark, central tail feathers are concealed by the greatly elongated upper tail coverts, which are golden green with blue or violet iridescence. The two median feathers, longer than the entire body, form a long, gracefully curving train which hangs below the bird while he perches upright on a branch and ripples gaily behind him as he flies."

The female quetzal is far less colorful than her mate. Her upper plumage is green like the male's, but her head is dark, smoky gray with no trace of a crest. Her upper tail coverts are also green and elongated but to a much lesser degree. Only her lower belly and under tail coverts are red, and her outer tail feathers, instead of being pure white, are narrowly barred with black.

The quetzal is a bird of the mountain cloud forest. It dwells in the cordilleras from the State of Chiapas in southern Mexico to western Panama, a distance of 1,000 miles. The two races of *Pharomachrus mocinno* are separated by the gap in the cordilleras in southern Nicaragua. In the southern part of its range it nests from 5,000 feet to perhaps 10,000 feet. But in Guatemala and Chiapas, where winter weather is felt, this nesting zone lies between 4,000 and 9,000 feet.

The quetzal is a trogon. True to its trogon nature it is a quiet bird except when nesting and is frequently found motionless among the jungle foliage. Like others of its kind, it feeds on a wide variety of insects, small amphibians and lizards, and on fruit which it yanks from trees with a twist of its bill while suspended in flight. Its flight is swift, its wingbeats rapid.

I had chosen to look for the quetzal in Costa Rica for one reason: there is an active and illegal trade in live quetzals there. Costa Rican law now protects the quetzal, but exporters simply claim that their birds came from across the border in Nicaragua. So birds are shipped from Costa Rica to zoos and aviaries all over the world.

I had been unable to find quetzal experts in Mexico or other Central American countries who could show me nesting sites. But in Costa Rica it was different; nothing sharpens the wits like money. Here a poacher—who may, admittedly, be doing the best he can to feed his family—can make two weeks' wages by catching a pair of quetzals. And they are caught easily with a burlap bag on the end of a bamboo pole as they incubate their eggs, for they nest in holes in the trunks of dead trees.

I reasoned that since men would be locating nests when the season began, it would be a simple matter to pay them to reserve a nest or two for me. As it turned out, it was not that easy. I was told on my first day in Costa Rica that nesting quetzals would be located within a week. In fact, it took me 29 days just to see my first bird. Although an average of 100 pairs of quetzals had been collected each year for the past ten years, this year not a single pair had been obtained.

Day after day, then, I went out into the cloud forest, sometimes alone, sometimes with a poacher; but we neither heard nor saw the birds. Often I was shown old trunks where quetzals had been caught year after year. Still, we saw no evidence of the birds. It was distressing as well to know that my guides were the men who had caused the disappearance of the birds.

When I consulted an animal dealer about the lack of quetzals, he insisted, "plenty birds . . . the birds will come." There was no doubt about it. It was just a question of time. But the birds didn't come. In fact, the quetzal seemed to have become testimony to the exploitation of a country's natural resources. These resources, which include the cloud forest and its flora and fauna, are falling to the machete and chain saw for conversion to dairy farms just as fast as roads push into the jungle. There has been no plan to save any of this natural beauty, not even the tops of the mountains that hold the heavy rains. No one comprehends the significance of what is happening.

A year of preparation went into my expedition; time and money had been committed. And I am stubborn, besides, in such matters as these. But as the days passed into weeks, I often considered quitting the whole venture and going home. Then each evening I looked at a couple of hundred rolls of unexposed film and countless other items—evidence of that long preparation. The thought of wasting this effort kept me in the field with the hope that somewhere the birds would be found.

Then on the 29th day, about the time I thought I would be finishing my project, I wrote in my journal:

"Yesterday I spoke with Juan Herrera, a poacher, at his house. Carlos and Juan were both there. They said they had been out together yesterday and had seen quetzals on a *finca* (farm) nearby. I asked to go the next day.

"We left a dirt road and walked for about fifteen or twenty minutes when Juan said we could start to look for the birds. A narrow strip of pasture ran uphill. It was bordered on both sides by forest. For the first time since my arrival in Costa Rica, I was expectant.

"There had been a little sunlight when we set out but clouds had since moved in. This deadened the jungle greens, but it made shadow and movement more visible. To someone who is not an old hand at birdwatching, it is hard to explain just how quick a glimpse can be. To the trained, attentive eye, the movement may be at the corner of one's vision; it may be colorless; it may pass at 1/100th of a second; it may have occurred through an opening in the jungle 100 yards away. And yet I knew I had seen something different. I knew I had seen a big bird with an ample tail, longer than that of the band-tailed pigeon that dashed overhead.

"I turned to Juan and raised my palm to him, signaling silently for him to stop. He had not seen it. We waited for a full minute. Nothing moved. Still we waited. Then I turned to him and shrugged. We could go on. But he didn't move, so I turned back to the trees. At that moment a large, emerald-backed bird with crimson below flew across our view through a gigantic oak about 50 yards away. A female quetzal! She never stopped.

"Right behind her appeared the sight I had longed to see. A magnificent male quetzal braked in front of a small, thinly-leaved tree about 40 yards away, its streaming tail floating out behind it. The sun had reappeared moments before. The bird sat motionless in full view for five or ten seconds watching us, his crest up, his back catching the sun, a crescent of crimson visible from the side. And then he was gone. The clouds immediately closed in on us again. When I turned to look at Juan, I saw only the image of a hungry dog unable to reach a bone."

This pair of birds saved my sagging morale. I decided then that all things were possible, that a nest could be found. Perhaps this pair was about to breed. News of my sighting improved my wife's spirits as well.

Lynn had flown to Costa Rica with our 3½-year-old son a week after I arrived. By that time I had located a house at 6,000 feet in quetzal territory, making it unnecessary to commute from a city to the forest. The house belonged to former President León Cortés and had been built for him in Los Cartagos 30 years before. It was vacant and we were able to rent it. The owner also owned the farm on the slopes above the house and instructed the manager to provide us with food, fresh milk and anything else we needed.

Alexander Skutch did his year-long study in an area "about two miles below the hamlet of Vara Blanca, on the northern side of the Cordillera Central of Costa Rica, along the old trail leading from Heredia across the continental divide down through the forests to the Río Sarapiquí, an affluent of the San Juan." By coincidence only, we were two miles above Vara Blanca on the same road.

By local standards we were living in a mansion. But there were certain elemental features missing—refrigeration and heat. And there was a wood stove in the kitchen which my wife announced she would not use. So one of our first purchases in San José was a one-burner Coleman. But when she discovered the wonderful utility of that wood stove, it was seldom out. It kept the kitchen shower-bath-warm when it was a damp 65 degrees outside; it kept water near a boil in a well to one side. And it dried clothes in a jiffy.

A few days after my first sighting, a poacher came by the house to say that a nest had been located. I asked him to take me to the spot immediately. The nest was at the top of a rotten trunk about twenty feet from the ground. The opening looked freshly renovated, but the birds were never seen here again. This trunk stood in a pasture, with a large shrub at its base and a small tree beside it, but otherwise it was in the open, completely exposed. The nearest forest was 100 yards away.

The quetzal's forest is composed of lofty oaks, which form a canopy 100 to 150 feet above the forest floor; alders almost as tall but not so massive; and a variety of smaller trees. Members of the laurel family, including the wild avocado, are important food trees for the quetzal and are plentiful. The forest is watered by abundant rainfall and in all seasons is bathed in cloud-mist much of the time. The epiphytic vegetation is hard to imagine. Each large oak upholds a mass of vegetation measured not in pounds but in tons. In addition to the orchids and air plants, there are mosses, ferns, herbs, shrubs, and even small trees. In fact, the epiphytes most certainly weigh more than the foliage of the host.

Then one week after seeing my first quetzal, a laborer on the farm behind the house casually mentioned that he knew where a pair was nesting. One would have expected him to come running with the news, but such is the makeup of these unexcitable people. Just as casually, I asked if we could go see the birds. He agreed. He said it would take us only half an hour to get there. If the nest was this close to Los Cartagos, why hadn't someone else found it already? There were many other questions I wanted to ask, but my limited Spanish stood in the way. And as we hiked uphill together, I grew less and less certain that a nest would be found.

Our route crossed lush pastureland, where giant trunks, evidence of the felled forest, lay strewn about the fields. Cows ambled out of our way through ankle-deep grass. On a steep slope we came to a plot of burned-over forest that would soon be pasture. We climbed through it to the edge of the cloud forest and stopped. My guide pointed to a trunk with two holes about fifteen feet off the ground. One of them looked fresh. Then the guide pointed slowly into the dull green forest to the iridescent green of a silent, motionless male quetzal. Without a word we turned back several yards, sat down and watched. In a few minutes the male flew to the hole. He clung there for half a minute, then entered. His body disappeared, but six or seven inches of his long tail plumes hung out the hole and waved like fern fronds in a breeze.

So I had found it, that doubtful entity—the nest of the quetzal. And everything about it was ideal for the photographs I wanted. The male had a perfect tail. The nest was only fifteen feet from the ground. The eggs had not yet hatched, for the bird had nothing in his mouth. The nest was at the edge of a clearing, providing the hope of daylight shots in the late afternoon. We were only a half-hour from the house; I would be able to go home for lunch. Then, too, packing about 50 pounds of camera and lighting gear to the nest each day, even with a porter, made this short trip look particularly good. Finally, as I surveyed the site, I noticed that the trunk leaned toward the clearing. Without a tower, my line of sight was still at a right angle to the trunk, and my pictures would give the appearance of being at eye level with the bird. There was nothing more I could possibly ask for.

My good fortune didn't seem possible. But after lunch, and after recounting all the details to my wife, a horrible irony occurred to me. I have come to Costa Rica because of the expertise of the quetzal poachers. Now that I had located the only nest known to exist in the area, how was I going to keep poachers away? These men made a good part of their living robbing nests of quetzals. To what ends would they go to get mine?

The men at the *finca* said they would have a blind built for me in two days. But I couldn't wait for one hour and I returned that afternoon to the nest. As I started the climb through the charred forest, I noticed two men and a dog behind a tree about twenty yards from the trunk.

Poachers.

Soon I was close enough to recognize one of the men. The other was a young assistant. If the female is caught, the male will often not enter the nest. The male must be taken first. I asked the question that would tell me everything. "Donde está el macho?" Where is the male? He said he didn't know. I set down my tripod and mounted my camera. He got the idea. I told him I had been photographing the birds for several days. A few minutes later he left.

I stayed at the nest until dark that night, then went immediately to the manager of the farm and asked for his help. He let me hire two of his men, and the three of us began a dawn-to-dark watch at the nest. For the next two days I waited impatiently for the blind to be built.

This generation is not the first to hunt the quetzal for its plumes; the poachers in Costa Rica, however, are the first to catch them so ruthlessly, so efficiently, and without regard for the future of the species. Quetzalcoatl, the cultural hero of both the Mayas and the Aztecs, was symbolized by the head of a serpent adorned with the tail feathers of the quetzal. The rulers in both cultures demanded headdresses made of quetzal feathers. But since the birds were considered sacred, they were freed after the long plumes were removed. According to Aztec legend, Quetzalcoatl was supposed to return as god-king in 1519 to rule them. When in that year Hernán Cortés sailed into Vera Cruz harbor, it was not surprising that the first gift Montezuma sent him was a magnificent headdress of quetzal plumes. That headdress is now in the Museum of Vienna.

Today the quetzal is honored in many ways that do not deplete its numbers. It is the national bird of Guatemala. The "quetzal" is the unit of currency in that country. And Quezaltenango, Guatemala's second largest city, means "the place of the quetzal." The colors for Mexico's flag are said to have been chosen from the colors of the quetzal; the bird itself is pictured on the flag of Guatemala.

But the business of poaching goes on in Costa Rica today. Zoos want live birds, of course; are willing to pay several hundred dollars a pair; and few worry about the source of the birds or the way they were obtained. Yet the quetzal is considered a bird of liberty throughout Middle America because people think it will not live in captivity. And although certain zoos have kept theirs for years, most of these delicate creatures fail to survive when caged, hence the demand is never-ending. Too, there is a substantial tourist trade in quetzals;

visitors to Guatemala buy many skins from taxidermists, although there is no live export trade from that nation.

Even before the blind was completed, I began my observations. Dr. Skutch's notes—recorded in a 1944 issue of *The Condor*—were an enormous help. The incubation pattern he described was soon evident. The female sits through the night and again in the middle of the day. The male relieves her in the morning and in the afternoon. This male was very irregular in its habits. Usually he arrived about 5:30 A.M., but was often an hour late; it was much harder to guess how long he would stay. Although he was replaced by the female before 8:30 A.M. on one occasion, he usually remained on the eggs until 11 A.M. For his second session, he once began at 11:30; another time he failed to return until 3:30 in the afternoon.

These irregular hours made photography particularly hard. Except for the tail-tips of the male, the quetzals were not visible when in the trunk. They could only be photographed easily as they clung to the hole for a minute or more before entering. And for a chance at a midair photograph, I had to crouch in the blind at-the-ready for long periods of time. The days passed slowly.

If the wind was not blowing or if it was not raining, the quetzal's arrival call —a one- or two-note thrushlike whistle—could be heard by both an observer and the bird on the nest. Immediately, the head of the nesting bird would appear in the hole. A few moments later it would fly off. Sometimes the two left together, calling to each other through the forest. But in a few minutes one would be back for its turn on the nest.

Twice I watched the male wing in through the trees to a perch about 25 yards from the nest and then, without a single call note, fly directly to the nest hole. Then he flew off and waited for his mate to exit. I watched the female do the same thing on one occasion.

The following are my notes from one day in the blind: "Monday. Arrived at 6 A.M. Male already in. We made too much noise in setting up, for his head appeared in the hole. First time this has happened. Didn't fly off. We retreated. (Have the impression the male is more nervous than the female. If I rattle tripod, squeak sneakers on floor inside blind, his head pops up in hole.)

"Female called to male about 7 A.M. but he didn't leave nest. About 11 A.M. I got impatient and hungry and gave the double-whistle call note. The male's head came up into the hole before I could whistle twice. He kept his head out for about two minutes, then flew off. The female wasn't around so he came back about five minutes later and went inside. She appeared in another five minutes and relieved him (about 11:15 A.M.). Female stayed in nest until relieved by male at 4:45 P.M."

How does the male protect its long train? Stories have claimed that the quetzal has two entrances to the nest. Then the male would not have to turn around in the nesting cavity. Skutch discredited this view, and the birds I saw used only one hole although there was another just below where a second cavity had been started. Skutch found evidence, however, that quetzal plumes frayed and broke during the nesting season. Poachers and animal dealers could not confirm this. The plumes of this Costa Rican male remained in excellent condition during incubation.

Indeed, after the first few days of feeding, the parents do not enter the nest but feed the young from the outside. As another protective measure, the males avoid dragging their plumes across a rough surface by frequently falling backwards from their perch. And these trogons' adeptness at plucking fruit from trees while in flight certainly eases wear on that tail.

Fifteen days after the first reports that the quetzals were nesting and ten days after I had begun taking pictures, I decided to wait for the eggs to hatch and take a much-needed rest. Skutch had said that quetzal eggs hatch in seventeen or eighteen days. Certainly the big event was about to take place. So I decided to take my wife and son down to San José.

But that morning just before the bus arrived, I received a cable from my office. I had some urgent business back home and would have to return. We decided to spend two days in San José; then Lynn and Jimmy would wait for me at the house while I flew back to Miami. I expected to be back in a week. My plane was scheduled to leave at 11 A.M. Sunday. I had time to take Lynn and Jimmy back to the house first, then go back down the mountain in the taxi to the airport.

We stopped at the little town of Los Cartagos to check with my porter, Miguel. Miguel's wife said there was trouble with the birds. My heart sank. I suspected an understatement. In a few minutes Miguel returned. Since the taxi driver spoke Spanish and English, I learned the whole story. At noon the day we left for town, one of the poachers came by Miguel's house and asked where I was. He said I had gone to town but would be back in a couple of days. Miguel was suspicious. His afternoon at the nest passed uneventfully, but that night he heard dogs barking in the pasture above his home and in the direction of the nest. He decided to go to the nest. As he approached, he saw two men flee the site. The next morning he climbed up the trunk and reached in. Nothing was there but egg shell. The young had hatched that day. The men had taken the female and the young.

As we flew dejectedly home, I thought often of how Costa Ricans are destroying the most beautiful part of their landscape. They do not possess major Maya or Aztec ruins; they have no towering Andes peaks, no glaciers, no spectacular waterfalls. But they do have the mist-shrouded cordilleras, pocked with volcanoes and draped with hauntingly beautiful cloud forest. These forests, inhabited not only by the quetzal but by other strange and wonderful fauna and flora, are rapidly being converted to pastureland. Around Vara Blanca the transformation is almost complete; 80 to 85 percent of the forest has been cut in four decades. In terms of the age of the forests or even the age of man, that is a day's work.

If Costa Rica were an exception, we might take heart. This is not so. It is more prosperous and more developed than most Central or South American countries. Therefore its problems—a burgeoning population confronting its natural areas and natural resources—are more acute. Attitudes are the same and the future looks as bleak for one country as for another.

Miguel told me that when he went back to the quetzal nest the next day the male was calling, calling for his mate. He stayed for some time, but the calling of the male never ceased. That bird was also calling to Costa Ricans. Miguel heard it and was moved. But will enough of his countrymen hear it in time?

PARROT! PARROT! FLICKERING OUT, BY EDWARD R. RICCIUTI

Can man save a nearly extinct species whose survivors have dwindled to two dozen, whose habitat has been decimated, and whose few nests face almost certain destruction by predators? The odds seem insurmountable. But because the answer is so important to many other tropical birds, thousands of dollars and countless man-hours are being expended to rescue Puerto Rico's only native parrot.

Rain pounded through the forest canopy, spattering the long, narrow leaflets of the sierra palms and rousing the legions of tree frogs hidden in unnumbered havens. The frog chorus, rising from the shrubbery near the ground and from the cups of the bromeliads perched on the branches above, provided a piping counterpoint to the monotonous drumming of the rain. Clouds of mist moved thickly through the forest, enveloping the slender palms and gnarled palo colorado trees, then spilling over the lip of the valley at the edge of the palm grove. The rain increased into the kind of driving downpour, common in the Luquillo Mountains of Puerto Rico, that sends chill streams of water sluicing down one's collar.

As the passage of the mist momentarily revealed the crown of one of the palms, a flurry of activity stirred its leaves and a series of harsh squawks erupted from within. The squawks increased in volume and frequency, and it was evident that they came from more than one creature. The noisemakers were not visible, however, until two birds, each about a foot long, burst from the palm crown and flew quickly into the mist-flooded valley. The calling from the palm lessened somewhat with their departure but continued for a few minutes more, until one bird, and then two others, abandoned their shelter and flew with rapid wingbeats into the mist. The echoes of their calling lingered for a moment, but then only the rain and frogs sounded in the forest. From the edge of the slope no birds were visible. They had vanished into the murk below.

The birds were Puerto Rican parrots (*Amazona vittata*), and on that rainy afternoon in April 1968 they were foraging near the picnic groves and restaurant in the central recreation area of the Caribbean National Forest. The only tropical national forest in the United States, it covers 28,000 acres of the rugged Luquillo Mountains, an hour's drive southeast of San Juan. It is best known as the Luquillo Forest or simply, according to tourist promotions, the rain forest. Many times I have walked its valleys and hillsides and each time it has thrilled me, but the sights and sounds of that rainy April afternoon will dominate my memories of the place. The occasion had a vaguely spectral quality. The tall palms, wraithlike in the mist, the sudden appearance and departure of the parrots, the fading echoes of their shrill calls—all seemed grimly appropriate, for even as the parrots fed there in the forest their species was dying.

The Puerto Rican parrot, once common through most of its native island and the nearby islet of Culebra, already may be doomed, although a handful of the birds remains in the wild and in captivity. According to the latest count, fourteen parrots survive in the Luquillo Forest and ten more are held captive. Three live in a wood-and-wire aviary at the Patuxent Wildlife Research Center of the U.S. Fish and Wildlife Service, at Laurel, Maryland. Two of the Patuxent birds were rescued from years of unproductive captivity in a zoo at Mayagüez, Puerto Rico, and the other was captured as a young bird early in

1972. The seven other captive parrots are kept in Puerto Rico at an installation maintained for the Patuxent researchers. All but one of these, taken as a nestling, were hatched from eggs removed from parrot nests.

In the face of admittedly miserable odds, the U.S. Forest Service, which administers the lands ranged by the parrots, and the Bureau of Sport Fisheries and Wildlife have embarked on a long-term effort to save Puerto Rico's native Amazon (as the parrots of the genus *Amazona* are called). For the first stage of the program a biologist was sent into the Luquillo Forest to observe its parrots for three years. The second stage, now under way, involves more field study and a long-shot attempt to breed the nine captive birds.

Thus far the effort to save the Puerto Rican parrot has cost about $100,000, most of which has been federal money. The World Wildlife Fund also contributed $15,000 to the project, which has consumed the time of several highly competent wildlife biologists. At first glance the entire venture might raise some questions, even if one admits that almost no species should be allowed to vanish without some effort to prevent its loss. A critic certainly might query the advisability of spending so much on a species whose doom seems inevitable. Moreover, it is unlikely that the disappearance of the Puerto Rican parrot from the fastness of the Luquillo Mountains will harm the region ecologically. Nor is the bird anything special from an esthetic point of view. It is, of course, colorful—bright green, with a dash of blue on its primaries and a red band on its forehead—but many other threatened birds are more beautiful.

The fact is, too, that the Puerto Rican parrot is only one of nine very similar species of Amazon parrots native to various West Indian islands. Seldom does a critically endangered species have so many close relatives. Therein, however, lies the special importance of the Puerto Rican parrot. Most of the other island Amazons are caught in the squeeze of expanding human population and the disturbance of nature that accompanies it, although none are in such bad shape as the Puerto Rican bird. What is learned about the Puerto Rican parrot and its slide toward extinction may help avert a similar fate for its Amazon cousins. And there always is the chance that captive breeding will succeed, with the eventual release of captive-bred birds to the wild.

There is something else that makes the Puerto Rican parrot especially worthy of scrutiny. If one views the species objectively it represents a perfect textbook case: it is the victim of several classic ecological pressures leading to extinction, any one of which might be enough to push a species over the brink.

Puerto Rican parrots were victims of excessive hunting. They were hunted in pre-Columbian times by the island's Taino Indians, and after the Spanish conquest by Spaniard, Indian, African, and probably every other strain of humanity that arrived in Puerto Rico. Some of the methods used to capture parrots were especially cunning: histories of the island tell how a boy, wearing a large straw hat to hide his face, would climb a tree with a live parrot in his hand; the parrot's screeches would attract other parrots, which would then be caught with lassos. The parrot was hunted for table meat and also for its reputed powers to enhance human virility; a soup made from the bird was believed to produce the desired effect.

Islanders also viewed the parrot as a threat to corn, chickpeas, and other crops, giving further impetus to the slaughter of the raucous green bird. And as agricultural land on this mountainous, 3,435-square-mile island became increasingly scarce, the lowland forests that were the parrot's preferred habitat were destroyed and the bird was pushed into mountain refuges much less favorable to its survival. Once in the mountains the parrot fell victim to a more rigorous climate and to a gang of introduced predators—the roof rat (*Rattus rattus*), feral cats, and possibly the mongoose (although some researchers who have studied the parrot debate this because the mongoose was not introduced on the island until 1877, after the decline of the parrot had begun). More recently the parrot has suffered drastically from the oddly mushrooming population of a natural competitor, the aggressive, noisy pearly-eyed thrasher (*Margarops fuscatus*), which takes over parrot nest holes.

Although various hawks occasionally have been seen making passes at adult Puerto Rican parrots, most of the predation on the parrot is inflicted upon its eggs and young. Both are eaten by rats and, apparently, by the thrashers, which even if they do not consume a parrot's offspring may toss them out of the nest. Until a few decades ago the thrasher was primarily a bird of dry, scrubby lowlands, but now it thrives in the moist mountain forests of the Luquillo region. The thrasher's adaptability may have sounded the death knell for the parrot.

That the Puerto Rican parrot was in any trouble at all, however, was not even indicated until the late 1870s, when people first noticed that the species had vanished from wide areas where it once had been abundant. Within the next few decades, Puerto Rican parrots became confined to two regions—the haystack hills of the island's karst country (in the west, between the mountain town of Utuado and the seaside community of Arecibo) and the forest of the Luquillo Mountains. By the 1930s the calls of the parrots sounded only in the latter range.

Even so, the Puerto Rican parrot received little attention until the early 1950s, when an official of the U.S. Forest Service in Puerto Rico, Dr. Frank H. Wadsworth, became concerned about the species' status. In fact, if the Puerto Rican parrot is saved, by some miracle, much of the credit should go to Dr. Wadsworth, director of the Institute of Tropical Forestry in San Juan. Dr. Wadsworth believes in the philosophy that the Forest Service is responsible for the fate of those species of wildlife whose populations are limited entirely to lands under its control. The parrot fits this category nicely; it has been years since any Puerto Rican Amazons have been seen even feeding outside Caribbean National Forest boundaries. And largely because of Wadsworth's urgings, wildlife biologists began to look more closely at the parrot.

The first significant investigation of the parrot's situation began in 1953 and lasted three years. It was conducted with federal and commonwealth funds by wildlife biologist José A. Rodriguez-Vidal of Puerto Rico's Department of Agriculture. Vidal tramped after the parrots and produced a report containing most of what is known about their feeding habits, nesting, and range, plus a gloomy picture of the predation that threatened the species. Yet there seemed to be hope for the parrot—Vidal estimated there were about two hundred parrots in the forest and indeed counted this many in one flock. Within ten years, however, estimates of the parrot population generally halved Vidal's count. Meanwhile, another biologist, Victor Marquez, was tracking the parrots through the forest. In the parrot's behalf he took on a couple of weighty foes, the Army and Navy. Marquez vigorously protested the use of the parrot's range as the site of detonation tests by the Navy and of maneuvers by the Army's Special Forces.

Eventually, the military was barred from infringing on the parrot's domain, and in 1967 the U.S. Department of the Interior declared the species endangered. Things seemed to be looking up for the parrot. Members of the Natural History Society of Puerto Rico, which uses the parrot as an emblem, kept regular watch on the wild flocks and their nests. Some particularly enlightening observations were made by the late Nathan Leopold (a society member, ornithologist, and convicted murderer in the 1924 Leopold-Loeb case in Chicago), who after his release from federal prison in 1958 moved to Puerto Rico and became an authority on its birdlife. Local newspapers featured the parrot with headlines such as "Island's Parrots May Be Saved" and "Rare Parrots Have Last Laugh."

For a time, indeed, it seemed as if the parrot would become something of a cause on an island where preservation of wildlife has never fired the popular imagination. All the while, however, the parrot population was careening toward oblivion, a fact that was made appallingly clear after the Bureau of Sport Fisheries and Wildlife sent Dr. Cameron Kepler to the Luquillo Forest in the summer of 1968. Kepler searched the forest for a month and a half before seeing his first Puerto Rican parrot. Shortly after his arrival he organized a team of volunteer parrot-watchers, who fanned out across the forest to census the bird. The result was dismal; Kepler estimated that only twenty-four birds remained. As he completed his study during 1971 his estimate dropped to fifteen parrots, and he predicted that the species would not survive in the wild for much more than another decade, trapped as it was in the hostile environment of the Luquillo Mountains.

This mountain range is vastly different from the sheltered lowland forests where the parrot once thrived. It contains some of Puerto Rico's highest peaks —El Toro, which rises 3,524 feet, and El Yunque, a towering 3,496 feet. The name Yunque is said to be derived from the Taino Indian word *yuke*, meaning "white land." When seen from as far away as San Juan, the peaks of the Luquillo Mountains fit the name, for they are mantled with white clouds.

The name Luquillo is also of Indian derivation. In Indian legend Yuquiyu was the good spirit, who from his mountaintop home watched over the welfare of the island. The mountains that bear his name are a basaltic formation that rises sharply six to ten miles from the Atlantic. The peaks rob the winds of one hundred billion gallons of moisture yearly, producing more than two hundred inches of rainfall in some parts of the forest. The abundance of moisture gives rise to the lush tropical rain forest.

Tradition says that Christopher Columbus' son Diego led the first explorations of the range. For much of the sixteenth century, however, a walk in the rain forest must have been a hazardous undertaking, for a stroller might well have ended up a meal; the forest served as a stronghold of the fierce Carib

Indians, cannibalistic warriors who raided the northeast coast of Puerto Rico in their great dugouts, terrorizing Taino and Spaniard alike.

Today a main highway, Route 191, cuts through the forest, and tourists can visit a number of scenic overlooks and recreation areas and hike moderately steep trails to some of the higher peaks. Deep in the interior, however, the landscape is little changed from the days when the Caribs roved it. High valleys sweep to the horizon and streams of clear, cold water surge down rocky hillsides, pooling behind piles of moss-coated boulders.

Although the entire forest is popularly called a rain forest, it actually is a composite of four considerably different forest zones. At the top of the highest peaks grows a forest that fits its rather poetic name, elfin woodland. There the trees are crabbed and crooked and not much taller than a man. Their branches are draped with mosses kept wet by the continual mist that pervades the woodland. Their aerial roots, spread over the true soil, are carpeted with a layer of moss; underfoot the ground is springy, rather like in a bog.

Below the elfin woodland are three forest zones that are closely tied to the ecology of the Puerto Rican parrot. From the lower fringes of the elfin woodland to about 2,500 feet grows a forest dominated by sierra palm (*Euterpe globosa*). From January through June the parrots flock to this zone, the palmbrake, and gorge on the thin-fleshed fruits of the palm. At 2,500 feet the palms thin out, except in and around wet ravines. Now the dominant tree is the palo colorado (*Cyrilla racemiflora*), gnarled and red-barked with leathery leaves. The palo colorado grows to about three feet in diameter and seldom exceeds fifty feet in height—a mediocre size compared with some of the giants that grow in the next zone down the slopes. Nevertheless, the palo colorado is venerable, for its age if not its size. Growing amidst the pink-and-white begonias that fleck the forest floor, the palo colorado trees were ancient when the Spaniards first came in search of wood for the homes and furniture of San Juan. They are so old that they are quite hollow. Cavities, where limbs have fallen from the trunk, and the hollow interiors of this tree serve as the only nest sites of the Puerto Rican parrot. Sometimes the birds nest deep within the hollows; one nest discovered by Leopold was fifty inches within the tree.

At 2,000 feet the palo colorado forest gives way to one in which great tabonuco (*Dacryodes excelsa*) trees tower forty feet and more above the sixty-foot-high canopy. White-barked, with a five-foot diameter, the tabonuco gives its name to this zone, which is the true rain forest. More than two hundred different types of trees grow in the tabonuco forest, where thick, woody vines of lianas lace the canopy and thread down through the branches. Orchids—red, yellow, and brown—create dabs of color in the canopy, growing with bromeliads and other epiphytes. Thirty-foot-high tree ferns grow here, too, their slender, unbranched trunks, leafy only at the top, qualifying them as trees.

Puerto Rican parrots feed in flocks on about fifty different wild fruits, eating mainly the pericarps. If a fruit grows in clusters, like grapes, a parrot will snip off the entire cluster, hold it with one foot, and consume only those fruits on the cluster that are ripe. The parrots migrate through the forest seasonally, according to the location and ripeness of the fruits. All of their movement, however, is within a tract of about 3,000 acres on either side of a ridge complex that is the major east–west divide of the Luquillo Mountains. It is in many ways the most spectacular part of the range, including El Yunque and other peaks almost as stately, with windswept cliffs and boulder-strewn valleys. The ridge has prongs that separate three large river valleys: the Espíritu Santo, which runs northwest; the Icacos, running south–southeast; and La Mina, a smaller stream which stretches to the northeast. The parrots regularly cross the ridges between the valleys when foraging.

Nearly in the center of this region is the recreation area where I stopped in April 1968. After a morning of searching the rough Espíritu Santo valley for parrots without succees, I headed for the restaurant at the recreation area and a late-afternoon meal. By the time I reached the restaurant, showers were dousing the area. My clothing was spattered with mud, and the cuff of one trouser leg was dripping as the result of a misstep into a rivulet. Feeling a little embarrassed among the neatly dressed diners, I mentioned to the waiter that I had been searching the forest for parrots.

"The parrots?" he said with a shrug. "Oh, yes. They were making noise outside a few minutes ago." Trying to appear calm, I left the restaurant, walked up an overgrown path where large land snails moved slowly over the worn stones, and stopped by a palm grove. Bananaquits buzzed in the brush, and a few tree frogs called, but I heard no parrots. The rain had increased, and I was about to go back to the restaurant when the mist parted and I saw and heard the parrots for the first time. That night I thought happily about my good luck, for I am not usually so fortunate in such matters. The next day my luck held, for when I returned to the recreation area I saw three parrots flying over the parking lot. They settled in some trees in a steep ravine, called for a few moments, and then headed off into the forest.

I have accepted the fact that this was the last time I would ever see wild Puerto Rican parrots. Even if the captive birds breed it is questionable whether released birds will survive in the wild. Young parrots appear to learn the routes to feeding areas from their elders. What happens if no adults remain in the forest when captive birds are released? The same situation could apply if eggs are removed from wild nests and the young reared in captivity for eventual release. The chances of getting young from eggs collected in the wild, however, are better at present than those of obtaining young from the captive birds.

Suppose captive birds are released and attempt to nest? While plenty of palo colorado trees grow in the Luquillo Forest, there is a lack of trees suitable for parrot nests. The best nest trees are older individuals in which large hollows have developed. Many older trees were cut for charcoal during World War II, and most of the best nest trees that remain grow in deep valleys far from the palmbrake.

This is a critical point, because when parrots are incubating their eggs and rearing young they feed in the palmbrake on the fruits of the sierra palm. They therefore must leave their nest for long periods of time. When it nests the Puerto Rican parrot merely cleans out a hollow and deposits the eggs within. Usually the species lays three eggs and only the female incubates. One female observed by Kepler traveled for as much as sixty-two minutes to her feeding ground from her nest, leaving her eggs untended for a third of all daylight hours.

The young thus left are in the midst of many enemies. The large, old palo colorados also draw the thrashers, which are unique in their family for their hole-nesting habit. Rats are attracted to the decaying wood. Kepler tried to encourage the parrots to forsake the palo colorado by providing them with nest boxes. The only birds who took up residence in the boxes were pearly-eyed thrashers.

Observations of the fate of known parrot nests constitute a litany of disaster, increasing in severity with the passage of the years. Vidal found sixteen nests containing thirty-three eggs during his study. Rats destroyed six eggs, thrashers two, and eight eggs were infertile. Fourteen of the seventeen fledglings produced by the surviving eggs flew off, one was drowned when water filled its hollow during a rainstorm, one was killed by a rat, and another died when its tree fell.

Vidal watched a pair of parrots leave their nest and two eggs when confronted by thrashers in 1955. The thrashers appeared outside the nest, flying around it and uttering harsh calls. They continued to buzz the parrot nest, harassing the parrots, and within a few days drove them off. The remains of eggs littered the ground and the thrashers already had started to set up housekeeping in the hollow three days after they had arrived.

Avian predators destroyed four of the five nests Kepler reported finding during his three-year stay in the Luquillo Forest. One of the predators was probably a Puerto Rican screech owl, and thrashers accounted for at least two of the destroyed nests. One nest, however, produced three young. The day after all were fledged, Kepler saw five parrots not far from the nest. The group consisted of a pair followed by a line of what appeared to be the three fledglings.

Leopold, when I talked with him in April 1968, reported finding two young Puerto Rican parrots in a nest only a few weeks earlier. Within a week after the nestlings had hatched, only one remained, and in another week a thrasher had replaced it in the nest cavity.

Storms also seem to have taken their toll of Puerto Rican parrots. Kepler believes that one particularly bad storm in 1968 wiped out a substantial portion of the forest's parrot population, and while hurricanes usually bypass Puerto Rico, it probably would take but one to wipe out the species in the wild. On completing his research, Kepler concluded that captive breeding was the only way to preserve the Puerto Rican parrot. Thus, in February 1972, mist nets were placed along a flyway used by parrots, and two of the birds were captured in the nets. The birds were placed in carrying cases while Forest Service personnel attempted to arrange for the papers necessary to get the parrots to Miami's Crandon Park Zoo, where they would be held in quarantine. Snags developed in making the arrangements, and for two days the parrots were held, within their cases, in the forest.

When the parrots' way through the maze of bureaucratic paperwork eventually was cleared, a helicopter picked up the birds in their cases and ferried them to the airport at San Juan. It was necessary to use the helicopter to minimize the parrots' contact with domestic fowl, thus avoiding the risk of

Newcastle disease, which now is prevalent in Puerto Rico. Both parrots, however, had to be tested for the disease, and one died during the test, which requires the taking of considerable blood. (Both the live bird and the one that had died were found free of the avian disease.)

The bird that remained alive was flown from Miami to Baltimore on May 30th. It made the trip in the pilot's cabin, where the crew could keep an eye on it. From Baltimore the parrot was taken to Patuxent, where the two birds obtained from the Mayagüez Zoo were already in residence.

Both of the zoo birds are believed to be female, for during the eighteen years they were together at the zoo several infertile egg clutches were produced. The new arrival is young, and federal biologists are holding their breath; unless the youngster is a male the proposed breeding program is in real trouble; thus far, the bird has not been sexed, nor demonstrated male behavior. On the plus side is the belief that the Puerto Rican parrot lives more than twenty years and can reproduce throughout most of that period.

Meanwhile, the Bureau of Sport Fisheries and Wildlife has sent Dr. Noel Snyder to the hilltop home in the Luquillo Forest that was used by Kepler. Dr. Snyder has taken the latest counts and is rearing the nestlings in an aviary facility within the forest, focusing much of his attention on the nesting habits of the parrot.

Ironically, as the Puerto Rican parrot declines, other parrots and parakeets have become established on the island. A few years ago a number of Hispaniolan parrots (*Amazona ventralis*), close relatives of the Puerto Rican species, were freed in the Mayagüez area on the west coast. This species is spreading through the island, and biologists say there seems to be no reason why it will not thrive. Canary-winged parakeets (*Brotogeris versicolorus*), a South American species, also have been introduced in Puerto Rico and are commonly seen in the San Juan area. A flock of introduced parrots, of uncertain species, has been seen within the confines of the Luquillo Forest. Many Puerto Ricans who see the Hispaniolan bird believe they are seeing their own parrot, something which has not helped the Puerto Rican parrot's case at all. Furthermore, competition from a relative is the last thing the Puerto Rican parrot needs, although it does not appear that the Hispaniolan bird has invaded the territory used by the Puerto Rican parrot.

In August 1972 I spent another day searching unsuccessfully through the Luquillo Forest for Puerto Rican parrots. I returned to the recreation area and walked to where I had first seen them. The forest was quite silent and unusually dry, for the island was suffering from a severe drought. Three green anoles lapped droplets of water off the cream-white efflorescence of a sierra palm. Bananaquits scolded nearby. The dry weather had silenced the tree frogs, and I saw only one land snail. For a while I waited, remembering the parrots' calls. This time there was only the sound of the wind in the crowns of the palms.

HAUNTED SANDS OF LAYSAN, BY GEORGE LAYCOCK

On a coral atoll far out in the Pacific Ocean, a visitor encounters the shadows of men—misguided, evil, and good—whose arrival in earlier years had enormous and sometimes catastrophic impact on the islet's wondrous birdlife.

From the gently rocking dock of the U.S. Coast Guard cutter *Buttonwood* we could see, lying off to the east, the historic bird island of Laysan. Unlike some of the other rocky islets and atolls of the Leeward Islands in the Hawaiian archipelago, Laysan scarcely rises above the surface of the ocean. From this distance, in the early morning sunlight, it was only a thin yellow line between the sea and the deep-blue sky. But that unimpressive stretch of coral has long been known as one of the world's most productive seabird nurseries. Thus, small groups of people have been coming to this remote part of the mid-Pacific for decades.

Earliest of the ornithologists to visit Laysan were Henry Palmer and George C. Munro, who spent eleven days there in 1891; Walter Rothschild then wrote a three-volume report on their pioneering expedition, although he personally never visited any of the Hawaiian islands. Sailing aboard the U.S. Fish Commission steamer *Albatross*, Walter K. Fisher, C. C. Nutting, and John O. Snyder landed on Laysan on May 16, 1902, and stayed for a week; Fisher wrote a sound and detailed report on the island's birdlife.

Of all the intrusions on Laysan Island, none brought greater change than the arrival of Max Schlemmer. In 1890 the Kingdom of Hawaii granted mining rights on Laysan to a guano company which dispatched Schlemmer from the main islands to manage the operation. As he sailed from Honolulu with his family and worldly belongings, Schlemmer must have had only the vaguest idea of how life would be on an island less than two miles long.

He saw Laysan as it had been through centuries—low sand dunes rising no more than forty feet above the high-tide mark, and blanketed with the dark greens of thick-growing *Scaevola*, a flowering shrub peculiar to these islands that in some places was shoulder-high. In the heart of the island lay a mile-long lagoon, a shallow basin of water saltier than the surrounding ocean. And on the north side of this pond was a tiny pool, the only source of freshwater on the island except for rain.

A long gentle slope extended down to the lagoon's edge, and here the main cover was *Eragrostis*, a coarse-bladed bunch grass growing in clumps two to three feet high.

Everywhere over this scene were seabirds, some of which are present on Laysan each month of the year. Schlemmer, looking across his new domain, saw clouds of sooty terns mixed with soaring albatrosses and tropic-birds, fairy terns, boobies, and as evening came, thousands of petrels and shearwaters. This extravaganza must have amazed Schlemmer, and as he tried to sleep that first night on Laysan, the calling of the terns mingled with the deep-throated moaning of the shearwaters certainly gave him long wakeful hours to ponder the wisdom of coming to this lonely place to live and work.

Laysan was indeed a frontier where men were cut off from the rest of the world the moment their ship steamed out of sight. There was no radio, no regular postal service, no medical help, and no way of obtaining emergency supplies. The guano workers on the island would truly learn the meaning of isolation. Yet Schlemmer lived there fifteen years, and his son Eric, born in 1904, was perhaps the only person ever to have claimed Laysan Island as his birthplace.

Schlemmer's ship had brought lumber, with which he built a modest frame house on the ridge above the landing, plus several small outbuildings used in the mining operation. The rest of the wood went into crossties for a short stretch of track reaching across the sands. Along these rails, carts carried guano from the deposit to the beach, where it awaited shipment to Honolulu.

But Schlemmer also saw other possibilities in his island. He brought a few coconut seedlings to plant beside his house. He imported a few guinea pigs and turned them loose. He brought a supply of tobacco seed and planted a patch.

Then Schlemmer decided Laysan needed some animals to supply meat. There was all that greenery growing there and not doing anyone a bit of good—and it would take a world of rabbits to eat that much.

Word went back to Honolulu on a visiting ship that Max Schlemmer wanted some Belgian hares, the big domestic rabbits that produce a lot of fine white meat and good-sized skins as well. So one fateful day in 1902, along with a supply of flour, salt, bacon, cloth, and hand tools, there arrived on Laysan's beach the first rabbits ever to reach that Pacific island. The number of rabbits brought ashore in that first shipment has been lost to history, but it was small, for Schlemmer imported rabbits three times that year and the next, and they totaled only eight or nine. But eight or nine rabbits, as events—and rabbits—were soon to prove, can go a long way.

By 1906, with the guano business rapidly sliding downhill, Schlemmer had packed up his family and belongings and had shipped out for Honolulu. He left behind some weathered buildings standing in the shade of two scrawny coconut trees, a few feral guinea pigs, plus a vigorous and fast-expanding colony of multicolored Belgian hares, hopping through the *Scaevola* bushes and nibbling contentedly at the native vegetation.

The rabbits shared the island with the seabirds, whose descendants still come to Laysan to nest. But there were also a few birds that lived on Laysan the year around, some of them known nowhere else in the world. These endemic species included the teal-sized dark-brown Laysan ducks which fattened on brine flies swarming around the edges of the lagoon. There were Laysan finches, yellowish, sparrow-sized birds that nested in the *Eragrostis* clumps. There were red-tinted honeycreepers, and skulking millerbirds, about the size of house wrens. And running through the grass were strange little rails that had evolved only one place on earth.

The Laysan rails scurried around the abandoned buildings like tiny domestic chickens. Their wings were short and the birds were incapable of flight. They survived because the vegetation provided escape cover from larger birds and because there were no predatory mammals or reptiles to pursue them.

The Schlemmers had been gone from Laysan only a few years when President Theodore Roosevelt, early in 1909, signed an executive order declaring the Leeward Islands to be the Hawaiian Islands Reservation, one of the earliest of America's national wildlife refuges. The same year a band of Japanese plume-hunters ran their boat up on the shore of Laysan Island and took up residency in the old Schlemmer home.

These new intruders arranged their tools, stacked their shipping crates in one of the sheds, and set to their grisly task with unequaled efficiency. Their major victims were the thousands of albatrosses that historically returned to Laysan in incredible numbers to nest, but the plumers also took feathers of several other species. They found it exceedingly simple to walk among the unafraid seabirds and knock them on the heads with sticks. To gather the wing feathers, they usually cut off the entire wing, sometimes killing the bird, sometimes not. Soon dead and crippled seabirds littered the coral sand.

Word of the depredations on the new federal refuge leaked out and the revenue cutter *Thetis* was dispatched from Honolulu to apprehend the poachers. Government agents swooped in on the beach and the bird-killers, having no place to run, were soon captives. The whole band, feathers and all, were taken back to Honolulu on the *Thetis*. Behind them was a desolate scene, the weather-beaten buildings once again empty—surrounded with trash now, and the decaying bodies of thousands of birds, around which swarmed multiplying flies. Meanwhile the rabbits, more abundant than ever, spent their days in petrel burrows or in holes they themselves dug, emerging in the evenings to continue cutting away at the disappearing vegetation, bringing Laysan steadily closer to its day of biological reckoning.

Among those saddened by the turn of affairs on Laysan was ornithologist C. C. Nutting, professor of zoology at the University of Iowa, who had visited the island in 1902. Two years later, on a visit to Iowa City, he showed lantern slides of the amazing courtship dance of the albatrosses. In the audience was a nine-year-old lad named Alfred M. Bailey. "I went home that night and dreamed about albatrosses," he told me recently, "and ever since I've been interested in them."

In 1911 Dr. Nutting influenced the U.S. Biological Survey to send a party to the Leeward Islands to make a museum collection of the native birds there. Professor Nutting handed the assignment to lead this party to an assistant professor, Homer R. Dill, who was shortly enroute to Hawaii in the company of a few assistants.

Dill and his group sailed out of Honolulu April 17, 1911, on the *Thetis*. Several days later, when they came within about fifty miles of Laysan, they began seeing increasing numbers of albatrosses, petrels, and terns around their ship. They stayed on Laysan until June 5th, taking their turn at living in the old Schlemmer place. As they came ashore, desolation greeted them. "Our first impression of Laysan," Dill later wrote, "was that the poachers had stripped the place of birdlife. An area of over 300 acres on each side of the buildings was apparently abandoned. Only the shearwaters moaning in their burrows, the little wingless rail skulking from one grass tussock to another, and the saucy finch remained . . . Here on every side are bones bleaching in the sun, showing where the poachers have piled the bodies of the birds as they stripped them of wings and feathers. In the old open guano shed were seen the remains of hundreds and possibly thousands of wings which were placed there but never cured for shipping, as the marauders were interrupted in their work."

The clubs, nets, and other tools of the bird-killers still littered the ground. "Hundreds of boxes to be used in shipping the bird skins were packed in an old building. It was evident that they intended to carry on their slaughter as long as the birds lasted."

But what astounded the professor from Iowa most were the rabbits. He was surrounded by rabbits. They had taken over Laysan Island. The vegetation was gone from large areas and the sand was free to move before the winds. It may well be that the visit of Professor Dill in 1911 coincided very closely with the maximum population of rabbits, and that the invading mammals were at that moment reaching the point where further breeding would so heavily cut into their food supplies that the rabbits would threaten their own future. "They were very fond," wrote Professor Dill, "of the green juncus that grows near the lagoon, and, while they are eating, their bodies are concealed among the thick growth and only their ears show." In the evenings the island seemed to be a garden of ears.

When Homer Dill returned to Iowa he carried the carefully skinned and packed remains of the rails, finches, and other birds collected to form the planned museum exhibit. But he also carried a warning. Unless an official party could be dispatched to Laysan soon to attack the rabbit hordes, the future was indeed bleak for that amazing bird island.

To this was added the opinion of Professor William A. Bryan of the College of Hawaii, who had joined the party for the first week of its Laysan expedition. "If active steps are not taken by the government to check or exterminate the rabbits on Laysan, it is only a matter of a very short time indeed when they will reduce this green island to a barren heap of white sand."

Because of these warnings, the U.S. Biological Survey organized still another expedition. This one would have a gruesome mission. In charge was a former governor of Guam, Commodore G. R. Saulsbury. The ornithologist aboard was George Willett. The youngest member of the team was Alfred Bailey who, years before, had dreamed of albatrosses. By 1912 the 18-year-old Bailey was a sophomore at the University of Iowa. Recently I visited with Dr. Bailey in his office in Denver, where he is the director of the noted Denver Museum of Natural History. "It would be nice," Dr. Bailey told me, "to be able to say that I was chosen because of my skills as a young naturalist, but I was the expedition cook." But he was also an expert taxidermist, as well as an experienced and self-reliant outdoorsman—an experienced hunter and a crack shot with a rifle. The expedition shipped out aboard the *Thetis* for Laysan, and three days before Christmas they stepped onto the beach. They had become the new tenants of the disintegrating buildings erected by Max Schlemmer.

Before them lay a staggering assignment. They had brought only two .22 rifles, one of which was Bailey's personal gun. "We also took along two or three ferrets," Dr. Bailey told me, "thinking these might help chase the rabbits out. We took only males. But when we went ashore and saw how many birds were in burrows, we put the ferrets back on board the *Thetis*." They had brought 6,000 rounds of ammunition, but there were probably more than that number of rabbits on Laysan at the time.

The rabbits at first were so tame that some could be caught by hand. Bailey kept score of the numbers killed. On their best day the rabbit population was reduced by 254. Toward the end of their tour on the island the rabbits became increasingly wary, and the men knew they were going to fail in their mission. Ammunition was running low, and time was running out. Thumbing his aging journals written more than half a century ago, Dr. Bailey said, "We killed 5,020 rabbits while we were there, and four guinea pigs. It wasn't a pleasant job. But it was one that had to be done. At the last we had a rule that anyone who made a poor shot on a rabbit had to run it down instead of using another shell." Complete elimination of the rabbits during this visit proved impossible. Starvation would eventually confront the ones remaining.

Dr. Bailey's journals also tell the sad tale of Laysan's birds at the time of his visit. The Laysan duck had become the world's rarest waterfowl—only seven remained. The Laysan rails still scurried from one shadow to the next, while beautiful honeycreepers still sang and millerbirds still skulked. All of these endemic species—unlike the traveling seabirds—found their food only on Laysan. The vegetation that supported the insects on which some of them fed, and which provided nesting and escape cover, was vanishing. With the rabbit population still substantial, the future for these resident birds was dim. So in the last days of their tour on Laysan, Willet told Bailey to capture as many of the flightless rails as possible. He penned them in one of the sheds, and on the day of departure 50 Laysan rails went aboard ship for release on Midway, where they flourished for many years.

During those lonely weeks on Laysan, Alfred Bailey made an excellent set of pictures of his favorite birds, the albatrosses. The party also collected birds for museum exhibits, but steadfastly resisted the temptation to take the Laysan ducks. Although only seven of their kind were left, there was still hope that they would somehow survive the rabbit tragedy that men had visited upon this coral island.

Following my visit with Dr. Bailey, I had one more call to make in my efforts to unravel the patchy history of Laysan Island. In Washington I talked with Dr. Alexander Wetmore of the Smithsonian Institution. Of all those who visited Laysan with the early scientific groups, only Dr. Bailey and Dr. Wetmore are still alive. Ten years passed between the time Dr. Bailey's group left the island and the arrival of Dr. Wetmore.

At the age of 37, Dr. Wetmore, already one of the world's most widely traveled and knowledgeable ornithologists, organized a party to cruise for four months through the Leeward Islands under sponsorship of the Biological Survey and the famed Bishop Museum in Honolulu, and to concentrate especially on the best-known bird island of the chain, Laysan. In Honolulu, Dr. Wetmore sought out a tall, gangly young man who had once lived on Laysan, Eric Schlemmer, and signed him on as a member of the twelve-man party. Schlemmer had not been "home" since his family left the island many years before. The group left the Honolulu harbor on April 4, 1923, on a World War I mine sweeper, the *U.S.S. Tanager*. Aboard were excellent photographers, scientists with varied interests, plus general helpers, including young Schlemmer.

Also in the baggage was equipment for one more attack on the rabbits—if necessary. In addition to rifles and several thousand rounds of ammunition, Dr. Wetmore had purchased a ton of fine leafy alfalfa hay in San Francisco, and had it compressed into compact bales. "I put it aboard with my baggage," Dr. Wetmore recalls with a smile. Included was a supply of poison.

"I don't know whether we should report all the gory details," Dr. Wetmore commented. He was leafing through the yellowing pages of his old journals, verifying facts as he talked. "But getting rid of the rabbits was absolutely essential to the wildlife of the island. We didn't use more than a bale of the alfalfa. We mixed it with poison, and to protect the birds that might have picked it up otherwise, placed it deep in the rabbit burrows."

During his first half-hour on the island, Dr. Wetmore could do little but stand in awe at the swirling clouds of seabirds. Then, when he began inspecting the island, he was struck at once with the desolation. Only remnant stands of vegetation remained. Petrels and shearwaters, once safe in their burrows, were now trapped with each windstorm. The old buildings were still there, more weatherbeaten than ever. Two coconut trees still stood beside the old Schlemmer house. In the limited shelter of a coral outcropping, Dr. Wetmore found three of the little Laysan honeycreepers, all that remained of a once vigorous population. The millerbirds were gone. And as for the Laysan rail, only the mummified remains of the last of the species were found.

The elimination of Laysan's remaining rabbits began immediately. There were perhaps no more than 500 rabbits left—skinny, starving individuals that came out in the evenings, vainly seeking greenery to satisfy their hunger. By the end of the fourth day the expedition had killed more than 250 rabbits. Already, the scientists could see the difference. Scattered plants, relieved of the incessant gnawing, had begun showing signs of renewed life. With his camp established and his party at work, Dr. Wetmore left Laysan aboard the *Tanager*, bound for a brief survey of the islands to the west.

"I returned the afternoon of April 29th. There had been stormy weather throughout most of the western trip." For three days before his return, gale-force winds had swept across the barren sands of Laysan. "But on the date of my return," he added, "everything was calm again, except for the usual trade wind." But the storm brought tragedy.

What about the three honeycreepers? Dr. Wetmore promptly searched for them around the coral rocks—without success. They were never seen again. This was a rare and sad event, for a naturalist had witnessed the extinction of a species. A few days earlier, Donald Dickey had photographed the last living Laysan honeycreeper.

There was still a glimmer of hope for the Laysan rail. If Dr. Bailey's team had not moved a seed stock of the flightless rails to Midway Islands, this species, too, would have been extinct. Now, Dr. Wetmore had brought eight rails back from Midway to their ancestral island. He released them on Laysan and watched as they scurried about, seeking places to hide. Exposed to view as they were on the now barren dunes, the rails were picked up one by one by frigatebirds. After a few days, no rail was ever seen again on Laysan. The species did prosper on Midway, however, until World War II. But increased military activity on the atoll introduced large numbers of rats. The rails on Midway soon vanished. The rabbits of Laysan had wrought the extinction of three species.

Dr. Wetmore's expedition saw fewer and fewer rabbits as each day passed on Laysan. There were times when they did not find a single rabbit for three or four days. "I went out at dawn," Dr. Wetmore told me, "to check for them. The wind would die down at night, and rise again in the morning. If you got out early before the winds came up to cover the tracks, you could see where the rabbits might still be living." Finally he could find neither rabbits nor tracks. If the *Tanager* party left any rabbits behind, they too soon perished, victims of the biological disaster their ancestors had visited.

As they were preparing to leave Laysan, Dr. Wetmore noticed one of the ship's sailors playing on the beach with some kind of animal, and he walked over quickly to investigate. "What the sailor had brought ashore," Dr. Wetmore recalls with a smile after all these years, "was a pet rabbit that he kept on the *Tanager*. I told him to take that rabbit, get back on the ship, and never come ashore on Laysan Island again."

During his visit to the Leeward Islands, Dr. Wetmore also landed on Lisianski, 150 miles farther west. Rabbits had once been released here also, but they had devoured their food sources and starved to death. He then visited Southeast Island in Pearl and Hermes Reef, where he found—and exterminated—still more rabbits, which were wilder than those on Laysan.

As had others before me, I stood one evening on the low ridge where Max Schlemmer had built his frame house, and silently marveled at the multitudes of birds. Hundreds of thousands of wings filled the sky, and the voices of the seabirds created a thunderous din.

Laysan's vegetation has recovered over the years. The old buildings are gone at last. The coconut trees are gone, too. The only evidence of the guano industry are a few remnants of weather-beaten cross-ties lined out across the sand, where carts once carried their guano burden through nesting colonies of albatrosses.

A more recently planted grove of coconut trees grows at the eastern end of the shallow lagoon. In the low vegetation between the coconut trees and the lagoon, hundreds of Laysan albatrosses with their gleaming white breasts and clean black backs raise their young. And nearby, the little Laysan ducks, now numbering perhaps two hundred, slip out of the dense cover of the *Scaevola* in the late evening sun.

Where the trail leads up from the beach, through thick-growing native vegetation, there stands a large sign to warn that Laysan Island is part of the Hawaiian Islands National Wildlife Refuge, and that unauthorized visitors are forbidden to come ashore. One reason is the ever-present fear that some new foreign animal, whether rat, cat, or mongoose, might find its way to this wondrous island which we have reserved for the birds.

MAN AND GULL,
BY FRANK GRAHAM, JR.

The herring gull, a familiar sight along our North Atlantic coast, once suffered grievously at the hands of man. Commercial eggers robbed its nests while poachers slaughtered the adult birds so that their feathers could decorate fashionable millinery. Today, thriving on man's garbage, herring gull populations have exploded, and these lovely seabirds have become not only a pest but a predatory threat to other species.

Rising just off the coast of eastern Maine is a lump of rock and turf called Petit Manan by early French explorers of the region, but almost ever since referred to by local people as 'Tit Manan. One of the tallest lighthouses on the Atlantic Coast stands on the island. Terns and a few laughing gulls nest among its rocks and rank vegetation. Herring gulls nest on a smaller island nearby.

From afar, Petit Manan Island seems to exist in lonely grandeur, undulating on the swell if the haze creates an optical illusion, a misty apparition untouched by man's dinginess. But no lives remain isolated from human impact today. The succession of ironic circumstances that finally affects this island illustrates in miniature the results of man's heedlessness along the world's coastlines.

One of the loveliest of all sights, to me, is a white gull soaring on motionless wings against a blue sky. It is as if the bird has gathered to itself the sum of heaven's light. Perhaps across the ocean Yeats had a gull in mind when he sang: "I would that we were, my beloved, white birds on the foam of the sea."

The herring gull—the common "seagull" of our North Atlantic coast—is a splendid creature in its breeding plumage. Its feathers are of the purest white, except on the wings and back, where a rich silvery gray accounts for its specific name, *Larus argentatus,* and the tips of its wings are marked in black and white. But the herring gull once aroused a meaner form of admiration so that less than a century ago there were men who believed it would soon disappear from our shore.

Gunners slaughtered the bird for the millinery trade because its feathers and even its wings were used in the decoration of women's hats. Late in the nineteenth century, so great was the gulls' scarcity that dealers paid 40 cents apiece for adults and 20 cents for the brown immature birds. Eggers searched out gulls at their nesting places on the islands and collected their eggs by the barrel. (The distinguished British naturalist Niko Tinbergen vouches for the tastiness of herring gull eggs, recalling his own egging expeditions "culminating in boiling or frying the eggs on a little fire of driftwood on the beach or, better still, scrambling them raw with some brandy and sugar.")

Few herring gulls at that time bred south of the Maine coast. Its islands supported many more people year-round than they do today, and by shooting the birds, disrupting their nesting cycle, and collecting their eggs, local residents severely limited the gull population.

Herring gulls declined all along the Atlantic Coast, even in those regions to the south where nonbreeding gulls had once been common. Edward Sturtevant, an ornithologist in Rhode Island, reported that he did not see a herring gull there for four summers during the 1870s. E. H. Forbush ventured the opinion that as "summer people" spread to the islands they would ensure the gulls' extirpation.

And then, slowly, the situation changed. Congress and the state legislatures passed laws to protect gulls and many other birds. The National Audubon Society stationed wardens on several Maine islands to protect the breeding gulls that remained. Because of altered social and economic conditions, the human populations abandoned many of the islands. The old people who persisted in their poaching and egging dwindled away.

Given half a chance, the native gulls proved themselves as adaptable as the English sparrow and the Norway rat. Tidal scavengers to begin with, the gulls took advantage of man's filthy habits and began to congregate around his garbage dumps and fish canneries, where they found almost unlimited quantities of food. Thus ample food and suitable breeding places, which are the chief requisites for a flourishing species, became available to the gulls. They experienced a population explosion. One of our most beautiful living things became a pest.

Habits as well as numbers establish a species' pesthood. When not in their breeding cycle, the gulls' main pastimes are feeding and loafing. In many places along the coast, the gulls took to feeding on garbage dumps, then flew in large numbers to local reservoirs, where they bathed and loafed for the rest of the day. Garbage from the dump stuck to the gulls' feet, and it was inevitably added, along with their droppings, to the public water supply. Sometimes their droppings spread fish parasites among the local ponds. On the islands their growing numbers crowded out terns and other seabirds.

In the 1940s, Dr. Alfred O. Gross, a noted ornithologist at Bowdoin College in Maine, devised a scheme to deal with the gulls' booming population. On behalf of the U.S. Fish and Wildlife Service, Gross sprayed freshly laid eggs on Maine islands with a mixture of high-grade oil and formaldehyde—the oil to suffocate the embryos and the formaldehyde to prevent the eggs from rotting and bursting and thus alerting the incubating adults to the fact that all was not well.

The twelve-year program was amazingly effective in view of the wide area over which it was carried out (over 900,000 eggs were sprayed) and man's remorseless dumping of garbage and fish offal. The breeding gull population, which had been doubling every twelve to fifteen years, declined in Maine during the period 1944–52.

But the results were not sufficiently spectacular for the Fish and Wildlife Service. Apparently its biologists expected a sharper decline in the gulls' numbers because they had underestimated their longevity. Adult gulls have no endemic diseases and few predators; it is now known that the average life-span of those gulls reaching maturity is about fifteen years. (A herring gull banded on June 29, 1930, by Dr. Olin S. Pettingill, Jr., at Duck Rock Island, near Monhegan, Maine, was found dead 36 years later on Lake Michigan's Little Traverse Bay, 800 miles away.)

Given several more years and a wider application of his principles, Gross might have been able to bring about a general stabilization of the East Coast gull population as the older birds died off without being replaced. But while he had reversed the gulls' increase in Maine, they were extending their breeding colonies rapidly southward along the Massachusetts coast, a development that may be attributed in part to Gross' disturbance of their original nesting islands. Thus the spraying program was abandoned in 1952.

The gulls immediately renewed their explosive increase all along the coast.

That trend continued until very recently, when another dramatic shift seems to have occurred.

In the summer of 1967, a station wagon crammed with camping and scientific equipment appeared at our home in Maine, and a blond young British ornithologist named Jeremy Hatch presented himself to us. He had heard in town that my wife and I might be sympathetic to a study of terns he was making.

Did we have a boat we could lend him to use during his studies on Petit Manan? We did, and we located an outboard motor to push it along. During that summer and the next we kept ourselves acquainted with Jeremy Hatch's investigations on Petit Manan and learned certain facts that we came to feel transcended the study of birds apparently remote from most human concerns.

Petit Manan, low and treeless and about 330 yards long, lies three miles off the coast. Its only inhabitants at the time were the three Coast Guardsmen who manned the lighthouse (the light is now automated) and the nesting colonies of seabirds, chiefly three species of terns—Arctic, roseate, and common, perhaps 3,000 in all. Terns, with their long, slender wings, are among the most graceful of all flyers; indeed, they are sometimes called "sea swallows." The Arctic terns are said to have the longest migration route in the world, some of them flying nearly from one polar region to the other and back again during the year. All in all, they are one of the coast's chief adornments.

At low tide, Petit Manan is connected by a shingle bar to its smaller neighbor, Green Island, which is uninhabited except for nesting colonies of eider ducks, herring gulls, and great black-backed gulls. Living on Petit Manan day after day, watching the birds from a distance with binoculars, Hatch was able to confirm many of the fears that other ornithologists have expressed recently about the future of Maine's tern colonies.

The incessant raids by the larger gulls on the terns' nests (simply bits of grass and twigs and shells scraped together on the ground) were devastating. As Hatch watched, a gull would swoop in on an untended nest, disregarding the terns that rose from surrounding nests to mob it, and seize a downy chick. Still mobbed by the shrieking terns, the gull would get back into the air, feathers flying as the terns pecked at its back, and gulp down the struggling chick in mid-flight.

Curiously, the gulls did not molest the terns' unhatched eggs. On other islands gulls have been seen smashing and eating tern eggs, and Hatch suspected the same thing might have occurred on Petit Manan before he reached there. "Perhaps late in the season," he wrote afterward, "the probability of striking an unpleasant rotten egg is so great that it is advantageous to seek the more certain delights of live chicks."

Hatch's meticulous observations confirmed the enormous toll. By clocking the number of successful raids each hour, he estimated that gulls devoured between 700 and 1,500 tern chicks on the island during the summer, a large proportion of those that might otherwise have survived to maturity. Indeed, tern colonies are known to be shrinking and vanishing all along the New England coast, and such predation by gull colonies swollen to artificial size by man's wastes apparently is a prime reason.

What is happening on the Maine coast is a reflection of events elsewhere. In

Western cattle feedlots, the heaped concentration of grain laid out for the domestic animals draws great flocks of blackbirds and starlings to eat up the operators' profits and contaminate the cattle's feed with their droppings. In Ohio, farmers plant endless fields of corn smack in the middle of red-winged blackbirds' ancient migration routes, then demand large-scale poisoning programs to protect their investments. And perhaps the ultimate indignity has occurred in India, where the Parsi burial towers attract clouds of vultures. One of these towers was moved after an aircraft flew into the massed vultures while trying to land at a nearby airport and the copilot was killed.

The threat that birds pose to men and their flying machines is directly responsible for the most comprehensive study yet made of herring gull populations. For man has invaded the element once dominated by birds, and the two sides, in effect, are tangling over the issue of *fliegensraum*.

The hazard has intensified since the introduction of high-speed jets. In a simpler era a pilot, even on landings and takeoffs, might be able to maneuver his plane to avoid flocks of birds that strayed into his line of flight. Today the speed of planes is so great that there is not time for either birds or planes to change direction. Moreover, the powerful jet and propjet engines suck birds into their openings, sometimes with fatal results.

In 1960 an Electra's engine ingested a flock of starlings at Boston's Logan International Airport, causing the plane to crash with the loss of 62 human lives. Seventeen others died at Ellicott City, Maryland, in 1962 when their plane hit two whistling swans. Two men died when a Beechcraft collided with a loon near Bakersfield, California, in 1963. The crew of a private jet fortunately escaped injury when gulls clogged an engine near Cleveland in 1968, but the $1.5 million craft was demolished. And, in a minor miracle itself, when a C-47 landed at Washington National Airport in 1963, a gull fluttered out of an engine cowling and flew away!

It is difficult to assemble accurate information about nonfatal bird strikes by aircraft, but both their number and the resulting financial loss are considerable.

"It isn't mandatory to turn in reports of these strikes," says James T. Morse of the Federal Aviation Administration, "and naturally the commercial airlines don't like to talk about the matter for fear of upsetting their passengers. The information we get is only the tip of the iceberg. The airlines don't like to divulge their financial losses, or even how long their planes are laid up from these collisions. That might upset their stockholders. After all, it's tough to lose a half-million-dollar engine because it's sucked up a couple of birds."

Civilian aircraft reported 537 bird strikes in 1970 and 566 in 1971. However, not a single commercial airline gave the FAA any estimate of damage costs, though most of the cases involved jet engine damage due to bird ingestion, and though the airlines reported many of the planes were out of service for repairs. Apparently there were no civilian deaths or injuries from bird strikes during those two years.

The great majority of collisions occur at altitudes under 2,000 feet, generally when the planes are landing or taking off. Military planes compound the problem because their maneuvers very often restrict them to low levels. In 1971 alone, the U.S. Air Force says there were more than 1,000 collisions with birds, 383 of which caused appreciable damage to the planes. A pilot and his crewman died when their F-101B ingested a bird on takeoff and crashed in flames. Here is an official Air Force report of what happened when an RF-4C collided with a black vulture at 500 feet:

"During low level flight, pilot saw a bird and started to warn the navigator a second prior to impact. Evasive action was not possible. The forward left edge of the pilot's canopy failed. Pilot initiated a pull-up to vacate low altitude. He was not able to see, nor could he contact the navigator due to high noise level.

"At approximately 4,000 feet he determined he was in a 70–80-degree bank. He rolled wings level and tried to contact navigator. However, the navigator, unable to see due to bird remains smeared over his visor, and unable to hear, became disoriented due to high positive 'G' force of pull-up and ejected. He suffered a broken leg. Fortunately, the pilot elected to return to base and land. His parachute had been deployed by the bird strike and had separated without his knowledge."

Jim Morse of the FAA provides a Cold War note.

"We asked the Russians where their military aircraft had the most trouble with birds," he recalls. "One of them grinned and said, 'At low levels, when we practice coming in low to duck under the radar—just like you do.'"

The Electra crash at Boston in 1960 spurred intensive research into bird problems. Though starlings caused that tragedy, gulls—because of their large size and omnipresence at Logan Airport—became the focus of official concern. The FAA made funds available to the U.S. Fish and Wildlife Service to study the cause of bird concentrations at airports, and Fish and Wildlife, in turn, gave the Massachusetts Audubon Society a subcontract to carry out studies on the gulls at Logan. This brought Dr. William H. Drury, Jr., the society's research director, into the picture.

"We were fortunate that the Fish and Wildlife Service wasn't simply interested in the question of how to solve the problem," Drury says. "We could have documented that for them in a couple of weeks. They were also interested in the forces that combine to create a problem. That took a lot longer to answer, but in the process we added to our knowledge of herring gulls and to wildlife population studies in general."

Few men who have played a part in pest control policies in this country have looked at the problem as clearly as Drury did. Is there a pest problem? Then eradicate the pests, reply the single-minded control specialists. Right from the beginning, however, Drury and his colleagues saw that the solution when it came would be general and not specific. Only when man cleaned up his own mess would the problem resolve itself.

Meanwhile there were emergency measures to be considered at Logan. Seven hundred and fifty pairs of gulls had taken up nesting sites at the airport, while thousands more fed on the tidal flats and at sewer outlets nearby. From April 1960 to April 1961 observers counted 38 bird strikes involving various species, including dunlins, ducks, starlings, and a snowy owl. But by far the greatest number, 24 at least, were gulls.

"If the architects who designed Logan had set out instead to design a gull sanctuary, they couldn't have done a better job," Drury says. "The location was surrounded by city dumps and sewer outfalls where the gulls could feed. The airport had a dump of its own, and it was dotted with freshwater ponds and salt marshes where the gulls could loaf. Finally, it had long, isolated runways stretching into the harbor where the gulls could roost undisturbed at night. No wonder they flocked there!"

The Massachusetts Port Authority set about making Logan Airport less of a gull haven. It ordered the alluring vegetation and watering holes removed, "putting more of Logan under concrete," as one official said. The MPA also established a "gull patrol," which consisted of armed men who toured the runways regularly and frightened away the birds with exploding devices and occasional gunfire. For the most part, the patrol carried out its task in a professional manner. Only when someone shot an osprey by mistake did Drury fire off a sarcastic report.

Meanwhile, Drury had embarked on a survey of New England's herring gull population that is a classic of its kind. A detailed census during the 1960s indicated there was a winter population of about 700,000 herring gulls along the Atlantic and Gulf coasts of the United States. Most of the winter gulls were concentrated in metropolitan areas, where the omnipresent municipal dumps, sewage outlets, and fish piers tided them over the cold months. Those areas, of course, also were the sites of major airports.

One of Drury's counts, for instance, showed 110,000 herring gulls wintering in New England. Eighty thousand of them infested the major coastal cities. The rest of the gulls foraged along less heavily populated stretches of the coast, making an honest living. Drury noted there were large breeding colonies of gulls in the Cape Cod–Vineyard Sound area during the summer, but in winter the population dropped from 34,000 to 8,000 birds, most of them clustered around town dumps. The winter gull population at dumps and fish piers in garbage-strewn Boston Harbor was four times that of the Cape Cod–Vineyard Sound area.

Drury and his colleagues also made a comprehensive survey of the summer colonies on 270 islands from Cape May, New Jersey, near the southernmost breeding limits at that time, to eastern Maine and neighboring New Brunswick. Riding in Coast Guard planes, which flew at levels below 500 feet, they counted the gulls visually and by taking detailed photographs of their colonies. Ground parties also counted the nests on selected islands to check the accuracy of the visual and photographic counts.

The observers ultimately came up with a total of 135,000 breeding pairs of gulls along the Northeastern coast of the United States, and another 50,000 breeding pairs on nearby Canadian islands. This survey, then, had accounted for less than 400,000 birds. After taking the significant winter mortality into consideration, what had happened to the remaining gulls?

Drury knew that herring gulls do not begin to breed until they have reached their fourth or fifth year. Among the details provided by his various counts were figures showing that a third of the winter population was made up of immature gulls, still in their brown plumage. Other studies had shown that each summer perhaps 20 percent of the adults "took a year off" from breeding. Again, some of the birds counted in winter later retired to remote parts of Canada to breed.

The surveys also confirmed Drury's suspicions that earlier estimates, placing the average life-span of adult gulls at six years, were far too low. By working out the proportion of gulls in each stage of plumage he settled on a figure closer to fifteen years. This jibes with the facts known about the gull's remarkable population explosion that continued into the middle 1960s. Studies on the various nesting colonies show that, though production varies considerably, the total of offspring reared to fledgling age each year averages a little better than one for each breeding pair. A few years ago this rate meant that 200,000 young gulls were added to the population each summer. Only 25,000 young need to survive into their fourth year to maintain the present population.

As Drury and his colleague, Dr. Ian C. T. Nisbet, point out, many of the species that man designates "pests" have in an evolutionary sense been *selected* to be adaptable. These species usually are plants or animals occupying habitats that are subject to frequent modification in detail.

"For such a species, an attempt by man to suppress its population is merely another environmental change, to which it already has the capacity to adjust," Drury and Nisbet say. "Hunting, poisoning, and other such remedies at the point where they are 'pests' can have only a very limited effect because the birds adapt and become wary. The strategy of management is then to seek the weak links in the adaptive system, and to use them to make the species adjust in ways that will benefit us."

I had closely followed Jeremy Hatch's studies documenting the threat of the herring gulls' spreading population to other nesting seabirds. I had also been in touch with Bill Drury about his work relating to the hazards of gulls around military and civilian airports. One summer day in 1972 I joined Drury on the old lobster boat he has used for some years to tour the gull islands off the Maine coast. Most of the Northeast was still staggering under the ravages of Hurricane Agnes, but thick fog was the only impediment to our cruise on Penobscot Bay.

"It's really a nostalgic trip for me," Drury said as he picked his way through the fog between the islands. "The federal funding for our gull studies has run out, but I think we learned a lot out here."

He is a tall, light-haired, youthful-looking man of middle age, a skilled boat-handler, and a biologist who approaches his task with imagination and wit. "There were some variables in our selection of which islands to work on," he said. "We neglected Green Island over there because it's full of stinging nettles."

But there were many more "Green Islands" and "Green Ledges" for him to choose among, a nomenclatural repetition he explained by saying that greenery grows readily on those islands that have been heavily fertilized by gulls, and thus is an indication of their presence. Often the nearby islands where the gulls do not nest are comparatively drab.

Through the fog we detected Little Brimstone Island, small and treeless, on which there was a colony Drury had been observing since 1963. It was half tide. Water foamed rhythmically up over the island's lower rocks and then, still glistening white, dripped back into the surf. A dozen seals had splashed off some large rocks, yet remained in the cove rubbernecking at the intruders. Lobster buoys, painted bright yellows, reds, and greens, provided the only daubs of color in this monochrome world. We anchored in 25 feet of water.

"Gulls are ordinarily ground-nesters, so they adapted to nesting on the islands to be safe from animal predators," Drury said. "When the early settlers here began to take their eggs, the gulls adapted again and started building their nests in trees on some of the islands. They still nest in trees on Franklin Island, near here in Muscongus Bay."

We dropped into the lobster boat's dory and rowed ashore. A cloud of gulls rose from their territories, and crying loudly, circled overhead. When we had clambered over the wet and slippery rockweed at the island's edge, we saw the first speckled greenish-brown eggs on the rocks just above the high-water line.

"How about your own presence on the islands?" I asked Drury. "Did you have any effect on the birds' breeding success?"

He nodded. "There was some mortality, of course, when the parents flew off and left their eggs or chicks untended. We found that the disturbance was greater when we visited the islands only occasionally. But if we landed often the gulls got used to us and they didn't stay away from their nests very long. There would be some mortality in cold, rainy weather when the adults weren't around to keep the eggs and chicks warm. But on the whole the disturbance was small."

Some of the gulls nested in the thick vegetation that covered the crown of the island. Grasses, yarrow, tansy, ragweed, angelica, silverweed, and mouse-eared chickweed formed most of the cover. Close by on the rocks we saw dozens of sturdy nests, fashioned of twigs, grasses, seaweed, and miscellaneous debris. Often there were dim splotches of paint on the rocks next to a nest.

"We used to come on the island in June and count the nests. Then we'd make a mark next to each one—a splash of green paint meant there were eggs in the nest, and blue paint meant no eggs. On some of the rocks you can see a number of marks, one for each year there was a nest on that spot. It helped us keep track of the nests we'd already counted, and it gave us an idea of nesting sites and how successful they were from year to year."

Originally the gull colonies were located chiefly on the outer islands, where the production of young birds was not nearly as high as it became later.

"A gull population expands not by exceeding a certain density on an island, but by founding new colonies," Drury said. "Gradually, under protection in this century, they moved to the inner islands along the Maine and Massachusetts coasts, where they were closer to the fish piers and other sources of food. In any case, the gulls closer to shore apparently have always had better success raising their young."

"Do gulls make good parents?"

Drury grinned. "Gulls are like people. Some are good parents, some are lousy ones. Gulls have excellent hatching success with their eggs—perhaps as high as 80 percent. But about half the chicks die before fledging, most of them during the first five days. We found that the main reason is that many of the parents simply don't make the transition in time from incubating eggs to feeding and caring for the young." Thus, Drury noted, "The young die from neglect."

We ate our sandwiches on the rocks without going up into the weedy areas.

"Eiders nest in there, too," Drury said, "and we don't like to disturb them. You know, it's a funny thing. You often hear that gulls prey heavily on eider chicks, but I can't think of a single place where eiders nest on the Maine coast that doesn't have a gull colony alongside it. And the comeback of the eiders coincided with the gulls' population climb."

Below us, on the glassy black swell, clusters of tiny eiders followed the adults. Like the gulls, these large ducks once had been nearly extirpated along the Maine coast. A few great black-backed gulls stood about on the distant rocks. Drury and his colleagues are studying the relationship of the blackbacks to the smaller herring gulls, which they have displaced on some of the islands.

What happens to the young herring gulls when, after two months of varying parental care, they are ready to leave the island? Drury, drawing on his own research and that of others, is able to supply a few of the answers. About a third of the fledged birds die during the first month while they are learning to fend for themselves. A few of the young follow their parents to feeding areas along the coast, begging food from them or finding out what to search for on their own.

"Chicks inherit patterns of behavior such as searching, probing, diving, prying, and so forth," Drury said. "But they have to learn what to search for and what to eat."

Man has proved a godsend to these inexperienced birds. A disproportionately high percentage of the gulls foraging at municipal dumps, fish piers, and pig farms are immatures, most of which would not survive to enter the breeding population without this sort of help. Thus for years the gulls' numbers spiraled out of control. By perpetuating the dole, man aggravated local threats to other breeding seabirds, unhealthy conditions at reservoirs, and hazards around airports. We had, then, not simply a wildlife problem, but a socio-political one.

What is the situation today? Tentative steps have been taken to clean up the most obvious sources of trouble. Cities have converted a few dumps to sanitary landfills (though some gulls continue to visit these sites), and the federal government has allocated funds to help municipalities move dumps away from critical areas. An Inter-Agency Bird Hazard Committee now functions within the federal government to deal with the threat to military and civilian planes.

Improvements in aircraft design have already helped to some extent. Jet engines are placed higher on many of the newer planes, causing some experts to conjecture that they no longer suck up as many birds (or even rocks and rabbits) from runways. Experiments are going on at U.S. Air Force laboratories to see if white strobe lights will be useful at long range in warning birds off a plane's course.

Whatever figures are available, however, indicate the damage to both military and civilian planes is greater than ever before. Federal and local authorities have yet to use the leverage they obtained after the Electra crash at Boston. In sustaining claims for death and injury against the federal government, a U.S. District Court held that the authorities were negligent in failing to force the removal of "attractions to birds" near the airport. A section of the Federal Airport Grant Act reads:

"Airport hazard means any structure or object of natural growth located on or in the vicinity of a public airport or any use of land near such airport, which obstructs the air space required for the flight of aircraft in landing or taking off at such airport or is otherwise hazardous to such landing or taking off of aircraft."

The gulls' depredations among the eggs and chicks of other species remain severe. Drury and Nisbet advocate driving gulls off those islands where their presence poses an immediate threat to aircraft or to the survival of other sea-bird colonies. "A control program which involves eliminating gulls [locally] is an unpalatable prospect," Nisbet has written, "but the situation itself is unpalatable."

Meanwhile, Drury's final summer census, made in 1972, revealed that the herring gulls' breeding population had abruptly stopped its upward spiral in the Northeast. "It will be a while before we know what it means, but at least it looks as if the runaway population trend has reversed itself."

Drury can only speculate about the causes at present. He had hoped for another government grant to continue his studies on gull population, but no funds were forthcoming.

"Most studies are funded only in a crisis atmosphere," he said. "It would be valuable to pursue the problem now to find out exactly what may be keeping the gulls' breeding population at a *lower* level." It seems clear that there is a direct correlation between the breeding success of herring gulls and man's domestic and industrial garbage. The New England fishing industry, plagued by its antiquated equipment and the foreign fleets offshore, is on the verge of collapse. Fish offal is no longer available to the gulls in unlimited quantities during their breeding season. Perhaps, too, a subtle difference in the composition of garbage at municipal dumps recently has affected the gulls to some extent.

Even if the hungry adults are inclined to breed, they cannot sustain a large production of young. The closing of dumps here and there also seems to have caused a winter die-off among gulls in those areas.

Drury also believes that we may soon see a repetition of the movement away from the crowded Maine colonies that took place during the 1940s, although on a smaller scale. For the herring gull is spreading its range southward. Biologists recently have found the gulls nesting, mostly on man made dredge islands, at various points along the North Carolina coast as far south as the Cape Fear River. Moreover, great black-backed gulls have followed the herring gulls into North Carolina.

"Our present observations on the state of the herring gull population," Drury says, "suggest that it will be prudent to look for growth of gull colonies in the middle and south Atlantic states in the next decade. If such proves to be the case, we would anticipate an increase of gulls at and around the many commercial and military airports in the South."

Numbers of gulls rested quietly on the water just off Little Brimstone Island, waiting for us to leave. As I watched them rise and fall on the swell, I was reminded of Oliver Wendell Holmes' phrase "The gull, high floating like a sloop unladen."

Holmes' gull, like the fictional Jonathan Livingston Seagull of the best-selling book, has had millions of human admirers. Now our own shortcomings have brought us into a degrading conflict with this beautiful and resourceful creature. If the bald eagle is the symbol of our country's grandeur, the herring gull may come to stand for something far less noble in our national character.

NO DOVE OF PEACE, BY DURWARD L. ALLEN *If the passenger pigeon had been capable of scattering and nesting a few pairs at a time, it might survive today. But the species was utterly dependent on mob existence, and once the white man began a systematic slaughter at roosts, along flyways, and at nesting sites, the pigeon's extinction was as unpreventable as it was irrevocable.*

Flocks of early morning flew low, and the best shooting would be at John Winter's clearing just at daybreak. So the party hurried Indian-file down the woods path.

Bringing up the rear was William Mershon, who had to run a few steps betimes to match a twelve-year-old's gait to the stride of his elders. Dodging the veteran water spaniel that lurched by him on the trail and bearing the full panoply of a pigeon hunter took some doing, but it was no hardship to a country lad in the 1870s.

Flights of early April began while snow still spotted the north slopes. Daily now, living streams of burnished, long-tailed meteors skirted the openings, sailed low over hilltops, and swept on westward to some feeding place beyond the Tittabawassee River. At Saginaw, Michigan, spring came in on pigeon wings.

Guns were cracking at the Winter farm, and young William and his party joined in. By 6:30 the flight had vanished, and the hunters strung up their birds. The four long tail feathers of the cock were pulled and knotted together at the tips. Then the quills were stuck through lower mandibles and the birds tied eight or ten to a string. There would be potpies that night.

These were among hunter and sportsman William B. Mershon's vivid recollections of the passenger pigeon in its early abundance. The pass shooting in which he participated was undoubtedly the most respectable of the various methods by which the birds were taken—and there is indeed little that can be considered respectable in the history of this species.

Keenly observant and concerned for the beauties of the out-of-doors which were disappearing around him, Mershon became one of Michigan's famous conservationists. He wrote two useful books, one of which was on the passenger pigeon. In its introduction he made one of the most perceptive statements to be found in early accounts of this species:

"The habits of the birds were such that they could not thrive singly nor in small bodies, but were dependent upon one another, and vast communities were necessary for their very existence . . ."

It is likely that Mershon's succinct appraisal contained more truths than even he saw at the time, and it seems to merit more exploration in the reflected light of what is now known (or strongly suspected) in the fields of population physiology, behavior, and ecology.

The extremes of pigeon adaptation were, to say the least, biologically improbable. They involved conditions which would have sent most wild creatures into throes of psycho-social stress. The bird was a noisy, restless, rowdy mobster that survived and succeeded through sheer weight of numbers. Its life was an unending series of conventions, and between times a game of follow the leader—no matter where. It was always in a hurry and always late.

In winter the pigeons roosted in huge concentrations in forested areas of southeastern states. During the day they would be away on mass flights to feeding grounds—that is, where abundant acorns, chestnuts, beechnuts, or other tree seeds littered the woodland floor. There the flocks moved forward in an incessant flutter of wings, like an endless belt, with the hindmost birds finishing everything edible, then flying forward to drop on new ground in front.

Evenings, the long streamers of pigeons swarmed back to the roost, where they broke down limbs and whole trees with the weight of bird piled upon bird. Most animals could not have stood an hour of such crowding, but these feathered extroverts stacked themselves "in clusters," said Alexander Wilson, and kept the night air astir with their shuffling.

Sullivan Cook, a resident of northern Ohio, told how, as a boy, he paid a nighttime visit to a swamp roost. The weight of birds bent alders flat to the ground, and strange forms like haystacks which could be seen through the gloom turned out to be small elms and willows loaded with pigeons. At his brother's suggestion, Cook fired an old 12-gauge horse pistol into one of these masses. In the light of a tin lantern they picked up eighteen birds and saw others hobbling away through the brush.

A forest or swamp used as a roost bore the marks for many a year. The trees were racked, split, and dead. Undergrowth was blighted and buried under inches of guano. It was well the pigeons moved around—they left the country a shambles wherever they stopped for a while.

The movement north came with the first good weather at winter's end, and the migration was an awesome spectacle. Flights, made up of both solidly massed and loosely connected flocks, sometimes took a day or more to pass. They moved on a front that might be several miles in width and layered to a depth that cast a shadow on the earth. When, without warning, the feathered tempest poured out of the horizon, horses took fright, and people stood in wonder. The roar of the millions abraded the ear for hours; the air was filled with the sharp smell of them, and their dung spattered like hail on the leaves.

The nesting range extended across the Lake States to New England and north well into Ontario. One year the big nesting might be in central Wisconsin. The next it would be found in Michigan, Indiana, Ohio, or Pennsylvania. A "big" nesting might be like the one described by Michigan geologist Bela Hubbard: a stretch of forest 16 miles long and 3 miles wide—50 square miles with every suitable bough occupied by a dozen nests. Most years, it is likely that such a nesting, and "smaller" ones of a few million birds, were scattered across the north wherever there was a mast supply to feed them.

In the face of varying reports, experts have concluded that the pigeon had a normal clutch of one egg and nested only once a season. Thus its reproductive potential was minimum, yet its huge numbers attested to an incredibly successful environmental adjustment under primitive conditions. The total population in the forested eastern half of the United States has been responsibly estimated at from three to six billion. Somewhere in the recent past there was a sustained build-up to this level, which implies a phenomenally high survival rate, especially for a creature whose environmental niche was that of a prey animal.

On a flimsy platform of twigs, the hen pigeon incubated her egg through the night, while the cock joined his fellows in a roost in some nearby swamp.

At dawn, the males rose in a cloud and flew to the feeding ground, which might be 50 to 75 miles away. About 10 A.M. the males appeared over the nesting, and each spiraled down into the trees and practically boosted his mate off the nest, instantly taking over her job of incubation (and keeping the egg protected from marauders). The hens then went off to fill their crops, to return about midafternoon. Evidently the males fed again before going to roost, thus getting one meal up on the females.

The egg of the pigeon hatched in about 13 days, and for about a week the adults fed the squab on "milk," a rich curd secreted by the crop. During the second week, the parents came to the nest with softened beechnuts or other mast in their crops, which was regurgitated to keep the offspring stuffed and growing.

About 14 days after hatching, the squab was feathered out and equaled or exceeded its parents in weight. Then the breeding pair called it quits and took off for a change of scenery. Nearly all the birds in a nesting were on the same time schedule, and most of them left together—some observers said to another nesting farther north, and certainly to some area where berries or other provender would feed the myriads through summer months.

The squabs got hungry and finally fluttered to the ground. They were plump with fat, and this kept them going until they could learn to feed and fly. These tender young were a favorite ration with Indians and whites alike, and tons of them were smoked or salted for winter use.

The critical characteristic of the pigeon was its gregariousness. Early accounts do mention small nesting groups or individual breeding pairs. But these were a minuscule minority of the billions, an aberrant fringe whose breeding was not sufficiently successful to rescue the species in its final years. In primitive times the great nesting assemblage was the bulwark of survival. It was no part of a local wildlife community. In a year of abundant mast within flying distance, the huge flight suddenly settled into a suitable track of forest. In little more than a month, the breeders and young were gone again, and they might not return for many years.

A resident prey species which achieves great abundance will exhaust its food, pollute its environment, support an increase of natural enemies, and quite likely succumb to disease. But before any of this could happen, the pigeon was off to a new and fresh habitat. The various units of the highly mobile population used eastern North America much as the Barren Ground caribou uses its Arctic range. The migratory caribou herds may heavily overbrowse a local area of the slow-growing lichens, but they may not be back for many years, during which recovery can take place.

The relationship of the pigeon to predators was especially striking. Concentrations of the birds attracted a host of natural enemies, but these were so outnumbered they made little impression. What might be regarded as the "normal" dynamics of predator-prey relations—in which the meat-eaters would have a period of years to increase—did not apply at all.

The advent of the white man changed all the rules. The aggregations which had been the key to prosperity now attracted a systematized slaughter that grew in efficiency with each passing year. The birds were heavily shot, both roosting and in mass flights; but it was the nestings that supported the most profitable and damaging commercial enterprise. During the 1860s and '70s the business of killing and marketing pigeons built up rapidly, and toward the last some thousands of professional pigeoners would gather at strategic railheads in the North as soon as word went out that new nestings were located.

Regardless of original abundance, no animal could bear up under a regime of killing that increased year by year on the breeding ground. Nearly any species that can reproduce in reasonable safety will replace heavy losses that come in fall. But disturbing the breeding cycle causes a scarcity more quickly and certainly than any other kind of damage. The large flights of pigeons declined during the seventies and disappeared in the early eighties. By 1900, stragglers were being reported as novelties. In 1914 the last known passenger pigeon died in the Cincinnati zoo.

Efforts were made to give some protection to this bird, while there still was time. But regulations were unpopular, inadequate, and not enforced. Reading some of the arguments might well jolt us today, for it was pointed out frequently how important the pigeon traffic was to the back-country economy!

The environmental adjustments, population mechanics, and biological failings of the passenger pigeon are more reliably interpreted today than was possible in times past. The species might have survived if it could have scattered out and lived a few pairs at a time, like the mourning dove. But it could not; it was specialized hopelessly for mob existence. Its formula for being was all or none.

Without much doubt, this unalterable requirement was the final arbiter of its fate.

THE AUTHORS

DURWARD L. ALLEN, professor of wildlife ecology at Purdue University in Lafayette, Indiana, has received a number of national awards for his professional work and for his books, scientific papers, and magazine articles in the field of wildlife biology and conservation. He is a past president of the Wildlife Society. For years Dr. Allen and his students have been studying the wolf and its relationships with other species, notably the moose, on Isle Royale National Park in Michigan.

ROBERT ARBIB, editor of *American Birds*, the National Audubon Society's magazine for birdwatchers and ornithologists, won the John Burroughs Medal for his book *The Lord's Woods*, which tells of the wonders—and the demise—of an unspoiled tract of forest on Long Island. A past president of the Linnaean Society, he is also a coauthor of *The Hungry Bird Book* and *Enjoying Birds Around New York City*, and is currently writing the history of the annual Christmas Bird Count, first organized in 1900.

BROOKS ATKINSON is best known in the world of the stage; he was drama critic for *The New York Times* for thirty-one years and the newspaper's critic-at-large for another six years. He recently wrote a history of the theater from 1900 to 1970, entitled simply *Broadway*, and a major Broadway theater bears his name. But Atkinson began his journalism career writing about the out-of-doors, and a number of his books, including the most recent, *This Bright Land*, are concerned with nature.

ERWIN A. BAUER is a full-time freelance photographer and writer on out-of-doors and environmental topics. His home is in Jackson Hole, Wyoming, near Grand Teton National Park. He is camping editor for *Outdoor Life* magazine and is the author of two recent books of interest to camera enthusiasts: *Hunting with a Camera* and *Outdoor Photography*.

HAL BORLAND is one of America's most distinguished nature essayists. For more than three decades he has contributed perceptive nature editorials to *The New York Times*; his articles appear regularly in several magazines, among them *Audubon* and *The Progressive*; and he has more than twenty books to his credit, including *Hill Country Harvest*, which won the John Burroughs Medal, and *Seasons*, with photographs by Les Line. Borland lives on an old farm in the Berkshire Hills of Connecticut.

ANGUS CAMERON is editor and vice-president of the New York publishing firm of Alfred A. Knopf. High on the list of his special interests are prehistoric archeology and Greek and Roman history, while nature study, camping, fishing, and hunting consume much of his leisure time. He is particularly fascinated by the history and natural history of owls, and this led to his collaboration with artist Peter Parnall on a book about these nocturnal hunters, *The Nightwatchers*.

MARGARET CHENEY, for the past several years, has been living on and developing a small farm near San Juan Bautista in central California. This project provided the material for her book *The Meanwhile Farm*, recently issued by a new West Coast feminist publishing house, Les Femmes. She has traveled widely, living at times in the Middle East and rural England, and her varied writing interests range from conservation to the motivation of violence.

JEAN CRAIGHEAD GEORGE, a roving editor for *Reader's Digest*, comes from a family of famous naturalists and is the author of many nature books for young readers, several of which have won national awards. Among them are *Julie of the Wolves*, recipient of a Newberry Award; *My Side of the Mountain*, which became a critically acclaimed motion picture; and her series on "The Thirteen Moons," exploring the relationship between climate and biological events. Her most recent book is *Going to the Sun*.

FRANK GRAHAM, JR., lives on a hill overlooking a picturesque bay in Maine's easternmost county, and in summer the sky above his home is constantly populated with soaring herring gulls, many of them en route to and from the area's sardine canneries, where they find abundant food. Graham's several books include *Where the Place Called Morning Lies*, a personal view of life and environmental issues in Maine; and *Man's Dominion*, which traces the history of the conservation movement in America. He is an *Audubon* field editor.

LOUIS J. HALLE has had a multifaceted career. He is noted for his writings about birds and nature, among them *Spring in Washington* and most recently *The Sea and the Ice,* on the antarctic and its wildlife. But he is also an authority on international relations and political philosophy, having served on the Policy Planning Staff under Secretaries of State Dean Acheson and John Foster Dulles and as director of strategic studies at the Graduate Institute of International Studies in Geneva, Switzerland.

JOHN HAY is president of the Cape Cod Museum of Natural History and visiting professor in environmental studies at Dartmouth College. Grandson and namesake of the Secretary of State under Presidents William McKinley and Theodore Roosevelt, he is the author of several books inspired by the wildlife and seasons along the Atlantic shore. They include *The Great Beach,* which won the John Burroughs Medal, and *Spirit of Survival,* a personal and natural history of terns.

FRANK HEPPNER, an associate professor of zoology at the University of Rhode Island, in Kingston, worked for several years in Washington state under the distinguished avian physiologist Donald S. Farner. In recent years Dr. Heppner has been studying the reasons geese fly in V formations and how starlings make turns. He finds starlings fascinating and says they would be cherished as cage birds if they were not commonly regarded as pests.

JAMES A. KERN makes his livelihood selling scenic and agricultural land in Florida. At heart, however, he is an adventurer and naturalist whose photographic expeditions have taken him to Borneo, India, Africa, the Philippines, the Canadian arctic, and to the mountains of Costa Rica in search of the legendary quetzal. Several years ago Kern founded the Florida Trail Association, which has completed three hundred miles of a hiking footpath through the state.

LOUISE DE KIRILINE LAWRENCE has lived in the fir and spruce forests near Ontario's Lake Nipissing for four decades, writing of the region's birds and other life-forms with both scientific precision and lyrical reverence. Her book *The Lovely and the Wild* earned the John Burroughs Medal. Born in Sweden, the daughter of a naturalist, she served as a translator to an American military mission during the Russian Revolution and was a Swedish Red Cross delegate to the Volga region during the famine of 1922 before emigrating to Canada to join the Outpost Nursing Service.

GEORGE LAYCOCK, an *Audubon* field editor and a highly respected reporter on environmental and natural history affairs, has twenty-eight books to his credit. They include *Autumn of the Eagle,* nominated for a National Book Award; *The Sign of the Flying Goose,* the story of the National Wildlife Refuge System; *Alaska: The Embattled Frontier;* and most recently *The Birdwatcher's Bible.* His articles have appeared in a wide range of national magazines.

HAROLD MAYFIELD has pursued dual careers throughout his life—business and ornithology. But he retired early as personnel manager for Owens-Illinois to devote his full attention to the latter, in particular the preservation of the endangered Kirtland's warbler. Mayfield is the only person to have been elected president of three principal North American ornithological organizations, including the American Ornithologists' Union. He recently completed a monograph on the red phalarope, based on five expeditions to the arctic.

ROGER TORY PETERSON is the world's most famous ornithologist. Artist, still and movie photographer, author, lecturer, traveler, authority on the birdlife of every corner of the Earth, Peterson originated the *Field Guide to the Birds* in 1934. Today, millions of birdwatchers carry copies of the several editions. He has received many honors for his work, including the Audubon Medal of the National Audubon Society, the Arthur A. Allen Medal from the Cornell University Laboratory of Ornithology, and the Brewster Medal of the American Ornithologists' Union.

GEORGE PLIMPTON, in his literary pursuits, has been led into adventures that most men, like Walter Mitty, only dream of. He has quarterbacked the Detroit Lions and the Baltimore Colts; boxed the light-heavyweight champion of the world, Archie Moore; pitched in Yankee Stadium against the National League All-Stars; spent a month on the professional golf circuit; played forward for the Boston Celtics. And in nonathletic endeavors, Plimpton has been gunned down by John Wayne in a Western movie, worked as a circus aerialist, and played in the New York Philharmonic orchestra.

AUSTIN L. RAND retired five years ago after a distinguished career as chief curator of zoology at the Chicago Natural History Museum. He is now research associate at the American Museum of Natural History's Archbold Biological Station in Lake Placid, Florida. Dr. Rand has written innumerable scientific papers on bird systematics, zoogeography, behavior, and ecology; coauthored *Handbook of New Guinea Birds*; and is the author of several popular books, including *Stray Feathers from a Bird Man's Desk, American Water and Game Birds*, and *A Midwestern Almanac*.

EDWARD R. RICCIUTI is a former editor of *Animal Kingdom*, the magazine of the New York Zoological Society. He has written ten books and many magazine articles on natural history for both adult and young audiences, including *Killers of the Seas*, about creatures in the world's oceans that are dangerous to man, and *To the Brink of Extinction*, a profile of seven threatened species.

FRANKLIN RUSSELL was born in New Zealand, educated in Australia and England, and worked at a wide variety of jobs before settling into a career as a freelance journalist—a career that has taken him into nearly every other part of the world. His evocative nature writings include several books about Canada's maritime region, among them *Argen the Gull, The Secret Islands, Searchers at the Gulf,* and *The Sea Has Wings* with photographs by Les Line. *Season on the Plain,* Russell's most recent book, is a narrative of the interdependent life of East African animals.

GEORGE B. SCHALLER has gained worldwide fame for his studies of mountain gorillas and lions in Africa and tigers in India. Research zoologist for the New York Zoological Society, he won a National Book Award for his scientific monograph on the lion. But the fascinating personal stories of his studies have been revealed in his popular books, *The Year of the Gorilla* and *Golden Shadows, Flying Hooves,* the latter of which tells of his three years on the Serengeti plains of Tanzania conducting close-up observations of the great African predators.

GEORGE MIKSCH SUTTON, professor of zoology emeritus at the University of Oklahoma and dean of American bird artists, has traveled from the arctic to the tropics with notebook, brushes and canvas, and a battered old paint box given to him a half century ago by his mentor at Cornell University, the great Louis Agassiz Fuertes. The many books to his credit contain not only his sensitive watercolors of birdlife and its habitat and, occasionally, mammals, but also wonderful stories from his expeditions. Among the most recent: *High Arctic, At a Bend in a Mexican River,* and *Iceland Summer.*

EDWIN WAY TEALE for the past sixteen years has lived on an old farm of one hundred and thirty acres in the northeastern corner of Connecticut. Trail Wood is the name of his personal sanctuary, and it contains two brooks, a small waterfall, a pond, woodlands, wild meadows, stone fences, and a treasure of living things to observe and write about. Which he did in his most recent book, *A Naturalist Buys an Old Farm,* the twenty-eighth title by the author who won a Pulitzer Prize in nonfiction for his four-volume series on "The American Seasons."

JOHN K. TERRES, a distinguished naturalist and former editor of *Audubon,* is the author or editor of some fifty books on natural history, including the prestigious "Living World" series on North American wildlife. He is currently putting the finishing touches to his life's work, *An Encyclopedia of Birds.* Terres's first book, *Songbirds in Your Garden,* has sold more than half a million copies since it was first published in 1953, and he won the John Burroughs Medal for the chronicle of his walking adventures on a long-abandoned homestead in North Carolina, entitled *From Laurel Hill to Siler's Bog.*